THE NATUR[illegible] USES OF LOTTERIES

The Luck of the Draw:
SORTITION AND PUBLIC POLICY

Series Editor: Barbara Goodwin
University of East Anglia

A major new series on the
use of randomisation
in education, politics
and other areas of public policy

The Political Potential of Sortition, Oliver Dowlen
978-1845401375 (cloth)

The Athenian Option, Anthony Barnett and Peter Carty
978-1845401399 (pbk.); 978-1845401405 (cloth)

The Nature and Use of Lotteries, Thomas Gataker (ed. Conall Boyle)
978-1845401177 (pbk.)

A People's Parliament, Keith Sutherland
A Citizen Legislature, Ernest Callenbach and Michael Phillips
978-1845401085 (pbk.); 978-1845401382 (cloth)

Justice by Lottery, Barbara Goodwin
1845400259 (pbk)

imprint-academic.com/sortition

THE NATURE AND USES OF LOTTERIES

A Historical and Theological Treatise
Second edition:
Reviewed, corrected and enlarged, with additional answers to some further arguments by the author

THOMAS GATAKER

Originally published in 1627

LONDON
Printed by John Haviland

Modernised with notes and bibliography by
CONALL BOYLE

IMPRINT ACADEMIC

Published in the UK by Imprint Academic
PO Box 200, Exeter EX5 5YX, UK

Published in the USA by Imprint Academic
Philosophy Documentation Center
PO Box 7147, Charlottesville, VA 22906-7147, USA

ISBN 9 781845 401177

A CIP catalogue record for this book is available from the
British Library and US Library of Congress

Contents

Preface to 2008 edition

Preface to Gataker's *The Nature and Uses of Lotteries* **by Conall Boyle**

"Puritan divine approves of gambling!"

Had there been tabloid newspapers in 1619, (or again in 1627 when the 2nd edition of this book was published) this is the sort of headline that might have been seen. The Reverend Gataker did indeed go against the settled views of his contemporaries and make the case for a limited form of gambling (or 'gaming' as its proponents coyly call it). This would have been enough to make his book notorious, but there is much more in this book than the use of lotteries in gambling. Gataker looked at the whole range of uses of lotteries from settling disputes between businessmen to criminal trials where a lottery would decide guilt or innocence. This book stands out as a remarkable early attempt to understand the full range of possibilities for the use of lotteries and the moral implications of doing so.

So who was this man Gataker, who was prepared to say such controversial things and defy conventional wisdom? A full biography can be found (also available on-line) in Brook (1813) *Lives of the Puritans.* A shorter more modern biography* describes him thus:

"**Thomas Gataker** was born in London on September 4, 1574, the son of a clergyman, Thomas Gatacre, who had served in Parliament during the reign of Queen Mary. A bookish child, gifted with an impressive memory, Gataker began his education early, earning his B.A. degree from St. John's College, Cambridge in 1594 and his M.A. three years later. During his Cambridge years, Gataker also developed significant relationships with important Puritans. He was ordained by 1600 (the precise date is not recorded) and proceeded to B.D. in 1604. Before entering into a benefice he served as tutor in the household of Sir William Cooke; he continued to live with the Cookes after being appointed as preacher at Lincoln's Inn in 1601. Between his Puritan father, friends and the influence of his college professors, Gataker became increasingly committed to the Puritan cause. Declining several prestigious academic and ecclesiastical posts, Gataker dedicated himself primarily to scholarship and to pastoral ministry, an increasingly

* from a website edited by R W Cooley, University of Saskatoon, Canada

difficult vocation, as 'times proved more troublesome than formerly they had been'.

"Gataker's Life as a Puritan Clergyman: Defined broadly, Puritanism is the form of Protestantism that existed both inside and outside the Church of England in the sixteenth and seventeenth centuries and viewed the English Reformation as an incomplete work in progress. Seventeenth-century Puritans were Calvinist in their theology, adhering to the doctrine of predestination that increasingly fell out of favour with authorities in the Church and State from the mid 1620s until the outbreak of Civil War in 1640. They were the 'hotter sort of Protestants', keen to purify the church of the remnants of 'Popish superstition'. Nearly all opposed the increasingly ceremonial liturgy of the Church of England under Archbishop Laud; some objected to clerical vestments, kneeling for the sacrament, ornate church decoration and the institution of episcopacy. By the broad definition, Thomas Gataker was certainly a Puritan, though a comparatively moderate one.

Gataker began his service in the ministry as a family chaplain. He then served as preacher at Lincoln's Inn for a decade. During those years Gataker had several opportunities for preferment, but he resisted them all. In 1611 the newly-wed Gataker settled in the parish of Rotherhithe in Surrey, where he preached for more than forty years. After many years of pastoral ministry, Gataker was appointed, in 1643, to the Assembly of Divines at Westminster, called by the English Long Parliament to reform the worship, doctrine, government and discipline of the Church of England. Gataker helped to draft the *Westminster Confession of Faith.* On matters of Church government he took a moderate position, advocating a mix of primitive episcopacy and Presbyterianism.

"Life as a Scholar: Gataker showed a predilection for Classical learning at an early age. Early in his career he was offered a Lectureship in Hebrew at Sidney Sussex, which he declined. His first published work, *Of the Nature and Use of Lots* (1619), provoked some controversy for its alleged advocacy of gaming. In all, Gataker produced dozens of works, including sermons, theological and controversial tracts, tomes on grammar, a biography and pamphlets on political and moral matters. He contributed to the comprehensive Westminster Commentary on the Bible, a major work of Presbyterian scriptural exegesis and prepared dedications for the works of others, occasionally editing volumes penned by his clerical colleagues. Gataker's most enduring work is his edition of Marcus Aurelius's *Meditations* with commentary, on which he worked for forty years. The work is praised by modern scholars as one of the monuments of seventeenth-century Classical scholarship. Gataker worked up until his death from fever at age seventy-nine on July 27th, 1654, leaving three works yet to be published. He outlived four wives and a son, but was survived by a sister, a son and a daughter. Gataker was buried in his church with no stone to mark his grave."

This brief description leaves out much of the excitement which surrounded Gataker's long life. Born during the reign of the firmly protestant Queen Elizabeth, as a teenager in London he would have experienced the turmoil and horror which the threat of the Spanish Armada posed in 1588. Religious upheaval had been significant in the life of Thomas's father, also a Thomas, but he spelled his surname in the more traditional form of Gatacre. Brook's *Lives of the Puritans* tells us that Thomas senior (1531 – 93) was from a well-off family in rural Shropshire. They were 'zealous papists' and did not take well their son's conversion to the new reformed religion of Henry VIII. To draw him back into the old religion he was sent to the Catholic University of Louvain. It was to no avail; Thomas senior persisted with his views, going on to be an ordained minister in the established Church, becoming vicar of the London parish of St Edmunds in Lombard Street. He is also recorded as being an MP during the reign of the staunchly Catholic Mary I. At the time Mary was married to Philip of Spain and it was he who would later send the Armada against England in a doomed attempt to depose Elizabeth and return the country to the old religion. (Later, Gataker (junior) would preach *An anniversarie memoriall of Englands delivery from the Spanish invasion: delivered in a sermon on Psalm xlviii. 7, 8* published in 1626, but presumably given in other years too.)

Following the death of Elizabeth in 1603 and the installation of James Stuart as King James I, religious matters remained unsettled. Thomas Gataker (junior, author of this book) had by then become a preacher at Lincoln's Inn, which was a centre for lawyers in London. Following the failed Catholic plot in November 1605 by Guy Fawkes and other 'Gunpowder Plotters' to blow up Parliament with King James and his sons within it, there was a great trial in London of the remaining plotters in January 1606 followed by their gruesome executions.

In 1611 Gataker moved down-river to his parish at Rotherhithe, where he was to remain as incumbent until he died 43 years later. Far from being a backwater, Rotherhithe was a busy port, one of the principal landing points for London itself*. Among his parishioners were many sea-captains and their families. One such was Christopher Jones, who captained and part-owned the *Mayflower* when it set off in 1620 initially from Rotherhithe. Their mission was to deliver the Pilgrim Fathers, a group of Puritans who felt they could no longer practice their religion in England, to Chesapeake Bay in Massachusetts. There they eventually succeeded in establishing a religiously pure colony. Captain Jones returned later with the *Mayflower* and is buried in the churchyard of St Mary's, Rotherhithe.

It was about this time in 1619, at the age of 45 that Gataker first went into print with the first edition of this book. Thereafter his rate of publication was substantial, but, according to Willen (2007) it falls into two bursts: The first burst lasted up to 1627 when he published many texts on religious themes. One of these, *Marriage duties* from 1620 seems still to be of interest and it can be read as a semi-

---

* Rotherhithe today is a delightful enclave in East London, with the Mayflower Pub a pleasant stop-off, after visiting the nearby church-yard of St Mary's where Gataker was vicar. The church you see today dates from after Gataker's time.

modernised text at: http://www.usask.ca/english/gataker/gat_intro.html (from where the brief biography of Gataker, above, was taken.)

With the advent of Bishop Laud such puritan works fell out of favour. It was only later in 1640 with the turmoil which came before and during the English Civil War that Gataker was able to resume his publications. This War which broke out in 1642, was seen as a power struggle between King and Parliament, but it was also a battle about the form of Protestantism to be adopted, with Cromwell's Puritan tendency prevailing in the end. Gataker was, as stated above, involved in defining the forms of worship for the new dispensation. But his revolutionary zeal had its limits: when it was proposed to execute the King for his crimes against the State, Gataker and others were moved, in 1648, to pen a defence of His Majesty in a letter which was sent to Cromwell and his Council. Despite this opposition, Gataker lived on in his ministry until he died. Finally at his funeral, the eulogy which was preached by Simeon Ashe (pub. 1655) was titled: *Gray Hayres crowned with Grace.*

Publications by Gataker and others on lotteries and other matters

Using entries from the British Library (BL) catalogue we can follow the publishing history of books on the subject of uses and abuses of lotteries around this time. Prior to Gataker's 1619 first edition *Of the nature and use of lots* (the original title), the Rev James Balmford had, in 1593, published *A Short and Plaine Dialogue concerning the unlawfulnes of playing at Cards or Tables, or any other game consisting in chance, etc.*. When in 1619 Gataker published his work, Balmford saw fit (in 1623) to re-publish his work, adding: *With a reply to the criticisms of Thomas Gataker in his "A Just Defence"*. Clearly some form of dialogue had gone on between these two reverend gentlemen, because Gataker's: *A just defence of certaine passages in a former treatise concerning the nature and use of lots, against such exceptions ... as have been made thereunto by Mr J. B[almford], etc* was also listed as published in 1623, although given an earlier date (in 1623) by the BL catalogue. Then finally in 1627 came the second edition of Gataker's *Of the nature and use of lots... Enlarged with addition of answer to some further arguments; by the author.* which forms the basis for this current updating and editing.

For most of the rest of his life Gataker's publications stayed with religious themes, but close to his death, he engaged in one last controversy which touched on his earlier theme of the unlawfulness of the use of divination. Annoyed by the comments of Lilly*, a widely consulted astrologer, concerning the use of alma-

* William Lilly (1602 –1681), was a famed English astrologer and occultist of his time. He was particularly adept at interpreting the astrological charts drawn up for horary questions. He caused much controversy in 1666 for allegedly having predicted the Great Fire of London some 14 years before it happened. For this reason many people believed that he may have started the fire, but there is no evidence to support these claims. He was tried for the offence in Parliament, but found to be innocent.

nacs, he produced his rebuttal (Gataker, 1653) ... *his vindication ... against the scurrilous aspersions of ... W. Lillie. ... wherein the pretended grounds of judiciary astrologie and the scripture proofes produced for it, are discussed and refuted.* Gataker was sounding off again in 1654 (published posthumously) with *A Discours apologetical, wherein Lilies lewd and lowd Lies in his Merlin or pasqil for the yeer 1654 are cleerly laid open ... his shameless slander fullie refuted ...*

Even after he died, Gataker's views on lotteries was still capable of provoking a response, this time by Leonhard van Ryssen of Utrecht, Holland in 1660: *Veritas secundum pietatem de Lusu Aleæ, a ... T. Gattakeri vindicate.* The curiously named Increase Mather* of Harvard University tried, in his 1687 anti-gambling treatise, to use references to Gataker to support his case for a total ban on gambling, claiming that Balmford had refuted his case and that Gataker had recanted. A mis-reading I think, but such academic disputation is nothing new. As late at 1773, we learn that the great Dr Samuel Johnson "amused himself with reading Gataker On Lots" rather than exploring Scotland (Boswell, 1784). Boswell continues: "on our return he told us, he had been so much engaged by Gataker, that he had never missed us."

Gataker makes a re-appearance in 1865 in the highly influential *History of the rise and influence of the spirit of rationalism in Europe* by W E H Lecky: "The first writer, I believe, who clearly and systematically maintained that lots were governed by purely natural laws, was an English Puritan minister named Gataker, in a work *On the Nature and Use of Different Kinds of Lots* [sic](London, 1619) – a well-reasoned and curious book, teeming with quaint learning." Later in 1971 Keith Thomas picked up on Lecky's ideas with his *Religion and the decline of magic* which was a set text on many university courses. He too, refers to Gataker, who he says, was the first systematic exponent of the modern view that lotteries any more than any other events were not any form of divine providence.

So this present work of Gataker on the nature and uses of lotteries (or *Of the nature and use of lots* to give it its original title) "stands in a class of its own [amongst his religious publications] and was arguably his most original work" (Willen, 2007). It is a surprising exception to the much greater corpus of his overtly puritan religious writings, but shows a remarkable opening of a mind to a practical reality which he discovered around him.

Why Gataker undertook this book

Why Gataker should venture into such contentious territory is not obvious. In his Introduction he explains that he had a two-fold necessity to write about it: Firstly, because many of those who had heard him preach on the subject had urged him to commit his ideas to print. But he also felt a necessity to defend himself against

---

* Increase Mather was also a major figure in the Salem witchcraft trials. Gataker too, condemned 'witchery' (see Ch 11, §7), but as a form of lottery used to predict the future, not the witchtcraft of consorting with the Devil through 'familiars' like domestic cats.

"unchristian slanders and uncharitable censures to tax and defame both me and it". This does not explain why he got involved in questions about the use of lotteries in the first place, nor why he concluded: that using divisory lots was acceptable; that gambling was not in itself wicked; but that special or extraordinary lotteries to divine God's will could never be justified.

Towards the end of Chapter 9 he explains this in more detail: that it was only by private study of the Bible that he produced his conclusions, never intending to publish. Later, he says, he was induced to publish for **four** reasons (Gataker is very fond of enumerating arguments and reasons!): Firstly, he wants to neither widen nor narrow the interpretation of scripture – this is surely a dig at Balmford and the other 'adversaries' who took a too narrow view. Secondly, god-fearing Christians he knows partake innocently in games of chance and want to be reassured that such normal activity is not sinful. Thirdly, using a lottery to decide the serious matter of dividing up property was, as Gataker acknowledges, his first encounter with the use of lotteries. If a total ban on religious grounds was enforced, then this useful tool would be unavailable to settle disputes. This, as Gataker puts it "required me to narrowly search and sift out the nature of lotteries in general." Fourthly considering the vehemence of those who rail against any use of gambling he felt that a more charitable view should be put forward: that such games which are so widely used perhaps should be discouraged but should not be condemned.

Here we see the mind, not of an over-zealous puritan, but a moderate, rational modern man at work. In later life Gataker achieved a reputation for assertive argumentation (Willen, 2007), which is also apparent here. But the reasonableness also shines through when he had encountered the moderate practice of gambling being used by members of what Willen calls the 'godly community'. It is tempting to think that using lotteries to decide contentious issues may have first come to his notice among the sea-captains at the docks in Rotherhithe when they were dividing the booty from an expedition. More likely it was from the lawyers at Lincoln's Inn that he had his first experience of this device, with litigants seeking spiritual advice on the use of lottery to decide their disagreements. His reaction was not to jump to conclusions, nor accept the conventional puritanical wisdom as preached by Balmford. Instead he choose to study the question for many years and only formed conclusions when he was certain of his case.

Gataker's Language: my form of modernising:

My aim in modernising this re-publication is to make it accessible to a much wider readership, mainly because I believe that there is much in this book that is interesting and well worth learning about. In its original form, as published, Gataker's book is difficult to read, due to the spellings, unfamiliar use of letters but above all the archaic language. It may seem like sacrilege to modernise the expression of language of an author who didn't just live in the age of Shakespeare but also the King James Bible, those twin jewels of the English language. No it is even worse! Gataker lived close by the Globe theatre and could have walked there of an afternoon to take in a play, with the Bard of Stratford amongst the players*. Gataker must also have been acquainted with members of the committee who worked at King James's command to produce a user-friendly (as we would say) version of the Bible, although they were Oxford men and he had attended Cambridge University. Nevertheless, I am convinced that Gataker was writing, not a great work of literature, but an accessible guide and explanation for his own parishioners and other educated readers of the godly community of his own time. The fact that he wrote in English rather than Latin shows that it was intended, not for the pan-European intelligentsia, but as a guide for his own people. Converting his archaic language into 'newspaper-article' contemporary style is, I believe, in line with what Gataker wanted to achieve in publishing his treatise.

Some changes to the original text were quick and easy: letters such as 'u' could be replaced by 'v'; letter 's' in the form of cursive 'f' could similarly be treated. Gataker's spelling was antiquated, but generally consistent; replacing with up-to-date spelling was straightforward. Some strange features like the German double-ess *(ß)* cropped up in the second edition, but present no difficulty. (Gataker was also interested in the forms of language, writing a treatise about diphthongs in later life.)

Punctuation was another peculiarity: the comma was used where today the full-stop (US period) is normal. The apostrophe was never used, hence the construct 'Jonas his house' where we would say 'Jonas's house'. Gataker didn't use abbreviations in the main text, but footnotes are another story. Indicating footnotes (or marginalia as they are usually called in these antique documents) does not follow modern ideas. Although small superscript letters (sometimes numbers) were used to indicate a footnote, they appeared *before* item referred to, not afterwards as is customary. I explain in the Bibliographical Notes section at the end of this book what the nature and content of these footnotes was and how I have dealt with them.

But it is perhaps to the expression of the ideas and the language itself as used by Gataker where I have made the most drastic changes. All of us who laboured over the plays of Shakespeare are familiar with the difficulty of comprehending them, even after several re-readings. I have replaced some archaic words by modern equivalents, but they are relatively few in number. The English language has changed much since those days, not least in the way sentences are structured. Editing this book I was struck by the 'Germanic' style, with verbs coming at the end. This is the main alteration that I have made to the language of Gataker, generally turning the sentences around so that they are more easily comprehensible.

Gataker was guilty of writing very long sentences, with many conditional subclauses being interposed between the initial subject and the final conclusion. This

---

* although it would not have been proper for a divine to attend. In one diatribe, Gataker rails against "brothels and playhouses" obviously seeing little difference between them.

often comes across like an extract from a sermon. Tempting though it was, I have not condensed the text. I have retained every sentence, only altering a few sentences to break them up into shorter ones to ease the burden of understanding. I have generally retained Gataker's paragraph numbering, so if you want to compare my rendition with Gatker's original you will usually be able to identify it easily, although in some cases his paragraph numbers changed between editions. Gataker only numbered his sections: I have invented titles for each section and added them on; this I think helps greatly in comprehension (and in skipping over the dull bits).

Some explanation is called for with some of the words which I have changed:

'Casual', 'casualty': are used to denote randomness and a random event. Both of these words have acquired quite different meanings today and are capable of being confused with 'causality', so I have changed most of them to randomness or random event.

'Lots' as in the biblical *'casting lots':* again there are possibilities for confusion and misunderstanding, so I have changed this throughout to 'lottery'.

'Gambling' as a word was not in use in Gataker's time. His expression *'lusurious lots'* was so delightful, that I was very tempted to retain it. No! We must say what we mean, even avoiding the euphemistic labels of 'gaming' or 'sports'. Gambling is what it is and our modern word expresses precisely what Gataker meant.

Gataker's references

What you have here is less than half the book that Gataker wrote. His pages show large amounts of footnotes. Of course he needed to bolster his case by showing off his own great intellect. He was well known for his prodigious learning and this certainly shows in these notes. I have not included the full text of all these notes for a number of reasons: Firstly the practical: they are in small print and often very difficult to read. They are mostly in Latin, Greek or sometimes Hebrew, of which I have small knowledge and would not wish to burden the reader with*. Gataker uses a system of abbreviations for the names of the authors referred to, which he nowhere explains. Some are easy to identify, for example *Cic.* is surely *Cicero*; others not so: who is *Aret.,* who features quite regularly?

I have not ignored the footnotes altogether, despite the difficulties. Readers of this modernised text would, I imagine, still like to know the source of Gataker's information. As I see it, the footnotes fall into three groups: Biblical, Classical and Contemporary:

* Expecting great learning from the reader is a custom which persisted into Victorian times: J W Headlam-Morley's 1891 *Election by lot at Athens* had references not only in Latin and Greek but included French, German and Italian extracts, *all un-translated!* It is also a vital reference for those wishing to find out more about the true nature of the origins of democracy.

The Biblical references are perhaps easiest to deal with and are to be found in abundance, which is hardly surprising given the Reverend Gataker's calling. Although his references are as usual abbreviated, they are not difficult to decipher. Further, the system of *{Book Chapter: Verse}*, for example *(Proverbs 16: 33)* is still in use today and many websites give easy-to-use parallel versions of the Bible. (I have drawn on http://bible.cc/) One oddity is Gataker's version. Although, as mentioned before, he was around while the KJV (King James Version) Bible was being produced, he used a different, but very similar English translation. Often Gataker gives several citations for the same incident because they can be found in different books of the Bible. To keep matters simple I normally give a single reference; the other references can easily be found on-line. At other times Gataker seems to draw on Holy Scripture simply for a telling phrase or expression rather than factual support. I have not included these references.

Classical references also abound, with Gataker drawing on the ancient Latin and Greek authors. He is wont to give the full original text in its original Latin or Greek (the compositors of his book must have had a fiendishly difficult job in setting up the print for this treatise!) Such displays of erudition must surely have impressed what Gataker called his 'adversaries', who were also men of learning. Again, it would seem that many of these references were used for their turns of phrase, rather than any support they gave to the argument; these I have omitted. More important and included, are references which provide factual evidence, for example of the use of lottery selection in Athenian or Roman government. Because of the cryptic nature of Gataker's references, I have included these as a name only, thus *(Cicero)* without the publication details. For those who need to find exact references, accessible modern versions of the classical texts are a more practical method. Gataker sometimes uses a general description of 'heathen' about these writers which can be confusing because he also picks up on the behaviour of recognisably heathen people, such as the un-Christianised German tribes. Under the heading of 'Classical references' I also include the writings of the early Church Fathers, such as *Augustine*.

'Contemporary' relates to authors who lived in Gataker's own time, or in his recent past. Many of these were scholarly and writing in Latin which was then the norm throughout Europe. A particular problem for Gataker was how to deal with 'popish' (as he often styled them) writers, that is writers who still held to the unreformed Roman Catholic faith. If they were pre-Reformation then they could be admitted without qualm. But what if they were avowed Catholics, antagonistic to Protestantism, such as *Delrio,* reputedly the 'popish' cleric who brought the Inquisition to the Low Countries? Gataker in references warns of their popery, but is otherwise respectful of their knowledge and wisdom. This note of inter-denominational respect is, I feel, a mark of the progressive and tolerant nature of Gataker, perhaps even out of deference to the beliefs of his grandparents. This attitude of openness also allowed him to approach the use of lotteries with a similar un-prejudiced mind. Of course the writings of *Calvin* and *Zwingli* presented no such difficulty.

Perhaps the most interesting of the 'contemporary' references are those in English, generally not on any religious theme, rather describing interesting facts. For these authors I have made the greatest effort to identify who they are and what they wrote. For this the catalogue of the British Library is a great boon.

In the text I have identified references in italics: *(Proverbs 16:33)* for Biblical, *Cicero* for the Classical and a more conventional *Hackluyt (1560)* for the Contemporary. For some of these 'modern' references I have been unable to discover any information: for these I have used the somewhat infelicitous *n/k* meaning year not known; so, *Dartes (n/k)*. Others where the year is known with some uncertainty are shown as *(Landulfus, ~1498)*. All the information given in this section has been garnered from internet sources. No specific references for sources are given, but all can be easily double-checked using Google etc. Sometimes Gataker's spellings and abbreviations have made it difficult to precisely identify sources. I may have mis-identified a few, and there are still some such as *Dartes* and *Aret.*. which remain a mystery to me. (At least you will have an identifiable name in full, correctly spelled to work with. Good luck, and if you find any further information, I would be glad to hear about it.)

I have avoided the use of references in footnotes, a practice I find very distracting, although much beloved of lawyers and historians. **Any footnotes which appear are comments or explanations added by me to Gataker's text.**

Gataker's dilemmas: why his book was contentious

The main controversial themes:

Using divisory lotteries: To our modern understanding there seems nothing wrong with, by mutual consent, using a lottery to share resources. Such an arrangement can be efficient, avoiding the need for complex rules or the employment of arbitrators. It can be fair, giving each member of a syndicate an equal (or measured) chance. When it comes to sharing out burdens, lotteries can also be used with similar effectiveness. Even if scientific ideas about random chance would not be formalised for another half-century or more, there was then an intuitive idea what it meant. Gataker devotes much of the first two chapters of his book to explaining, as best he can what he means by 'chance event'. The problem with using such lotteries arose because, as Duxbury (p20) puts it: "…Gataker departed radically from the orthodox puritan opinion by claiming that it is not divine law but the laws of nature that determine the outcomes of lotteries." This contradicts, according to Duxbury (p18) Aquinas's position on the lottery which suggests that it was regarded in medieval times as a means of getting God to speak. Since God knows all outcomes then using a lottery is tantamount to inviting, even requiring God to adjudicate. As the oft-quoted Psalm has it "The lot is cast into the lap; but the whole disposing thereof is of the LORD" *(KJV Proverbs*

16: 33) It took a brave, or very intelligent, or maybe very conceited person to challenge this seemingly clear-cut biblical admonition. Gataker had some ammunition against his critics: he was able, for example, to quote the case of Calvinist ministers in Geneva being chosen by lottery to visit the sick when pestilence was rife.

Gambling: Making the case in favour of gambling and other games of chance was a much weightier challenge and indeed it occupies the entire middle half of the book. It was not just the case that gambling, which invariably makes use of some uncertain random event, seemed to involve the calling down of God for frivolous uses. The act of gambling was associated with many forms of debauchery and led to behaviour which could only be described as sinful. Objections to gambling and even laws to prohibit gambling altogether were not just a concern to right-thinking people 400 years ago; they are still of concern today and despite the ever-rising availability of gambling outlets there remain some who see gambling as essentially corrupting and sinful.

Gataker's core argument in favour of gambling was this: just because something is associated with sacred uses, does not mean all uses of it are sacred. His example was water: used in the sacraments for sacred use, it is also widely used for drinking, washing, flushing even. No-one would argue against the use of water in this way. Nor should the use of random chance in gambling be condemned, only the misuses that surround it. Recreation of all sorts is a necessity and so long as any recreation is not turned into a profession and is used in moderation it is good and can be beneficial.

Divinatory lotteries: The simple theological case is that the Bible gives several examples where some form of lottery ('casting lots' is the usual expression) had been sanctioned: these include dividing out lands, deciding on sacrifices, deciding what action to take in battle and many more. These were examples of what Gataker calls 'extraordinary lots', lotteries with explicit divine approval. Gataker does not accept that such divinatory lotteries have any place in contemporary life.

The argument is complex and perhaps the theological aspects may seem arcane and irrelevant. Firstly, Gataker tries to minimise the importance of many of the biblical cases cited, that they were not really extraordinary lotteries, or that they involved heathens. Hence the likelihood of a repeat calling by God to decide some issue using a lottery in our own times is so far-fetched as to render it unthinkable.

Gataker reserves fuller condemnation of those who deliberately call on God or the deity of 'Fortuna' to decide their fate. His arguments fall into two categories: calling down deities opens the door to the devil, who will gladly pervert its users: or, there is no power in the forms of divination used, so it is all a waste of time. Gataker does not try to resolve the contradiction between these two cases.

What you can learn about in this treatise

Of course the one thing that you will *not* fully experience is how different the English language looked and sounded 400 years ago. Curiosities of spelling have been ironed out and odd-sounding phrases and constructions have been straightened out. Verbs have been modernised with, for example, 'seemeth' replaced by 'seems'. The erudite look and feel of an early 17th century book with its dense marginalia in classical languages has all gone and if that is what you want to see, then you must go to one of the libraries which hold this ancient treatise. You can also find it on the website of Early English Books On-line (requires password access). However you will still find some of the archaic style of language in this modernised version, but not so much (I trust) as to interfere with your understanding of the argument that Gataker was trying to put across.

As a learned man of his times, Gataker was very comfortable with the classical Latin and Greek authors and you will learn a great deal about them in this book. He draws heavily on their writings and we get elaborate descriptions of the uses of lotteries in the governance of both Rome, but especially of Athens. Again, all of these examples are well known and can be found in commentaries of our times (for example Elster, Headlam-Morley, Dowlen, Barnett). But whereas writers of our times view this as drawing from the inspired wisdom of the originators of de mocracy, Gataker takes a more sanguine view of these 'heathen' authors.

He is also aware and gives good accounts of later uses of lotteries in the contemporary (to Gataker) government of Florence and Venice, although Gataker sees this as a merely 'divisory' aspect. It seems to have passed his notice that here, and especially at ancient Athens there was a template for a democratic society, an alternative to electoral politics. It is one of the great treasures of this book to realise just how much was already known about the use of the lottery as a democratic device at those times. There have been many modern attempts to do something about the malaise of democracy by introducing some element of random selection. Most commentators start with the ideas of Callenbach and Phillips in 1985, or the seminal book by Burnheim also in 1985. It would be invidious of me not to mention the works in this field of Goodwin (2005) and Sutherland (2004) (invidious because they are my editor and publisher respectively!). More recently (2006) O'Leary has added to this growing literature. Gataker himself did not have much to say about this. He observes that lottery-choosing of officials is to be found more in republics than monarchies. In the Putney debates which took place two decades later during the Civil War, Gataker would have been, I am sure, against the radically democratic ideas of the Levellers and supportive of the firm autocratic government of a king, or in his absence the autocratic Cromwell.

Of more technical interest in the book is how chance and probability were understood in those times*. It would be another half-century before Pascal and Fermat gave scientific expression to these concepts. Gataker, as Duxbury (1999)

* Stigler (1986) gives a good explanation of these development, including the ideas about probability extant at the time of Gataker.

said, stood on the cusp between an age which believed that everything was the result of direct divine intervention and the more modern view that God knows all, but only intervenes in special ways on rare occasions. This is especially apt when discussing the outcome of a random event which is then used for some ulterior reason: does God know all and control all? (old thinking) or is there a general providence at work where God is indifferent to such outcomes? (new thinking).

Statisticians would quibble with Gataker's habit of lumping together genuinely random events like the roll of a fair die, with the haphazard event of having one's hat blown off. This perhaps betrays a fundamental misunderstanding between scientific knowledge and the intuitive understanding of random events. It could be argued that Gataker, along with the ancient Athenians and even the man-in-the-pub playing cross-and-pile have a very good understanding of the unpredictability, yet fairness in chances of outcomes which a 'casualty' or random event produces an answer.

Cross-and-pile (a form of coin-tossing) is one of the many games of chance that Gataker refers to. His book should also be of interest to those who study the history of gambling. Some games which were used for gambling also involved an element of skill, or might not involve the wagering of money. Gataker includes all of these under the heading of 'gambling' (or 'lusurious lots' to use his expression). This may seem to cast the net too wide, scooping up innocent pastimes with the wicked, but Gataker argues that they all involve random chance, and the winner's prize is still valued even if it is not money. Another useful service which Gataker provides is to list all the laws which had been enacted in England against gambling (in this he was no doubt helped by his earlier incumbency at Lincoln's Inn, and his contacts with the lawyers there.)

One curiosity in this book about the use of lotteries is the complete lack of comment by Gataker on the state lotteries being organised in his own time: in 1567 Queen Elizabeth I established the first English state lottery. Prizes include cash, plate and tapestry, with 400,000 tickets offered for sale. In 1612 King James I of England, by royal decree, created a lottery in London. The proceeds were used to aid the first British colony in America – Jamestown, Virginia. Interestingly, Anglican churches held two of three winning tickets for the first draw. (Spofford, 1891; Farebrother, 1999). Further lotteries were held in 1627, 1631, 1638 to fund schemes to bring water to London. Is it possible that Gataker did not recognise these as games of chance?

For his long and unremitting condemnation of the use of divination Gataker brings forward many examples of the attempted use of this method. They form an amusing collection of fraudulent hocus-pocus. Again one might quibble that Gataker spreads his net too widely, including all forms of pretended magic, not all of which involve the use of lotteries. No doubt all those who read this book today would echo Gataker's admonition that trying to read the signs by looking at patterns in the entrails of animals is futile, because it does not work. God will not intervene in these trivial pursuits, however much He is invoked. But would we agree that such divination is also sinful, that giving a shred of credence to the daily astrological predictions is not just a bit of harmless (and useless) fun, but is also a bad thing to do? Irrationality remains rife in today's society, despite the best efforts of scientists to explain. Just as Gataker sermonised against the use of the occult, so modern-day alternative thinkers seem immune from this form of rationality.

But it is the defence of gambling for which Gataker's book is mainly renowned. In this he was a lonely voice making the case that moderate gambling as a form of recreation was not sinful and indeed could be beneficial. Again in today's moral climate this would not seem exceptional. The clergy no longer condemn gambling as inherently sinful and something which should never be permitted. But this change is fairly recent: traditionally and especially amongst the nonconformists gambling (and drink) were vehemently opposed. In that sense Gataker failed; he did not convince the clergy to accept gambling as a normal activity. But his arguments, based as they are on a mixture of pragmatism and theology still bear re-examination. It is a contentious issue and the easy availability of 24-hour casinos in every city again raises some moral questions.

Perhaps of less general interest is Gataker's discussion of divisory lotteries. This is a pity, not least because it is my own major field of particular interest in this treatise! I am sure no theological case would today be made against two consenting businessmen agreeing to use a lottery to divide out shared goods. To that extent Gataker's arguments have been superseded. But his (and my) case that this can also be a wise and practical method of deciding remains, and is worth exploring. Again it is the wealth of examples of this practice that may be the most interesting aspect of this section of Gataker's book. Some of these lotteries involve the selection of people for jobs within organisations. Here Gataker makes a particular distinction: while it is perfectly proper to use this procedure for government jobs, it must not be used for religious appointments. Again scripture seems to contradict him, but his explanation is that examples of appointments at the Jewish temple were not to select the priests, only to divide their tasks amongst themselves

Much of this book consists of arguments from the fields of philosophy or theology. I am sure Gataker's exposition was sound, because there were others, equally erudite who wished to dismiss his case, such as his arch-adversary James Balmford who would gladly have pointed out any mistakes. Whether the theological arguments remain of validity or even interest is moot. Clearly the blanket condemnation of the use of lotteries for any purpose is no longer the dominant view of religiously minded Christians. Perhaps the philosophical argumentation in this book may prove to be more resilient with the passage of time.

My experience and understanding of the text

My interest in this book stems from an obsession about what Gataker called 'divisory lotteries'. Many years ago I came across a paper by Aubert (1959) which included a description of the method of choosing the two *capitani regenti* – the rulers of San Marino. They were drawn from a short-list of 12 (six pairs) during a ceremony at the basilica each March. This led me on to investigate other uses of lotteries to distribute goods and bads, which culminated in 2003 when I began to investigate this as a research degree in the Economics Department at Swansea University, Wales. (Final M Phil title: *Who gets the prize: The case for random distribution in non-market allocation, 2006)*. As I trawled through the references, especially in Duxbury, Broome, Elster and Goodwin there were a number of comments about Gataker, with references back to this seminal work. According to Elster (1987) after Gataker there had been no significant work published on the general idea of the use of lotteries in social affairs for over 300 years.

So in undertaking this modernisation of Gataker and re-presenting for scholars and others to access and learn from, I can claim a good understanding of the ideas associated with divisory lots. I have in my time been a lecturer in Statistics and Economics. To encourage more interest in statistical ideas about divisory lots I produced a paper in 1998 which was read at the Royal Statistical Society, London *Organisations selecting people: How the process could be made fairer by the appropriate use of lotteries.* A knowledge of statistics is highly appropriate in understanding the nature of a 'fair' lottery. Gataker was writing half a century before Pascal and Fermat had established scientific ideas about probability and chance, so his use of words like 'casual' and 'casualty' are understandable if somewhat vague. With my knowledge of statistical theory I hope that have been able to correctly interpret and convey the meanings that Gataker intended.

My own upbringing in Ireland in the 1950s was intensely religious, being taught by Franciscan monks in a deeply catholic country. I no longer practice, but retain much of what I learned, which has helped in understanding Gataker. The effect of my lessons in Latin and Greek have long since faded, so translating the plethora of footnotes is beyond me. But the lessons in Christian doctrine may have been useful, if for no other reason than familiarity with concepts like 'occasions of sin' which Gataker sometimes alludes to (when discussing gambling). I am quite taken by the openness and lack of rancour with which Gataker refers to my co-religionists. Although the epithet 'papist' may be somewhat derogatory, for a man of his times he uses it sparingly and without malice (although in some of his later writings he inveighed against catholic doctrines such as transubstantiation).

Despite the best efforts of the Franciscan monks who were my teachers I would not claim to be in any way knowledgeable or expert in theology. Nor would I claim to understand (or at times sympathise with) arguments of a philosophical nature. I am admitting to this, because a great deal of Gataker's argument is of a theological and philosophical nature. In pursuing the modernisation of the text I hope I have not done an injustice to the arguments; in many cases I found these not to be easy to comprehend, so have rendered them as best I can.

In a somewhat unrelated sphere, I can lay claim to some significant knowledge of events which were happening in London and elsewhere in England whilst Gataker was preacher at Lincoln's Inn (prior to taking up his post at Rotherhithe). In 1605 a dastardly Plot was uncovered to blow up the Houses of Parliament, with the King and the Lords with them. The aim of the plotters was to restore England to Catholicism. I was interested in this as a historical event because of the religious angle. Even more interesting to me was that the plotters came mostly from the English Midlands. At the time in the 1960s I was a newly arrived immigrant working as an engineer in a car-parts factory in Birmingham. This led in 1994 to a guide book for walkers and cyclists *In the footsteps of the Gunpowder Plotters: A journey through history in middle England.* When the Plot was foiled, the remaining plotters fled through and past their great houses which lay in an arc to the South and West of Birmingham. There have been many conspiracy theories about this plot, which mainly centre on the machinations of the Lord Chancellor. What is inarguable is that the squashing of this plot was turned into an anti-catholic propaganda event by the wily English establishment. Sermons were regularly preached and bonfires lit to give thanks for the deliverance of Protestant England from the catholic menace.

So I have some knowledge of some of the topics Gataker discusses and of the times he lived in. I would acknowledge my weaknesses in the realms of theology and philosophy and apologise in advance for any misrepresentations I may have made. As to the other aspects of his work I believe I have particular understanding and expertise to be able to interpret what he is saying. Gataker produced a book on the subject of the uses of lotteries which is lucid, well-structured, and makes use of copious examples to underpin and illustrate his points. The theological arguments may be over-long and of much less relevance today, but the rest of the work is fascinating, full of delightful descriptions and asides. I was so taken with the work that I had begun the process of updating it so that it could appeal to a much wider readership. When Keith Sutherland of Imprint Academic asked me to prepare it for re-publication, under the editorship of Barbara Goodwin I was delighted to take up the challenge. It has been quite a slog (helped by the poor Summer of 2007!), but I hope others will find the Reverend Gataker's treatise as readable, entertaining and illuminating as I have. I would like to thank James Maw at Swansea for his unfailing patience and practical help; also Peter Stone of Stanford and Lyn Carson of Sydney for their useful and encouraging comments, together with all the other correspondents on the Kleroterian mailing list – a group of people world-wide, who are interested in the use of randomness in social affairs. The support and encouragement of both Keith Sutherland and Barbra Goodwin have been essential in seeing this project through to completion and I take this opportunity to thank them for it. And so, dear reader, (somewhat as Gataker himself puts it in his Introduction) I humbly hope that you will accept my poor and ineffectual labourings in modernising the work of that most erudite divine.

References used in this Preface:

Titles with * are being published/re-published by Imprint Academic along with this present work.

Ashe, Simeon (1655) with the title: *Gray Hayres crowned with Grace. A sermon preached at Redriff, Aug. 1. 1654. At the funerall of ... Mr. Thomas Gataker.* was published in 1655.

Aubert, Vilhelm (1959) Chance in social affairs *Inquiry* 2(1) 1959 1 – 24

Balmford, James (1593) *A Short and Plaine Dialogue concerning the vnlawfulnes of playing at Cards or Tables, or any other game consisting in chance, etc.* Richard Boile: London,

Balmford, James. (1623) *A Short and Plaine Dialogue concerning the vnlawfulnes of playing at Cards or Tables, or any other game consisting in chance, etc* Another edition.] [With a reply to the criticisms of Thomas Gataker in his "A Just Defence,". *Ellen Boyle: London.*

*Barnett, Anthony & Carty, Peter (1998) *The Athenian option: An idea whose time is coming* London: Demos

Boswell, James (1784) *The journal of a tour to the Hebrides with Samuel Johnson LlD available on-line:*
http://www.visionofbritain.org.uk/text/chap_page.jsp?t_id=Boswell&c_id=14

Boyle, Conall (1994) *In the footsteps of the Gunpowder Plotters: A journey through history in Middle England* Warley, West Midlands, England: Meridian Books

Boyle Conall (1998) Organizations selecting people: how the process could be made fairer by the appropriate use of lotteries *The Statistician* 47 Part 2, pp 291 – 321 London: Royal Statistical Society

Boyle, Conall (2006) *Who gets the prize: The case for random distribution in non-market allocation* M Phil thesis, University of Wales, Swansea

Brook, Benjamin (1813) *The Lives of the puritans: Containing a biographical account of those divines who distinguished themselves in the cause of religious liberty from the Reformation under Queen Elizabeth to the Act of Uniformity 1662.* (in three parts) London James Black Full text at: http://books.google.co.uk/books?id=-ZUrLyZm8F8C&pg=PA1&dq=lives+of+the+puritans

Broome, John (1984) Uncertainty and fairness *The Economic Journal* 94 Sept 84 624 – 632

Broome, John (1984b) Selecting people randomly *Ethics* Oct 84 p38 – 55

Broome, John (1994) Fairness versus Doing the most Good *Hastings Center Report* July-August 1994 p36 – 39

Broome, John (1990) Fairness *The Aristotelian Society* meeting 3 Dec 1990

Burnheim, John (1985) *Is democracy possible? The alternative to electoral politics* Cambridge UK Polity Press

*Callenbach, Ernest & Phillips, Michael (1985) *A Citizen Legislature A modest proposal for the random selection of legislators* Berkeley/Bodega, California Banyan, Tree Books

Cooley, Ronald W (supervising editor to on-line version of Gataker's *Marriage Duties briefly couched together; out of Colossians, 3, 18, 19* which includes the biography quoted here, as well as a Bibliography of books by and about Gataker. http://www.usask.ca/english/gataker/index.html

*Dowlen, Oliver (2006) *The Political Potential of Sortition.* D Phil Thesis, Oxford, New College

Duxbury, Neil (1999) *Random justice – on lotteries and legal decision-making* Oxford, Clarendon Press

Elster, Jon (1987) Taming chance: Randomization in individual and social decisions *Tanner lecture on Human Values, Brasenose College Oxford May 6,7, 1987 from* www.tannerlectures.utah.edu/lectures/Elster88.pdf

Elster, Jon (1989) *Solomonic judgements: studies in the limitations of rationality* Cambridge UP

Elster, Jon (1992) *Local justice: how institutions allocate scarce goods and necessary burdens* NY Russell Sage

Farebrother, Richard William (1999) A brief history of the British national lottery 1567 – 1826 *Chance* Vol 3 No 1 p27 – 31

Gataker, Thomas (1619) *Of the nature and use of lots: A treatise historical and theological*

Gataker, Thomas (1623) *A just defence of certaine passages in a former treatise concerning the nature and use of lots, against such exceptions ... as have been made thereunto by Mr J. B(almford), etc*

Gataker, Thomas (1627) *Of the nature and use of lots: A treatise historical and theologicall 2e*

Gataker, Thomas et al (1648) *A Serious and Faithfull Representation of the Judgements of Ministers of the Gospell within the Province of London. Contained in a Letter from them to the Generall and his Councell of Warre.* Delivered to his Excellency by some of the Subscribers, Jan. 18. 1648. [Dated Jan. 17, 1648. [o.s.] Signed by Thomas Gataker and many others.]

Gataker, Thomas (1653) ... *his vindication of the Annotations [on Jer. x. 2] by him published ... against the scurrilous aspersions of ... W. Lillie. As also against the various expositions of two of his advocates, Mr J. Swan and another, ... Together with the annotations themselves: wherein the pretended grounds of judiciary astrologie and the scripture proofes produced for it, are discussed and refuted.* (London, 1653.)

Gataker, Thomas (1654) *A Discours apologetical, wherein Lilies lewd and lowd Lies in his Merlin or pasqil for the yeer 1654 are cleerly laid open ... his shameless slander fullie refuted ... Together with an advertisement concerning two allegations produced in the close of his postscript; and a postscript concerning an epistle dedicatorie of one J. Gadburie.*

Goodwin, Barbara (2005) *Justice by lottery 2e* Exeter, Imprint Academic

Headlam, James Wycliffe aka J W Headlam-Morley (1891) (revised by D C McGregor 1933) *Election by lot at Athens* Cambridge: C U P

Lecky, W E H (1865 but re-published several times) *History of the rise and influence of the spirit of rationalism in Europe* London s.n. (available on-line)

Mather, Increase (1687) *A TESTIMONY Against several Prophane and Superstitious CUSTOMS, Now Practised by some in New-England, The Evil whereof is evinced from the Holy Scriptures and from the Writings both of Ancient and Modern Divines* Cambridge, New-England: Harvard printed in London 1687

O'Leary, Kevin (2006) *Saving democracy: A plan for real representation in America* Stanford CA; Stanford U P

Ryssen, Leonhard van (1660) *Veritas secundum pietatem de Lusu Aleæ, a ... T. Gattakeri vindicate* Utrecht

Stephen Stigler (1986) *The history of statistics before 1900* Camb. Masss, Harvard U P

*Sutherland, Keith (2004) *The Party's Over: Blueprint for a very English revolution* Exeter, Imprint Academic

*Sutherland, Keith (2008) *A People's Parliament* Exeter, Imprint Academic

Sheynin, Oscar *Probability and Statistics in the 18th Century* At: http://www.sheynin.de/download/italy.pdf

Thomas, Keith (1971) *Religion and the decline of magic* London: Penguin

Willen, Diane (2007) Thomas Gataker and the Use of Print in the English Godly Community *Huntington Library Quarterly* September 2007, Vol. 70, No. 3, Pages 343 – 364

THE NATURE AND USES OF LOTTERIES

A Historical and Theological Treatise
Second edition:
Reviewed, corrected and enlarged, with additional answers to some further arguments by the author

THOMAS GATAKER

Originally published in 1627

[I have omitted five pages of Latin and Greek text, including a dedication to Henry Hobart and others.]

Introduction

INTRODUCTION to the first edition

To the judicious and honourable reader:
I have been reluctant, knowing my own weakness, to publish anything in the press, despite those that know me best having often pressed me to do so, but they have never prevailed on me so far. Now a twofold necessity is imposed upon me to do something about it.This is partly from the urging of many religious and judicious Christian friends who have either heard about it while partaking of my public ministry or they have heard reports by others; there have been some who have requested to see some part of this weak work. All have continued to solicit the publishing of it. It is also partly and more especially by the iniquity of some others, who being of contrary judgement in some of the disputed particulars herein, and being intolerant of anything that seems to go against their judgement, have been more forward than was fit with unchristian slanders and uncharitable censures to tax and defame both me and it. It is as if, as *Augustine** puts it, "their private opinion is their public standard and the model by which every man was bound to mould his affections". There seemed to me no better and readier way to clear these unjust and undeserved aspersions, than by offering to open view of all what I had delivered before to but a few in an obscure auditorium.

So with this, good Reader, you have the same effect and substance that was then and there delivered, enlarged only with matters of history and humanity that would not have been fitting to pester the pulpit with, or encumber the auditorium either. How I first entering into this discourse and my motives for wading into it so far, I am unwilling to spend longer here than needs be, so I leave that to Chapter 9, §10 where I render an account of it.

If any shall surmise that writings of this kind may encourage too much liberty to be taken (a thing that needs little encouragement in this over-licentious age), I answer briefly. It is unfair that because of the looseness of some who are dissolute, that the consciences of those who are of a godly disposition should be entangled and ensnared. Also, if anyone should take more liberty than is given here by me, they must remain certain to keep within the bounds of piety, sobriety, equity

---

* *Names* in italics are references used by Gataker. For more details about these *names* see the Bibliographical Notes at the end of this book.

and charity. More than this I know not what can be required. I had no sinister purpose in view when I undertook this task (and I protest this before God's face and in his fear). I have not claimed or defended anything in this book, but what I am truly persuaded is agreeable to God's word. If any man can better inform me in this, I shall be right ready to listen to him. I have not neglected any means either by writing or in conference with others, as well as my own private labours that might further me in this.

There cannot, I know, but be many defects in this work. Whose work is completely free from them? For mine there are many, much more; too many I myself see and many more I am sure a curious eye may soon spot. If any, let them be shown to me in a friendly and loving manner (as some have already been by some; to whom I rest beholden for and I count that a special kindness). Where defects shall appear, first consider whether they are vital and fundamental, such as touch the very heart and life of the main matter, or minor so that the frame or foundation at least may stand firm. Remember too, that I deal in an argument that has been handled in a very confused way by most, and often not very soundly by the best, as any unbiased observer of this present discourse may very evidently see.

From you, (whoever you may be), I desire only to find an impartial reader, a judicious discusser and a charitable censurer. Do not condemn out of prejudice unheard what I propose, nor should what I prove be rejected because it is inconceivable or what I offer with the right hand should be not put down. In charity, may you continue with diversity of judgment even if you are still not satisfied (something that is lacking in this uncharitable age). The favourable acceptance of these my sorry first-fruits may encourage a weak beginner to attempt something further afterwards which may prove to be of better use. I commend both you and the others to Him who is the author of all truth, the clarifying whereof has been my main aim in this work. He vouchsafes a blessing and through His blessing of the labour (I hope) it shall not prove unfruitful.

Thine in Christ
T G

An Advertisement to the reader concerning this second edition

"Nothing", as *Cicero* said, "is begun and finished at once". Nor is any creature made by its first conception, as it is at birth, nor in birth is it near the extent of growth and strength that it is likely to attain in process of time. "One day teaches another", as the *Psalm 19* says, though in another sense. And more daylight is daily discovered by the diligent. In this regard, I am not ashamed to profess myself at one with worthy ancients such as *Augustine* who are said to "profit as they write and write as they profit". I have received some opposition on some of the points discussed in this treatise which caused me to think further. On reviewing it, in the second chapter especially, I have endeavoured to clarify some things and altered some others. I do not consider it any blemish on my first book if this edition comes forth somewhat better than the first. For myself, I now see things more clearly than before and have not altered anything in my judgement for the better. I have ever and shall always consider it an honour for a man to acknowledge his own error, rather than to discover the errors of others.

There are some things where I cannot yet satisfy myself, but neither these nor the former now altered are of any such weight as to alter the main matter which has been subject of so much controversy concerning the use of a lottery or a chance event* in deciding any non-weighty business. (Not all authors are agreed on their meaning when they mention 'lottery'.) I am not at all altered in my judgement in this point so far; rather I am much more confirmed in it because I see the prime defenders of the case against it have now wholly relinquished and given up the sole grounds on which all the main arguments produced by them and others were formerly established. They are wrong when they say: "In every lottery (or in every mere chance event) which is applied to decide any difference, there is an extraordinary and immediate hand and providence of God present". If this point is denied or not defended, then neither can that reference to it in *Proverbs 16:33* be explained, from which so much is urged in this argument. Nor can those positions be maintained from which is wrongly deduced that: "All lotteries are divine oracles, God's sentences, works of God's special providence etcetera and that in them God sits as a judge and gives His immediate decision. And that to use them is to appeal to His sentence". Since all of this is the sole medium of the principal arguments used against lotteries being used in this way, so if their ground-work fails them in this, it all falls to the ground. What new arguments have since been produced, instead of those where the weaknesses have been discovered, are answered sufficiently in Chapter 4, §1^, though briefly, for fear of over-burdening this book.

And this is all for the present I would with thee.

Farewell.

---

* The words Gataker uses here are 'lots' and 'casual event', which I have generally changed to 'lottery' and 'chance event', as explained in my Preface.

^ I have consigned this new section to an Appendix at the end of Chapter 4.

Chapter 1

What a lottery is, and on lotteries in general

§1. Lotteries: Used and often abused throughout the ages

The use of the lottery is very ancient and it has been frequently used by men of all sorts in all ages. Considering the things that are most in use, they are, by means of man's corruption often subject to abuse. It is not so strange then that the same fate has also befallen the use of lotteries. Having been much used, they have not been free from abuse. Having been used by so many, they have been abused by most. This is equally true for any of God's creatures *(Tim 4:4)* as it is for any civil or sacred ordinance. They may be good and holy in themselves but it would be fortunate indeed if they were not marked by a deep tincture or at least a slight stain from the foul hands or defiled fingers of most of those who deal with them. Just as the lawful use of an ordinance should be wisely discerned and warily separated from the abuse of it, so the use of it should not be wholly banished or abandoned because of its abuse. This will be the main matter that this whole treatise is aimed at. In the Chapters of this treatise I will first try to correctly consider and conceive what the nature of a lottery is in general; after that what are the several sorts of lotteries. The warrantable and unwarrantable use of a lottery may then become more plain.

§2. The origin and form of lotteries

A lottery may be defined or described as a chance or random event purposely applied to the deciding of some doubt. In this definition or description, as in all others, there are two things principally to be considered: the **genus**, as they term it, which originates the matter; and the **form** or specific difference of the thing defined.

The **genus**, or the origin of a lottery is said to be some random or chance event, because however a lottery may be used to give some kind of an answer, even so the outcome of it is mainly random. This is principally and necessarily required in the constitution of a lottery. Those people such as *Aquinas (1270),* who define a lottery as the doing of anything whatever so that some hidden thing may be discovered are therefore reaching a little too far. There are many things which can and may be done for the discovery of hidden and unknown truths which do not come within the nature and scope of a lottery. For example: a man suspecting his servant to be light-fingered, lays money in his way as a bait to tempt him and so tests his honesty of which he has some doubt. This is no kind of lottery.

We may omit many of the methods normally used by those in authority who have the power of judgement when identifying malefactors and discovering crimes. Just because they are uncertain does not make these processes into any kind of lottery, any more than it would be a chance event. Indeed, using a lottery will always involve some chance event. For example: A man could try to see if his servant is a thief or not by putting the servant's name on one scroll of paper, together with the names of others also on scrolls, all rolled up. All the scrolls are then placed on water to see which will unfold first. He might try thereby to determine and judge whether the party suspected is guilty or guiltless of that crime. This tends to illustrate the sayings of various good authors, that:

> "To use a lottery is to put a thing from skill and counsel to temerity and chance." (*Cicero)*;
>
> "A lottery is the child of chance." *(Euripides)*;
>
> "The result of lottery is not in man's power, but is such as accident casts upon us." (*Ambrose)*;
>
> "In a lottery there is no certainty." *(Cicero)*;
>
> "Lotteries are not carried by reason and judgement, nor by counsel and advice." (*Ambrose)*;
>
> "Chance and accident strike the chief stroke in them, (if we respect secondary causes)." *(Isocrates)*
>
> "When by some course of lottery a thing it is concluded or effected, it is by chance such and such a thing fell out or came forth." *(Plutarch)*

For example: It was not a lottery therefore but a mere mockery of one which Verres* once used when a priest was to be chosen by lottery at Syracuse. He caused all the tickets or tokens that were cast into the lot-pot to be signed with one and the self-same man's name. *(Cicero)* That was, of course, no lottery because there could be no accident or uncertainty in the drawing of the tickets so signed. But we will speak at more length in the next Chapter of real chance or accident.

The **form** or specific difference of a lottery is taken from the use and intent or purpose of the user or whatever this accident or chance event is applied to. This could be for the deciding or settling of some doubt, either the defining of some act to be done which is still undecided, or the discovery of some hidden and unknown truth in things done or suspected to be done already. It is this which distinguishes a lottery from all other chance events and accidents and that makes the

---

* Verres had been sent to run Sicily as its proconsul. He was corrupt even by Rome's remarkably low standards, selling guilty verdicts, shaking down entire cities, and even crucifying one Roman citizen for refusing to pay bribes. But what made Verres stand out was that he actually got prosecuted, by a rising lawyer named Cicero. This story can also be found in a novel *Imperium* by Robert Harris (2006) Arrow Books UK (A good read which paints a highly believable picture of ancient Rome.)

chance event so used to be justly called a lottery. Every lottery therefore is a chance and there can be no lottery where there is not a chance event. But every accidental outcome is not as a consequence a lottery. Many things fall out randomly and happen to people continually in the whole course of their lives. An example of this is the chance meeting of people in a way that they never imagined or dreamt of; or of someone lighting on a person in the street or at the market, whom they desired to speak with while going about other business; or of finding one thing while looking for another or even when not looking for anything at all.

These things and their like are chance events, but they are not lotteries; there is no lottery at all in them. These things may befall a man willy-nilly and will often happen many times whether he notices them or not. A lottery on the other hand depends upon the will and purpose of the user. By applying it to such ends and purposes the user makes a lottery of something which would otherwise, in it own nature, not be one. So a man who applies such an accidental thing or the accidental occurrence of any such thing to the discovering, defining, deciding, determining or directing of any unknown truth, uncertain event or unresolved course is using it as a lot and makes a lottery of it. This is what gives the very essence of a lottery to it. This agrees with the definition of a lottery given by some others who say: "A lottery is an accidental event which determines our purposes" *(Aret.)*, although that may be somewhat too scant a definition and include just one kind of lottery. Or: "A lottery is the settling of some doubt or uncertainty by a variable event or the disposition of some recognised thing that we propose to ourselves". *(Lyra, ~1300; Balmford, 1593)* This latter definition, though it does not so precisely point out the exact matter of a lottery, does, as we shall show later, fully include the proper use of a lottery and what may justly make a chance event to be so termed and esteemed.

§3. A warning against the false uses of lotteries

From what has been said so far about the nature of lotteries there may be a better definition or at least a description of a lottery, namely: that it is the deciding or settling of a doubt by some accidental event. So a lottery is not about a question or controversy of some sort or other, or a doubt of something to be done or not done, or by whom, or in what manner it is done, or some deliberation concerning something to be done or not done, or to be done either in this way or that. Whether this is to be decided and settled by a lottery is a matter of choice. There are many and sundry even an infinity of means whereby questions and controversies can be settled and in all of these it is only when some accident or chance event is made the choice for the settling of the doubt that we can properly term it a lottery. *(Perkins, 1592)* There are those *(Serarius, 1609)* who wander far from the right path in this point. They confuse the methods of voting or voices which were used anciently for the election of magistrates and officers *(Aristophanes)*;or in matter of legal judgements made by the casting of white or black beans *(Ulpian)*, or of beads, stones, bones or shells taken whole or hurled into a pitcher or other vessel prepared for that purpose. It was used to decide whether to acquit or convict the party on trial *(Pollux)*. This is what Alcibiades* *(Plutarch)* was probably alluding to when he said, "He would not trust his own mother with the trial of his life if he could avoid it, for fear she should unwittingly cast in a black bean for a white".

Lotteries have also been used for allocating some of the offices and places of employment in the state (*Aristophanes)*, as if they were of the same nature, which they are not. Others seem to shoot no less wide in this business and draw within the ambit of the lottery the proof of Aaron's right to the priesthood by that miraculous budding and fruit-bearing of his almond-tree rod. *(Num 17:8)* They also quote trials of quarrels in questions of right by duels and combats; and the canonical clearing of guilt [purgation] by the taking of the Host or the Eucharist; and also when fire and water were anciently used even in these parts; and by using divination to foretell fortunes by using men's names to tell who should prevail against another and the like. *(Delrio, 1618)* The means in these cases whereby the doubt or controversy is settled is not mere random chance and the decision of the doubt cannot therefore be properly termed a lottery.

§4. A lottery can be merely random or use chance deliberately

Let me add one further thing. It is not only necessary in the matter of lottery that the thing which is applied to the deciding of a doubt be random, but that it be applied thereto in so far as it is random. (I speak in regard of the person both using and the thing used.) So the lottery should not, either in it own nature, or in the conceit or counsel of those that make use of it have any special relation to the business to be decided thereby.

Two examples will help to clear my meaning here: If a man is requested to ride out on a rainy day with his friend and says "I will ride only if I am held up by no-one, otherwise I will not go out"; Or: If a man decides whether to take a journey or not by the outcome of being crossed randomly by a hare. *(Plutarch)*.

In both these cases a doubt is decided by a chance event, but they should not be considered as chance events because they have a peculiar relation to the business intended and whether convenience or inconvenience is affected by the one and presaged by it in the other. Neither is therefore a lottery. This is the point where some former authors like *Delrio (1618)* seem to fail when they say that divination by the flight of birds and by their eating or refusing their food are examples of lotteries. They are not, but it would be a lottery if a man is asked to accompany his friend and says, "we will draw cuts to decide whether we shall stay or go, or whether I shall go with you or you stay with me and put off your journey to some other time".

---

* Alcibiades was the brilliant but unscrupulous Athenian politician and military commander who provoked the sharp political antagonisms at Athens that were the main causes of Athens' defeat by Sparta in the Peloponnesian War (431–404 BC).

Another true lottery could occur if, on being upon their way together and disagreeing about their course, they refer the question and controversy between them to the flight of the next bird or the footing of some beast that has gone before them on the way. This is a matter of chance which can be regarded as merely random. In this respect when it is applied to decide a present doubt no-one will therefore, I suppose, deny that it is indeed a lottery. So we can thus see what both a lot and lottery is in general, namely:

A lot is some chance event purposely applied to the deciding of some doubt;

and,

A lottery is the deciding or settling of some question or controversy by such chance outcomes considered as they are such.

Chapter 2

Chance and random events

Chance or randomness lies at the heart of a lottery, with random events being the subject matter of lotteries. Because the nature of chance is so significant for our present concerns, this Chapter gives due consideration to clarifying the nature of lots and lotteries and the questions which need to be asked about them. Concerning 'chance' and 'random events' we will consider four things. The name of it. (Chance); The nature of the thing so named. Two distinct Acts concurring in it; and Certain conclusions or aphorisms concerning it.

§1. Chance: An acceptable term?

The term 'chance' or randomness may be utterly condemned by *Piscatorius (~1600)* and others and held to be foolish and heathenish. But it is a term that is used in the Christian Bible, both in the Old and New Testaments. In the Old Testament it was Solomon, the wisest man that ever was since Adam who said *(Eccl 9:11)* that "Time and chance befall all men or all things". This can also be found elsewhere *(Eccl 9:2)* in the Bible. In the New Testament it was our Saviour Jesus Christ, who told *(1 Corr 1:24)* the parable of the Jew, who while journeying to Jericho fell among thieves. As he lay wounded, half alive and half dead, a Priest is said to have "come by chance that way". The Evangelist Luke expresses in Greek what our Saviour would have spoken in Aramaic; he used the word which precisely matched that used by Solomon and springing, it may be surmised, from the same root. I might add that in many other references *(King 5:4)* the term 'chance' is also used in religious writings.

For example: Saint *Augustine*, one of the greatest early Church fathers, used 'chance' or 'fortune' rather often in his writings. He repented of this in his final work 'Retractions', saying that he disliked the use of the word because of its abuse by heathens. "It was they", he said, "who saw Fortune as a blind Goddess and ascribed to her what they should have given to God". He further explained himself saying that he meant nothing more by 'chance' than 'the chance event of things'. In this sense he acknowledged that it may be rightly used and not condemned by religion, nor would it be prohibited to say, "Peradventure such a thing shall be", or, "Perchance it may be", or, "Such a thing came to pass by chance or some chance event."

§2. The nature of the thing called chance

As to the nature of the thing which is called 'chance', there are some like *Olevianus* who say that it is nothing, just as the same was said by *Aristotle* of sin, and it therefore deserves no name. But even 'nothing' must have some name to express not so much what it is, but what it is not. Yet chance and random events are indeed something and may be defined as: Chance in a casual or random event is a contingency or an uncertainty not dependent on forecast and foresight.

Contingency or uncertainty, as I term it, excludes it from necessity and certainty. If there is necessity or certainty there can be no chance or randomness. Chance and certainty are mutually exclusive. That is why I add "not dependent on forecast and foresight" to the definition, to distinguish them.

Chance or randomness is thus both an aspect of the persons doing it and of the effects of doing it. In regard of the former, the ancient philosopher *Aristotle* commonly discerned among the causes in the ranks of those doing it an 'affection of an efficient', or an adjunct to the manner of doing it, rather than an 'efficient' cause of or in itself. In regard of the latter effects, chance or randomness is taken as figure of speech to signify the result which is effected. That is how I take it here and consider in the matter of lotteries as many authors such as *Masius (~1570)* use it and as Christian writers like *Keckermann (1612)* most usually understand it in these questions, that:

> **A chance or random event** is a contingent event, not directed or settled by any forecast or foresight and,

A contingent outcome is one that is uncertain or variable, as all grant it to be. Again the outcome of it is so uncertain that the uncertainty of it is not directed or settled by the skill, counsel or forecast of those it concerns or befalls. It may be effected and produced by known natural causes, but neither skill nor counsel can direct the causes which produce that effect, nor can foresight determine what the effect will be in particular. All else is mere conjecture.

To better understand this, I will classify all outcomes under three heads, which corresponds to the distinction of effects and outcomes which are used by the best writers *(Plutarch, Aristotle, Augustine)*, by necessity, by skill and by chance. The three headings are: (i) Necessary, (ii) Contingent but not Random (Chance), or (iii) Contingent and Random (Chance).

(i) Necessary are things that always fall out naturally in a certain and constant course and cannot do otherwise, unless some supernatural power countermand and over-rule them and the causes which are producing them. Such kinds of events are the motion of the heavens, the course of the sun, that a fire will burn combustible matter thrown into it and the like.

(ii) Contingent and not chance are things which are done one way, but might have been done some other way. The uncertainty here is settled by knowledge, art, forecast and skill, or by the advice, counsel, deliberation or free election of those whom they concern or befall. An example is a man walking along. He can go on or stand still, he can go forward or backwards, it being in his power and determinable by his own will and advice to do one thing or the other. Thus a man in a sword-fight may receive or avoid the stroke or thrust of his adversary using his skill and cunning.

So the two types of events so far, namely outcomes that are either necessary, or are contingent but not random are to be excluded from matters of the lottery. The third and last, which will now be dealt with, are the contingent and chance outcomes and are the only ones to be admitted as related to the matter of lotteries.

(iii) Contingent and random (chance) are such things that might fall out in a number of ways which cannot be settled by any art or forecast, counsel or skill in regard of the person to whom they are random, or whom they randomly befall. An example is a man travelling on his way, unaware of an imminent eclipse of the sun. He then spots it at exactly the same instant as he is in a river which he has entered to water his horse. The eclipse of the sun here is natural and necessary, his seeing or not seeing it is contingent or voluntary, his spotting it in that place when he was going along had nothing to do with it; it is merely random and accidental. Another example would be the slaying of Achab by accident. *(1 King 22:34)* This was when someone drew a bow at will, intending that his arrow should hit wherever it did, it being shot out at all adventure by him, the uncertain motion neither directed nor settled by the will or skill of the shooter to the mark that it hit. So the slaughter of the person that was accidentally slain was said *(Num 3:22)* "to be done suddenly, inconsiderately, not out of enmity, not of set purpose or by a train" and that the person that did it neither eyed nor saw him, nor was he seeking to hurt the person whom he slew. All these terms and phrases were used by the Spirit of God in that case. They tend not only to express the uncertainty of the outcome, but to remove also all knowledge and counsel, all foresight and forecast, whereby that uncertainty might be settled by the party that was agent in that act.

A further clarification*: Perhaps some further distinction may seem needful. Outcomes may, as was said before, be uncertain and undetermined either in regard of the thing itself and the causes producing it, or may, in regard of a person's notice, apprehension and direction of it relate to that purpose it is applied to. So an outcome, though necessary or contingent in itself, may yet may be deemed and termed random or chance, with such latitude of sense as the word is taken here and so may become a lottery matter. This can relate to the uncertainty of a person's knowledge, or its indeterminacy. This in turn could depend on any foresight or forecast of the outcome, either indirect or immediate. Some instances will make this clear:

As an example: Suppose (as in the example in Chapter 1) two men cannot decide which direction to take, so they agree to choose by events such as; the flight of a bird that crosses them, or if a stranger turns up, riding before them, goes to the right or to the left. But the bird would fly that way because some carrion that

* This is a new section added in the second edition, presumably to counter critics.

it either sees or senses attracts it. And the stranger would turn this way or that because it is convenient for the place that he is going to. But neither of the two men would have a forecast or foreknowledge of either of these events. So in this case the outcome may well be deemed randomly casual, though contingent, but only in itself. Even though the outcome was utterly unknown to both men, this event cannot be called a true lottery. The bird was led by natural instinct and looked for nothing but its prey. The man was guided by a deliberate purpose in the shaping of his course. Neither acted for the benefit of the parties in contention, nor did they wish to settle their differences.

Another example: Again, if the Roman poets *Seneca*, *Lucian* and *Ovid** are to be believed, massive things of themselves naturally and necessarily move downward, something which is true of all bodies whatsoever. Therefore any water that is poured out, or any spherical body thrown down on firm ground, will of necessity drop that way onto the ground. Where it finishes depends on the surface, so that the water let out or a ball thrown through a hole in a wall, when it lands on the ground, will of necessity go the way that the ground gives. It may look like the motion of the water or ball could be deemed random, especially to those who understand nothing of the site and posture of the soil. They may even try to use the outcome of which way the water or ball moves to decide some controversy between them. But this is no lottery, unless the ground was purposely prearranged so that the water or the ball might always go one way. A lottery could be fixed so that it could take one way only and the actual slope being equally unknown to either of them. And the same might be said of some question referred to the return of the flood (which both parties are alike ignorant of) by the turning of the tide.

Finally, it must be remembered that things past and done have now become necessary. Before they were done they might well have been contingent and indifferent as to whether they would be done or not done or done in this way or that. But there is no power in nature to change things that have been done, or to cause that which has been done to be not so, since that implies manifest contradiction. So the track of a beast which has already passed along one way may be utterly unknown and uncertain to two parties having a dispute. But making use of these tracks for a decision may seem like a random event. But the beast had no such end or purpose when being driven that way earlier, so a decision thereby of the question or controversy cannot be called a lottery.

§3. Two distinct types of chance events: Acts of man and Acts of God

Random or chance events (as in all things) can be seen in two main aspects: Acts of man (or other creatures) and acts of God. The acts of creatures including man can be either **reasoned** out, or **not reasoned** out.

---

* It would be another 40 or so years before Isaac Newton (also a Cambridge man like Gataker) discovered the laws of motion of the planets, and all other 'massive bodies'.

Of the **reasoned** chance acts of creatures, they can be settled merely by guess and conjecture, as in drawing of cuts, or more adventurously, by drawing out a ticket from those which have been shuffled and blended together, leaving no place for guesswork.

Of the **not reasoned** chance acts of creatures they could be decided in a particular circumstance using natural but uncertain events like the flight of a bird, or by the bird's feeding or refusing their food, or by it moving in some other circumstance. In so far as any art or skill is used, it has little to do with it. These events may take many courses and finish in many ways. This is similar to what happens when a blind man or someone who is blindfolded shoots an arrow at random; or when boys play at cross-and-pile [a form of coin tossing; 'heads or tails']. There might be many actions taken, such as when many dice or pawns are cast out of the same box or hand, or sundry balls or bowls thrown out of the same lap or arm. Here the result must of necessity fall out even more diversely and with greater uncertainty.

The other is an act of God who is the creator and who shows His providence or assistance either in a **general** way in ordinary random events, or in **special** circumstances and in extraordinary events.

God's **general** providence is, I say, ordinarily found here, as it is in all other things. For the prescience and providence, or, if you prefer it, the will, pleasure and omniscience of God extends itself in general into all things, even to the alighting of a sparrow or to the shedding of a hair. "God" as *Seneca* well said, "is the author of all things, be they random or other". "God is author, I say", the well distinguished *Augustine* also said, "of the action, though only the disposer, not the author of the evil, where any is, in it". If a providence of God therefore is in all things, then it is in random events also. And as it is in all things, so it must ordinarily be in random events and cannot be otherwise. If a sparrow may not fall without God's permission *(Matt 10:29)*, so much less is any man slain without God's providence, Who is therefore said "to offer the man that is randomly slain unto the hand of him by whom he is slain".

But sometimes there is indeed a more **special** divine providence in operation. This happens where God's secret will and purpose effects some special work of judgement or mercy for the glory of His name either in crossing his enemies or for the benefit of his beloved.

The Bible gives many examples: Joseph's brothers had cruelly conspired his death, which God prevented by having his life saved, but also that when he went to Egypt he was afterwards advanced in the service of the Pharaoh. *(2 King 12:22)* Another example is Ruth's happening upon Boaz in his field, who by that means came to take notice of her and by marrying her became one of the Messiah's progenitors. As when the 'dead' man was suddenly thrown into the sepulchre of Elisha, for fear of an on-coming enemy, but by God's admirable work, the man, a faithful servant of God, revived thereupon. (*II Kings 13:20)*

The same divine providence may well be deemed to be in those judgements (or calumnies as we commonly call them) of fire and water, plague and pestilence, sudden death, shipwreck etcetera. These were for the most part effected by ordinary means and natural courses. God's special providence acted through oxen and asses, wolves and wild beasts, yea and the very worms themselves too. (*Psal 104:21)* This providence must apply much more and in a more special manner over man, a creature made in God's own image and in such things that especially concern the life of man and in such things as may betide him for some special good or evil. If a poor sparrow falls not without God's permission, so much less would any man's life taken away but by special providence.

As an example: When a beam fell by chance and dashed out the brains of a notorious bad fellow, an onlooker, *Stratonicus* by name, broke out into a speech: "Sirs, there is I deem a divine power and providence, but whether there is or not, surely this beam might well persuade a man there is."

Of divine providence generally it was well said by *Augustine* that: "That which is commonly called chance, is yet by a certain course secretly guided: and that even in those things that we say come by chance or by adventure, respect ought to be had to a divine disposition". But in regard of this providence being put to use through random chance events to check up on the counsel given by men, Solomon commented *(Eccl 9:11)* that "The race goes not always with the swiftest, nor the battle with the strongest, nor bread to the wisest, nor wealth to the most skilful, nor grace to the most cunning; but time and chance befall them all". That is what the heathen man *Petronius* saw when he said: "Men ought not to rely overmuch on their counsel or forecast; for that fortune is God's providence by fortune". An expression in almost the same terms came from Solomon who said *(Proverbs)* that, "It strikes a great stroke and oft carried things across to that we expect". This is so in other chance events, including lotteries. Of these Solomon said *(Proverbs 16:33),* that: "The lot is cast into the lap, but each disposition of it is of God". Many divines* of great and of good note explain or have implied that the word of God as spoken by Solomon suggests that although there seems nothing more random than a lottery (when it is carried out as it ought), there is a divine providence in the disposition of it. This is the same as it would be in all other outcomes, of whatever nature and quality they be. But when you look what is said by Solomon about lotteries, you will find the self-same is said elsewhere of all of men's thoughts and ways and words and works and counsels and courses. They are all disposed by God and none are absolutely in our power to issue as we will.

As Saint *Augustine* said: "Those things that fall to us by lottery are given us from God". According to the *Psalm v5:* "The lines are fallen to me in a pleasant place and I have a fair heritage. I praise the Lord for it". (Though that is intended to be a metaphor, as the previous words show: "The Lord is the portion of my

* The names of the 'divines' referred to are too difficult to read here, but Gataker returns to this topic in Ch 7, §3.

part and of my cup; and the maintainer of my lot".) But so too whatever the manner of acquiring wealth, be it left by decease of friends, or got by travail and industry, or attained otherwise, or rest or sleep and a good wife and children which are said to be God's gifts and to come all from Him, who gives all things to all and worked all things for all and in all.

But sometimes there is a more special and immediate providence in extraordinary cases and on extraordinary occasions in these chance events. There was such a providence in the chance outcomes of the lottery whereby Saul was chosen (*1 Sam 10:21)*, whereby Achan was taken *(Josh 7:16)*, whereby Jonathan *(1 Sam 14:42)* was detected. It was also in a lottery whereby Jonah was once discovered *(Jon 1:7)*, done, as *Jerome* well said (and is equally true of all others) not by any power or virtue of the lottery itself, (for no lottery has any such natural power all in it) much less of the sort of lottery used by heathens and infidels, but by His will and providence that ruled or rather over-ruled the uncertainty of it. And in this case where *Bernard (~1120)* said: "That which seems chance to us, is as a word of God acquainting us with His will", which is true indeed in general if we consider God's decreeing of whatever comes to pass, for we know that it was God's will that it should be so. *(Lament 3:37)* We see it once it has fallen out so and His will is manifested by His work, either for the doing of the thing itself, or for the permitting of it to be done. Otherwise, to further understand the manifestation of God's will concerning something to be done or left undone by us, it is not true in general. For the word of God is shown in His will in this kind and this sense. But what about when a hare starts out before a man going on his way, or a bird flies beside him, or he treads in some unclean thing unawares and the like, is it any more than in any other act whatever? No, unless we give way to superstitious and frivolous conceits that make such accidents ominous. How is it that an extraordinary lottery cast by special instinct or express appointment of God is most true? How may we understand the speeches of the Ancients such as *Ambrose* and *Origen*, who call a lottery "a divine trial and a divine sentence" and say that "a lottery discovers God's hidden will to men and makes it known openly what God judges secretly". And also that "a lottery is a matter in man's doubting, manifesting God's will". All these sayings, if they are to be understood as God's will in what He would have done or not done of us must of necessity be limited solely to those lotteries when God Himself appoints some special means to be used to that purpose.

Four conclusions

§4. First: Do not confuse acts of God and acts of men

They are related but not part of the same set. It is wrong when considering random events and also lotteries, to confound the act of the Creator with the work of the creature. They are two different things, distinct in themselves, which ought not therefore be confounded in chance, random events, or indeed any other events whatever. Yet many seem to do so, even men of some note. As an example: *Cicero* reported of the old Academics, that fortune or chance are the same as God's providence and that they differ only in respect, and also that providence, fate or destiny and fortune or randomness are in truth all the same. Yet they can be distinguished, because the first includes the two latter. Providence is the cause of all things that are done; which is the Providence in respect of things done of necessity which is called fate or destiny and which in respect of things done casually or randomly is called fortune or chance. And therefore "That" (say they) "which to the wise and godly is God's singular Providence, to the foolish and profane is Fortune or Chance."

Lactantius, (and before him *Seneca*) confounded nature with God when he said: "Folly and error and blindness and, as Cicero confessed, the ignorance of causes brought in the names of nature and fortune". And again, "This overthrow of piety brought in Nature's name: for when men knew not by whom the world was made, or would persuade men that nothing was made by the Deity; they said that Nature was the mother of all things", as if they should say that all things had sprung up naturally of themselves; which by using such words, they confess their own folly, since Nature, severed from divine power and providence is just nothing.

A similar error is committed by those who define Fortune as a certain goddess which by various random strokes makes sport for herself by defeating men's purposes. They do not understand from whom those good or evil things come that befall them. A worthy man *Mornay (1581)* once said, when answering that objection of atheists and epicures, "what will become of Fortune if there is a divine providence in all things?" It is true indeed that we can speak of fortune, as the poet *Pacuvius* painted her, blind, standing on a globe, turned about like a weathercock with every puff of wind. But this is just a poetical figment, that may as easily be made out by us as it is drawn by them. Or it might at best be a symbolical emblem *(Clement)* which deciphers the great uncertainty of chance events. We shall say more anon. Again the same *Mornay* has said that if (with *Proclus),* we understand fortune to be a divine power which couples unlikely causes together so that they may work towards the same purpose, then we have to acknowledge such a power and providence not only in random events and things which are merely uncertain, but must acknowledge it in all other things whatsoever, even things that are most certain. For fortune is just a nickname for God .

But what if we consider the terms 'nature', 'fortune' or 'chance' in the same way that the Holy Ghost uses them? *(1 Cor 11:14)* Nature can be considered as a power or faculty within creatures distinct from God's providence in guiding and ruling and which often over-rules nature for those purposes as He sees good. So fortune or chance are also an affection or action of creatures, as distinct from the same providence with which God guides and disposes at His pleasure. In natural effects therefore, there is the work of the creature, which is true whether there is providence disposing it or not. But if the creature is left wholly to itself, then there can also be random events. They happen, but yet are ordered, as all other things, by God's providence either in general or special ways. So often things happen as they do as if there were there no providence at all, with the creature left to do its own work and will.

As the Schoolman *Aquinas (1270)* has not unfairly said, "there might be the use of some kind of lottery even though there were no providence at all to guide it", if the decision of the matter in question is referred wholly to the random motion of creatures, without any special providence of the Creator being required. In a word, if in random events we consider anything apart from the nature and the uncertain motion of the thing itself, there is nothing guiding it but God's providence. It is uncertain (I say), because it cannot be determined by us; rather it is determined by some natural cause or other. These two things, the act of the creature and God's providence accompanying it, though never sundered or severed, can even so be distinguished and considered separately and are not to be confounded with each other.

§5. Second: Being a chance event does not make it part of God's providence

The random nature of an event does not simply of itself make it a work of God's special or immediate providence. Sometimes there is a more special providence in many of the things that are not random but contingent only, than of the most things that are random. There are many unpredictable events which daily befall us, almost as many as are the number of times we meet people, or take footsteps, look this way or that and see a new variety of chance experiences with every unexpected object bringing a random event with it. But no-one would say that these are works of a special or immediate providence. And yet one contingent outcome among many may be random, even when it is not.

As an example: A man on going on his way may often have a hare cross his path, see many people unknown to him, find a piece of old iron, spy a covey of partridges, have his hat blown off his head and the like. These can all happen and all be merely chance. But a man, fearing that his friend is in some danger or forecast of distress, might force his company on the friend so that he does not travel. By being in his company this can be a means of saving his life by recovering him from a fall, or by rescuing from an assault. That would be a contingent outcome rather than a chance one.

And yet we can acknowledge a more special providence of God in the latter case that is not so much random, but contingent only, deliberately and voluntary undertaken upon mature counsel and forecast. The former then is, or may be merely chance and just happen unexpectedly without any forecast at all. It is true indeed that God's providence is manifested more in things randomly befalling us for good or evil, than in things that befall us contingently by means of men and their forecast and affection for us, or their hatred and malice. There are more things that fall out contingently than in things that are necessary. So how does the providence of God ordinarily extend itself to all of them alike and how is it that a more special providence can sometimes be found in some random events than in others? The same event can be either random or may sometimes be justly deemed as a more special providence of God than others, depending on the circumstances concurring.

Another example: A man travelling over Salisbury plain finds a pitcher of water left there and having no need of it or use for it would hardly take it to be a special providence of God. But if a man was exceedingly vexed with thirst, extremely distressed, as Sampson was *(Judge 15:18)* and ready to die for want of water to drink, was to find the same pitcher of water, just as Hagar was directed by God's angel to a well *(Genesis 21:19)*, he might well have taken it to be a sign of the special providence of God. He might also term the place where he found it, as when God's angel found the same in another place, "the well of the living God that looked after me when I was nearly lost". *(Gen 16:14)*

Only a very superstitious person would see God's providence in the first example and any pious man would judge so of the other. Yet both are equally random; the randomness of events therefore does not in itself simply judge them to be either. In neither of these cases could such an extraordinary or immediate providence of God be affirmed. This is what some seem to maintain not just in all lotteries, but in all random events as well. But there is a great difference between a pot of water left by one being weary of the burden and having no further use of it leaving it there; and the pot of water that Elias was presented with in the wilderness, which when the Angel woke him, he found standing beside him. *(1 King 19: 16)* The first is brought there by ordinary means; the other either conveyed there without any such means or created and produced suddenly in the place. So much for the idea that every random event, by being random, necessarily implies any such extraordinary or immediate divine providence, an idea that is thereby imagined by some.

A riposte to critics on* 'Being a chance outcome does not make it part of God's providence'. It has been objected that in the writings of good authors such as *Aristotle*, that nature, and chance or fortune are frequently seen as opposites. Causes working by nature are said to be distinguishable from causes working by chance and random events, and are thereby severed from natural effects. It may seem, therefore, that such random events are not effected by any natural cause or course and are to be referred to some extraordinary and immediate divine providence.

To this I answer: First, just as nature and chance are taken as opposites, so nature and counsel, nature and reason, nature and art, nature and force, are all similarly opposed by the selfsame authors (*Aristotle)*. As indeed, natural and voluntary are both agents and acts that are often distinguished one from another. And no man will, I suppose, either deny that voluntary acts and affairs which are managed by counsel, art or reason, or actions which are produced by external force

---

* New in the second edition. Gataker does not identify his critics here.

and violence, are usually effected by natural causes and courses. Nor would they infer that there is an extraordinary and immediate providence in all such effects. So if that distinction does not imply the one, neither does it imply the other.

Secondly, the purpose and meaning of these authors making such distinctions is not to exclude wholly the natural working of the creature [man] in producing the act or the work so effected, or to imply any concurrence of some supernatural power as being necessarily required in producing such outcomes. An exception for them are those outcomes which they term ‘natural effects’. But this is to sever the use of counsel and skill on the one hand and external force and violence on the other from such effects, as if it was either only flowing from a mere natural inclination and instinct in the creature, or that it was the creature’s purpose proceeding in a natural and ordinary course, and is either effected by it, or happens to it. Counsel and skill proceeds both from a natural power and ability in the creature and work also in a natural and ordinary course. External force and violence is something which may proceed from the natural power and ordinary work of some other creature.

So those authors are taking ‘nature’ in a more strict and philosophical sense than men are wont to do in ordinary speech. This is akin to the explanations of the cause of motion and rest in bodies which works constantly in a uniform course unless it meets with some impediment, rather than saying that it is all down to some supernatural power, which they will not deal with at all in their discourses. This ignores such inward grounds in reasonable men’s minds, be they native or acquired, which may work in many ways as advice and art do. As to other outward occurrences, which either force a creature out of its own course, or befall it unexpectedly, without its foresight and forecast, for example by violence or chance, are they the work of nature or the work of chance? In reply, the critics might say also, that: “Art does that which often Nature cannot do” *(Aristotle),* and that “by chance many times it comes to pass, that which by skill and counsel could not be encompassed” *(Pliny)* And that is their only meaning, because it is plainly acknowledged by these authors that even in random events, as well as in those which they are wont to call natural effects, an act of the creature working within the sphere and scope of its own natural endowments is producing these outcomes. They also reject the opinion of those that ascribed such outcomes to some supernatural power (*Aristotle)*, as if there is no reason in nature why such occurrences could be thus rendered. This is a frivolous conceit and unworthy to be refuted.

Lastly (thirdly), the thing itself shows that such random outcomes are usually produced by ordinary known causes and courses.

For example*:* If by chance a soldier opened an aposteme [abscess] in his enemy’s body with his weapon and so cured him of that which his physicians could not cure, what is here? An ordinary act of a military man in the field, during a fight while he is aiming his weapon at his adversary. By hitting him in that way, would he not lay open that part which was handiest to receive the stroke of his weapon? Yet by hitting that spot in way that he had not looked for, it proved beneficial rather than evil as was intended. It is therefore said to have fallen out by chance. How is it that, like the heathen *Valerius Maximus*, we deny a special divine providence here, but explain that it is the working of known secondary and ordinary courses, especially if the party that was helped had despaired of ever being cured and had gone out into the field for the purpose of losing his life. Weary of his life and desirous to be rid of it, he happened upon that unlooked-for boon, which was a means to prolong it.

Another example: Monstrous births usually ascribed to chance *(Aristotle)*; they deviate from the common course of nature. This is reported by *Timberlake (1603)* to be most frequent in those chickens that are produced and hatched by an artificial heat in Arabian and Egyptian furnaces. And yet despite what the philosopher *Aristotle* and the physician *Lemnius (1559)* say, ascribing such outcomes to chance, are they not also wont to render natural reasons for them?

'Chance' is the expression used when a man lights on treasure hidden in the ground, discovering it while digging perhaps to plant or to bury, or to lay a foundation for a building, or for some other such like purpose. The treasure may have been laid up there by someone who chose that place as fit for such a purpose and by no other means than an ordinary and natural outcome does it come to be discovered, as when it is necessary to dig the ground, not while searching for treasure.

It is chance if he meets someone at the market, who he wanted to speak to, but had made no arrangement to meet there. This means of happening on him may well involve several businesses lying both in the one way and therefore drawing them both together at the same time to the place where they then meet. But because neither of them intended it, this meeting is said to happen by chance.

The same may be said of many other chance outcomes. Because it appears to be chance in the ordinary meaning of it and in a way which is intelligible to the person so affected, yet some of the ancient philosophers *(Aristotle, Pacuvius)*, it seems, utterly deny that it is chance. Yet they are amiss. Chance or fortune is not a distinct kind of cause, but only an affection or adjunct cleaving unto it which accompanies some causes and so differences them from others by the manner of their working in producing some effects.

These philosophers would have ascribed this to the causes which produced them, not to fortune or chance, which are in truth nothing but expressions of the manner how such causes and effects are produced. Nor does the distinction of events into natural and random, any more than dividing effects into natural and artificial exclude ordinary methods of effect, or imply an immediate and extraordinary providence in such events or effects that are thereby opposed to the natural ones. The contrary does very evidently appear ordinarily in such.

§6. Third: What may be chance to one may not be chance to another. There can be forecast, foreknowledge or counsel which foresees, directs or disposes of outcomes for one person, but not for another, in spite of appearances. To better understand this, imagine that in a chance event two things occur: ignorance or lack of foreknowledge in anticipating them; and carelessness, or lack of forecast in directing them. These are the things that make the outcome uncertain and uncertainty breeds chanciness.

First: Lack of foreknowledge or foresight of a future outcome does not make an event random. There are some who have said that chance is founded on and depends wholly on man's ignorance. And that therefore if ignorance is absent, the more a man knows, the less he is subject chance; the less he knows the more he encounters it. It also looked that way to others such as *Mornay (1581)* who have said that ignorance of causes forged the term of Chance or Fortune. This is not the ignorance of the first and principal cause of all things, which is God, as some *(Anti-piscat)* would have it. They use that term knowingly and acknowledge causes in much the same way as the heathens imagined a blind goddess called Chance. This term is, no doubt, older than these authors' figment and was in common use before any such counterfeit deceit was dreamed up. This is due to ignorance of the secondary causes which puts such random occurrences into effect, or rather as I would prefer to call it, the ignorance of events and (as I said before) of what will be. But as I said before, this does not deny that chance is an affection of both efficients and of effects and that the ignorance does not usually proceed from the ignorance of their causes. But just because effects and outcomes are often better known than their causes, we may well know the one and be ignorant of the other. We may be able to see something stirring and not know whether it does so by internal might, or some external means. We may foreknow some outcomes too, not only by being told about them but also by observation, though we may not know the grounds for them. A fever may recur or the tide turn; we may be ignorant of the cause of either. In these things it was well said by *Aristotle* that "inexperience bred chance, just as experience begat art".

Nor does follow, as *Augustine* said that "chance is merely a thing whose cause or the means whereby it is effected is hidden from us. There are many things where we do not know the cause, yet we do not ascribe them to chance, nor are they random. Some uncertain outcomes are necessary, as that a loadstone [magnet] should attract iron and steel and direct the needle touched with it to the north. There is no known cause or certain reason that can (as yet) be given for this and yet these are necessary and natural, not random outcomes. Some outcomes are contingent only, as when the return of the plague happens in the ordinary course of a disease. That is not, properly speaking, random, but only contingent at the most, even when, as some are wont to do, out of ignorance of the true cause, suspect it is caused by some kind of spirit. Again there are many things that come to pass daily, where we do not know the cause of them; they seem random or chance to us, because we had not foreseen them.

An example is when a hare is startled by hounds and it crosses a man going about some other business. He is not ignorant of the cause of his own journey that way, nor of the cause of the hare's crossing that way at that instant, yet it may be a random event to him that a hare should then and there cross him. If a man knew beforehand what would befall him on his way, then nothing that happened would be unexpected to him. This is how the same thing may be random to one, but not to another, because it was foreseen and foreknown by the one but not by the other.

Another example was Saul's meeting with those that Samuel had foretold him about before. This was a chance event to those he met, but not chance to Samuel and Saul themselves. The one foresaw it by revelation from God, the other foreknew by relation from the first. *(1 Sam 10:2)*

Again, all counsel and forecast is excluded from chance events. Nothing that is done by advice, counsel or forecast, is done randomly by he who does it. "What is done randomly is done unadvisedly", as was well said by *Cicero.* And temerity is swayed by chance, but not reason or advice, as we have formerly shown. In common parlance we say of those that speak inconsiderately and deal unadvisedly and inconstantly, that "they deal as if they dealt at random, or went by lottery; and that they speak as if they drew cuts as to what they should say". And the heathen man *Seneca* said that wise men are less subject to chance (because they carry on their business by counsel and forecast) than are unwise persons, that thoughtlessly rush in. And again what is chance to one is not so to another, because of intentions and purpose of one person is not the same as another.

Examples are: Ahab's meeting Elias which was unexpected by Ahab, but not by Elias, who went of purpose to meet Ahab. *(1 King 21:20)* And Jephta's meeting his daughter and she him, was a chance event for him (he had not expected her), but was not a chance encounter for his daughter when she purposely went to meet him.[*] *(Judge 11:34).*

Then there are many things that may seem to be random events when indeed they are not and when it is thought that they happened by chance, when they are produced by art and advice:

One example is given by *Plato* who counselled the rulers of his imaginary state to couple persons together by trickery through the semblance of a lottery, so that they might seem to meet each by chance, when indeed it was done by cunning and fraud.

Another example from *Herodotus:* Darius got his horse to neigh after a mare which the horse had recently had been with at that place. This seemed a chance outcome to his competitors, who had agreed beforehand to settle the Empire on who-so-ever's horse first neighed when they next met there. But it was not

[*] The story of Jephta is based on a promise he made to God, that if successful in battle he would sacrifice the first living creature he encountered when he returned home. This was his beloved daughter of course. Handel turned it into a powerful oratorio.

chance, nor did it seem so to Darius, or at least to his groom who had previously made preparations for his horse to win.

An example by *Aquinas (1270): A* man sends his servant on an errand through a lane where he knows that he shall meet his mistress coming from market laden with goods. They meet accordingly, the one not expecting the other and suppose they meet by chance, when indeed it is not chance, but the good man's care in forecasting it for the ease of his wife.

Example *(Mornay, 1581)*: of the servant who finds money that his master had purposely laid as a bait to try his honesty, to see whether he will restore it or retain it. The servant thought it came there by chance, whereas it was placed there on purpose.

All of this is, in a word, cheating and a cunning conveyance using the idea of a lottery to make something seem to be random when indeed it is not, only being carried out by some fraud. This sort of thing is so common that among the Dutch it is reported to have grown into a by-word, "In Lottery is Bowery", that is, knavery or cheating.

So however it is that the ignorance of causes makes things seem random when in fact they are not so, yet it is rather the ignorance of events that indeed makes things so for many. They may prove to be random, but would not have been had they been foreseen by some means.

§7. Fourth: God cannot play dice.

There are no uncertain events for God because there is no ignorance in God. There is nothing that is uncertain for Him, nothing that comes contingently, but all things are necessary in regard of Him and His decree. *(Aquinas, 1270)* If indeed we respect human nature and its manner of working, then some things come to pass of necessity, some contingently and some by chance. But if we respect God's will and purpose, his prescience and providence, then nothing falls out contingently or by chance and all things come to pass of necessity; nothing is contingent, for in contingency is uncertainty. All things are certain with Him, who has already done what He will do or will have done *(Psal 104)* and with whom whatever ever shall be, is as sure as if it was done already. For there is no wisdom nor understanding nor counsel against God. He has disannulled the devices of the nations and has defeated peoples' purposes. But his counsel shall forever stand and his purposes shall always take place. *(Proverbs 21:30)* Nothing is random, because He sees all and knows all. He even foresees and foreknows all that ever shall be. For from the beginning of the world, yea from all eternity, God knew all His works. (*John 2:24)* His foreknowledge and prescience is co-eternal with Himself and His own essence and all the thoughts, words and works of all his creatures are as well known to Him as are his own. For "there is not a word in my tongue, but thou, Lord, wholly knows it", said David, "and thou understands my thoughts long before". (*Psal 139:3)* "And Thou alone knows all men's hearts", said Solomon. (*1 King 8:39)* And again, "All things are naked and broken up to him with whom we have to do". (*Heb 4:12)* He foresees and foreknows all things before they happen; He sees and knows all things past, present and future at once. As human beings on our way in the world, we can see those who go before us or with us, but we cannot see who comes after us. God is alone, standing aloft on a sentinel and sees all both before and behind under one view and at one instant. That is what the *Psalmist* seemed to allude to when he said, that "God looked down from heaven and saw all Adam's sons. From His place of abode He views all the inhabitants of the world and as He framed and fashioned the hearts of each of them, so He takes notice of all their works". Since God foresees all things before any of them happen, this means that none of them fall out uncertainly for Him. Not only does He foresee all things beforehand, there is also nothing that he never sees and as He sees it, He sees all things at once.

So, in regard of God, nothing can come by chance because all things are guided and governed and ordered by His providence and eternal counsel to such purposes as He sees best Himself. So even those things that seem most disorderly in themselves are ordered by Him. It is not only the best things that are all effected and wrought by Him *(Ephes 1:11)*; even the worst and the wickedest are all so ordered and disposed by His eternal counsel and unsearchable wisdom. Even those who do what He willed but had not forbidden, He fulfilled what He willed. Nothing therefore comes to pass but what God foresaw, fore-decreed, fore-knew and fore-ordained. There is nothing that comes randomly in regard of God, since chance necessarily excludes all fore-knowledge and forecast. That is what the heathen man *Olevianus* of old foresaw when he said, that "Nothing was a random event for God, though many things were with man". It is in this sense that we should take *Augustine*, when he reasoned thus against randomness: "Whatever is done by chance, is done unadvisedly; whatever is done unadvisedly is done without forecast or foresight". Therefore if anything in the world happens by chance then the whole world is not administered by forecast or foresight. Taken at its simplest this argument of *Augustine* might also exclude all contingency in regard of uncertainty, as all chance in outcomes. But this must necessarily be understood of outcomes only in so far as they relate to God (with whom, because He foresees everything before it happens and fore-determines how all things shall fall out), none of those outcomes that are random to us are random to Him and none are contingent to God of those many that are contingent unto us.

Nor does His providence, therefore, be it general or special, nor His ordination, be it ordinary or extraordinary, nor His cooperation, be it mediate or immediate, alter or change outcomes and occurrences, or make those acts or effects that either in their own nature, or in respect of contingent or random use, to be regarded otherwise, only except for God, for whom no act or outcome is truly and properly said to be such.

Chapter 3

The several sorts of lotteries

So far we have spoken in general about the definition of a lottery and of the random or chance events of which a lottery is one. We will now proceed to consider the several sorts and kinds of lotteries. In the definitions of lotteries I find much diversity among writers, some describing them under two heads, some three, some four, some to more, being uncertain how many.

§1. Those that describe types of lotteries under *two* heads:

Lyra (~1300) makes just two sorts of lotteries:

–Divisory lotteries used for dividing something between various persons.

–Consultative lotteries to determine what is to be done.

Divisory lotteries are said by Lyra "to be lawful and free from offence, if the outcome is committed to chance or the random motion of a creature, without greedy desire of gain. A Consultative lottery is unlawful if it depends on a result taken from any outside activity such as the motion of the planets or the operation of evil spirits. It might be lawful if it was based on the chance act of a creature. It could be lawful if it is expected that God or good angels wish it, and that it is done in cases of necessity, with due reverence and not as part of ecclesiastical elections".

Tilenius (~1610) also makes two sorts: Divine and Human:

–Divine lottery in a special manner appointed by God which we may not now use having no permission so to do;

–Human lottery which he subdivides into Divisory and Consultative, allowing the former to be used with some caution, but being wholly silent as to any censure on the latter.

Lavater (1586) and *Schindler (1612)* make two sorts, but in different terms: Divisory and Divinatory:

–Divisory lotteries are used (as before) for the division of possessions, legacies, spoils, offices, exercises, employments and the like. These are lawful and commendable.

–Divinatory lotteries are used to find out hidden and unknown truths and to foretell future events. They are unlawful and damnable.

They think the Consultative lottery should be included in the former, though in not quite the same way.

Serarius (1609) again make two classifications, but in another way: Consultative and Divinatory. His view is that the reasons for using a lottery are either for the bare knowledge of things past, present or future, or it could be wider and include anything which might be considered as deliberation and counsel. So some are Divinatory lotteries, some are Consultative lotteries. The divisory lottery may be referred to as this latter.

§2. Those that describe types of lotteries under three heads:
Aquinas (1270) makes three sorts: Divisory, Consultative and Divinatory.

–Divisory lotteries determine what each one shall have;

–Consultative lotteries inquire into what is the best thing to do;

–Divinatory lotteries try to search out what shall happen in the future.

Aquinas comments that "if the result is expected from the stars then it is false and vain. If it is from chance alone, as in divisory lotteries, then it is not wholly free from some vanity. But if there is some spiritual cause directing it, whether it be the Devil, or if it be God, then that in itself is not evil. But it may become sinful if lotteries are used when not necessary or without due reverence or when it involves the abuse of divine oracles or for ecclesiastical offices. In other situations, when necessary, it would be lawful to invoke a divine decision by lot, if done with due reverence".

Most of the popish writers follow Aquinas, apart from *Cajetan (1525)* and *Toletus (1610)* who limit it to the Consultative lottery only. Some such as *Malderus (~1610)* and *Delrio (1618)* condemn utterly both Consultative and Divinatory lotteries, except in case of either special command or instinct. They allow the Divisory lottery so long as it does no wrong or injury to anyone. *Peter Martyr (~1560)* describes the same sorts of lotteries and then passes the same censure upon them: that to expect a result from using chance or fortune is frivolous; using evil spirits is superstitious; and using the motions of the planets is ridiculous. It is from God alone that the only religious and lawful use of lottery comes. They can be used in case of necessity, reverently and religiously, without superstition, without fraud or collusion and without the abuse of divine oracles.

Peucer (1572) and *Krakewitz (~1610)* describe three sorts of lottery also, but in another way:

–Divine lotteries guided and governed immediately by God, which godly men use upon God's special command, not now warranted to us.

–Civil or political lotteries used for the ending of strife and lawsuits, or the sharing of goods, gifts and legacies, or the award of some honours and offices. These may lawfully be used with mutual consent and without coven [conspiracy] or fraud.

–Divinatory or superstitious lotteries are where men presume upon idle grounds, neither warranted by God's word nor founded on natural reason, to find out hidden truths and guess at future events. This is a satanical course and is expressly forbidden in scripture.

Perkins (1608) again makes three sorts of lottery but with a new twist:

–Civil or political lotteries are used for the dividing of bargains etcetera, to end strife.

–Sporting [gambling] lotteries commonly used for the setting up of bankrupts.

–Divining lotteries (sometimes known as divination) which are used in the foretelling of future events.

The first is warrantable when used in cases of weight and necessity and with the invocation of God's name. The two latter notable abuses have no warrant in God's word.

§3. Those that describe types of lotteries under four or more heads:

Estey (~1603) is alone in making four sorts of lot:

–Divine lotteries appointed and commanded to be used by God

–Diabolical lotteries used for divination and condemned by all;

–Political lotteries used to choose Magistrates in cases of war, tolerated by many;

–Gambling* lotteries used for sport and pastime, questioned by most and disallowed by Estey.

Lastly *Serarius (1609),* besides his former categories, draws up opposing pairs of lottery types: Serious and Gambling. This is akin to what others have done, as permitted and prohibited, or as lawful and unlawful, or as religious and profane. There are many other categorisations which are too insignificant to bother with. They are drawn from a great variety and diversity of sources. They concern those that work with lotteries, the instruments used in lotteries, matters which are disposed of by lotteries, the manner how, the places where, the times when lotteries were used and the like.

§4. My choice: two categories Ordinary lotteries (both serious and gambling) and Extraordinary lotteries:

Leaving these diverse and inconsistent divisions by various a authors, I will attempt to give a somewhat fuller and more exact classification than most of them have done, which is fitter and more commodious for the business in hand.

Lotteries, I say, should all be referred to under two heads and sorted into two ranks, namely Ordinary lotteries, which are commonly termed Divisory lotteries and Extraordinary lotteries such as the Consultative or Divinatory lotteries. The Ordinary lotteries may be subdivided into Serious and Gambling lotteries. These again may be distinguished by various differences as occasion shall require it.

* The word 'gambling' was not coined until the 1700s; 'lusurious lots' is the expression used repeatedly by Gataker in the sense of gambling or gaming. Despite his use of this delightful description, I have modernised it to the rather blunt 'gambling' for the rest of this book

TYPES OF LOTTERY (according to Gataker)

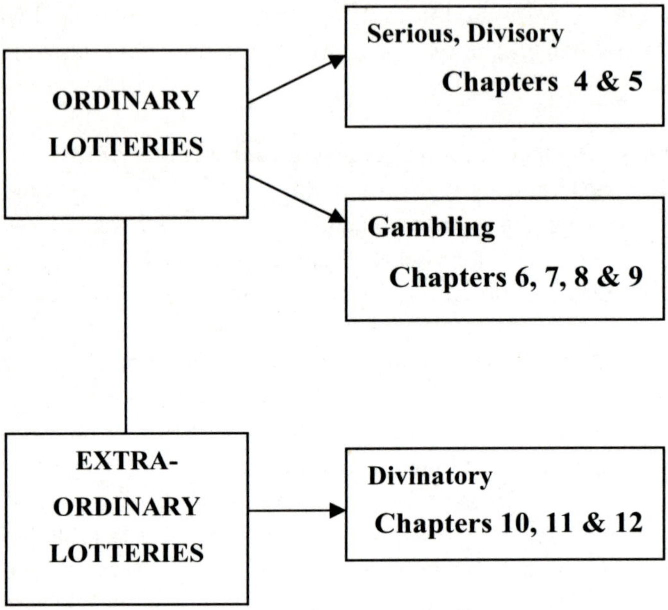

Gataker's schema for the rest of the book based on his classification of lotteries

Chapter 4

Ordinary lotteries for serious uses

§1. 'Ordinary' lotteries

Ordinary lotteries are those whose effect works in a fully ordinary or natural way by the person using them and used in them. No extraordinary power or divine providence is required for the direction of the action to which the lottery may be applied. One kind of ordinary lottery is that which is merely divisory. Here the matter in question and controversy can be decided by an uncertain motion or event of a person or thing. The use of it is decided by those who have it in their power to use it. Thus no special providence or extraordinary means is required to direct such an action in any particular manner. This kind of lottery may also be termed either civil or profane, taking the word profane as opposed to sacred, but in its better sense.

So where do we get the following definition: "That a lottery is a kind of consulting with God of rare use, lawful if used in situations where neither reason nor human advice can conveniently be had"? *(Aret.)* This describes nothing less than a consulting with God when such a lottery is used, without cause, reason, ground or occasion to do so. *(Aquinas, 1270)* But if there is no question concerning what a person would have done or not done, nor any doubt over the difficulty of doing it, then this does not require any special aid, assistance or divine presence or providence to settle it, any more than any other ordinary act or affair in this life. Nothing supernatural is expected or required in these ordinary, civil, divisory lotteries. They rest solely on what is within the natural power of the person using them and with the will and consent of the person making use of them. They are just as easy to put into effect as a man who has limbs can walk or who has sight can see. This will become evident by a diligent review of the several examples that follow in the later sections of this chapter*.

So ordinary lotteries are of two sorts; on the one hand there are the serious lotteries and on the other are lotteries used for gambling. *(Serarius, 1609)* I call a

* At this point in the second edition Gataker pauses. The case that an 'ordinary' lottery does not imply divine intervention must have been very contentious, and provoked counter-argument, for example from Balmford. To prove his case Gataker inserted no fewer than nine new pages of logic-chopping. If you want to follow this theological dispute, I have included his arguments as an appendix at the end of this chapter, rather than continue here, because I think it would seriously interrupt the flow of the discussion.

lottery serious when it is used in some serious business, be it great or small, weighty or light. Otherwise, an ordinary lottery which is a matter of mere sport or delight alone I would term 'gambling' and will expound on these in later chapters. Serious lotteries have sometimes been described by authors as 'divisory' because they are frequently used in the division of lands, goods, chattels, bargains, exercises, offices, employments and the like. As Solomon said: "The lottery causeth contentions to cease and parteth between the mighty." *(Proverbs 18:18)*

§2. Distributing sacred offices and duties by lottery

There is a great variety of examples of the use of lotteries both in Holy Writ and in profane writers. We may observe that lotteries have been used for the distribution of offices and charges, for the division of possessions, lands, goods, chattels and the like. When it comes to matters of office or service and duties which have been distributed by lottery, they have been used either for sacred or civil tasks.

For sacred tasks: Firstly, there are some who **mistakenly** find examples of choosing by lottery in scripture:

The Angels in heaven are said to have their charges assigned to them by a lottery which decides who shall rule in this or that province *(Dan 10:13)*, who attends to this or that person or who governs this or that Church. We should ignore this bold fancy by *Origen*, which he took from a reference to Moses in a mistranslation by the Septuagints *(Deut 32:8)*, which he himself mis-expounded. He writhed and wrested various parts of scripture for his 'proof' of this frivolous assertion. The same gross error was also put out by *Ambrose,* so that many who were otherwise of good note both in former times (*Bede)*, as well as in later days also (*Perkins, 1590; Schindler, 1612*) mistakenly followed him.

It is also a misinterpretation of a reference in the Gospel which says that "The High Priest in the Old Testament was elected by lottery". *(Luke 1:9)* There is evident proof to the contrary that among the Jews the high priesthood was selected legally and usually by descent *(Num 20:25)*, although this was indeed sometimes corrupted by force, favour or purchase. *(Macc 4:8)* But it was never, as we read of in *Baronius* done by lottery, apart from one occasion, just before the final utter ruin of both church and state.

There is the suggestion that the Apostles of Christ used a lottery to divide up the whole world amongst themselves to preach and to plant the gospel. This is a groundless conceit of that counterfeit *Prochorus*, although many agree with him. Prochorus also falsely claimed that the seventy-two disciples who should accompany and attend on each Apostle were chosen by lot, as the Levites did with their priests and that John's lot was to go to Asia.

But we pass from these fond figments to genuine examples: In the Jewish Church sacred offices were shared out by lottery for the readier manner of performance and more orderly execution of them. The divisions of sacred offices made among them by lottery were either General or Special.

General division of sacred offices: Genuine examples

The whole body of the Tribe of Levi was sorted out into ranks by lottery as follows: First, the Priests were all divided into 24 companies according to their families, which took their courses by turns, week after week in order. The order of their courses was settled by a lottery. *(Bellarmino, 1610)* This was done to take away all murmuring, so that none might complain or feel less regarded and cast behind others. Again, the Levites who were not Priests were also divided into 24 companies and appointed to attend on the priests: who, which and when was decided likewise by a lottery. Since everyone, great and small alike submitted themselves to the lot, there was no contention or emulation amongst them. *(1 Chron 25:8)*

In particular, for the Priests of each company who served at the same time, a lottery was cast by them for the sharing out of offices among themselves. This was done partly to avoid confusion and contention (for "God is a God of order and peace" *(1 Cor 4:33))* and partly to better settle the service. It is well known that no man has regard for what is everyman's charge (or as the saying goes "Where most servants, least service!"). So it was decided who should tend the Altar of Incense, who the Table of holy bread, who the dressing of the Lamps, who the Altar of Burnt offerings, who should feed the Fire, who should carry out the Ashes etcetera. All this is plainly reported in the books of the Jewish liturgies.

This explains what is meant when the Evangelist Luke said of Zachary, that being of the course of Abia and serving in his course, he went in by lottery to burn incense. (*Luke 1:9)* This passage has been misunderstood by many of the Ancients, including *Ambrose* who suppose this Zachary to have been the High Priest, which it is apparent he was not. The High Priest was given no particular course, nor did he live in Jerusalem, but had constant employment and continual abode at the Temple. (*Estey, ~1603)* When this Zachary was assigned by lottery to burn incense for the solemn Fast of Atonement, this was a time when only the High Priest could enter into the innermost Sanctuary not only with incense, but with blood also and that but once in the year. *(Hebr 9:7)*

It is also a groundless and uncertain conceit, though in a matter of no great moment, which continues to our times, concerning the time of our Saviour Christ's conception and birth. Some refer to it as in the Spring toward the end of our March *(Ambrose)* and others to Midwinter about the latter end of December, or the beginning of January *(Jerome)*. Most of the ancients referred His birth-time to our Spring, which was their harvest, about April or May *(Clement)*; and other later ones of great note *(Scaliger, ~1610; Broughton, 1588)*, upon uncertain grounds would reduce it to September or October in Autumn.

But to return to our Task. As the Priests shared the services among themselves by lottery, so the Levites did likewise for those that were Singers and those that were Porters. It was by lottery that the order was established for their musical and ministerial employment as singers and which gates of the Temple should be waited at and attended by the porters. *(1 Chron 26:13)* If there were too many to wait in the same place it is reported that they likewise took their turns by lottery, as well as for the nightly watch and for the daily ward. *(Psal 34:1)* Who should be singers, who porters, etcetera was, it seems, originally distributed by David, Nathan and Gad, with other principal persons assisting them, having warrant so to do from God. *(1 Chron 6:31)* Only the order and course of their employment in those offices was divided up among them or decided and settled among themselves by joint consent and general agreement using a lottery.

This is the origin of the phrase used by Simon Peter to Simon Magus, "Thou hast neither share nor lottery in this business". *(Acts 8:21)* This speech no more proves what that bastard *Prochorus* broached, that the Apostles shared among themselves by lottery, any more than does God's command to Elias to anoint Elizeus as Prophet in his own place *(1 King 19:16)*, (which was done, as the story showed, not by pouring oil on his head, but by casting a mantle on his back) prove that Prophets were either ordinarily or ever anointed in the time of the Old Testament (an opinion generally received without sufficient ground). Or that anointing of Kings was ever usual in Persia, because Cyrus was termed the Lord's anointed *(Esai 45:1),* or that material oil was poured upon our Saviour to that purpose, because he is called Christ and Messiah and is said to have been anointed by God. Anointing is to solemnly set apart and appoint, even where there is no material anointing at all, because men were sometimes installed by that ceremony into some sacred offices. *(Exod 40:13)* So a lottery is falsely used here for the right or the interest to deal in that holy business, which was not, except in Matthias' case disposed of by lottery *(Acts 1:26),* because sacred Offices or employments had sometime been thereby distributed.

Later post-biblical division of sacred duties

During a time of persecution, *Augustine* determined by lottery who among many of the pastors of people in a city should stay on and who should retire and preserve themselves for better times. This ensured that neither those that stayed might be taxed with presumption, nor that those that retired might be condemned of cowardice. This is also reported by some to be the practice to this day in the Church of Geneva, that a lottery is cast among their ministers, so that some of them are assigned to visit the infected at the pest-house in times of general infection by epidemical diseases *(Beza, 1564).*

§3. Distribution of civil offices in the Bible

As with the assignment of sacred offices, so too has the distribution by lottery of civil offices and matters of duty been ordinarily used among people. Two special examples are found of it in Scripture.

The first example is in a military matter *(Judg 20:9)*, in a quarrel among the Levites. One of them had had his concubine ravished, so that she died of it at Gibea in Benjamin. The other Tribes of Israel each resolved to go up against the Benjamites by lot. So it was conceived that a lottery should determine which

Tribe of the eleven should first go up against them. (They are said to have asked of the Lord at Shiloh and of the Priest that stood before him there, which Tribe should give the justice.) The meaning of this, as two worthy interpreters *(Peter Martyr, ~1560; Junius, ~1590)* rightly observe, is that a lottery decided which of each Tribe should be warriors and which purveyors, who should go forth to fight and who should be employed to bring in provisions to those that were out in the field. The state [regime] there was then popular, as one of them well noted and therefore it seemed best to decide by lot, which during anarchy could not otherwise easily have been settled without much tumult.

The second example is in organising a city: When some people returned from the Babylonian deportation, under Ezra's direction they organised a lottery amongst themselves to decide who should bear the burdens of charges and expenses, who should be employed in fetching and bringing in wood and who should spend their days in God's service on the Altar of burnt offerings. The times were then dangerous and the work was of some difficulty because their enemies lay in wait for them on every side. *(Num 3:46)*

There are also some Jewish writers *(Solomon, ~1090)* who affirm that a lottery determined which of the first born should go free by way of exchange with the Levites and which of them should pay a certain sum of money by way of redemption. But regarding the burden in regard of the firstborn there is no certainty of it in these words and the whole of the burden might as well have been raised from the general body rather than the firstborn.

§4. Distribution of offices: The Greeks:

In Theory: The use of the lottery was just as frequent among other nations as it was among the Jews. It was most commonly to be found in democracies or popular states *(Plutarch)* because they, it seems, saw justice in having the greatest equality and indifference within them, which they do without question. Such indifference may not always be allowable, nor may such equality always equate with equity. However the lottery is no stranger to any kind of state or form of government. *(Isocrates)* Its use in the most flourishing and best ordered states is not rejected, but admitted and approved by those state-masters or state-wrights (if I may so term them) *(Sallust)* that have plotted and moulded ideal states, as if they wrought them out of wax. They deemed that it would be for the best and likely to continue longest.

Plato in his imaginary model of a state intended that it would be the most exact and absolute in all points. He would have most of his magistrates designated yearly by lottery. Some offices were to be excepted such as the Chief Justice and the General when there was a war on against other military powers. The lottery was to be used to prevent and meet with the peevishness and waywardness of the multitude. For this reason Plato suggested that 360 men be chosen each year by popular vote out of the whole community. They would come from the four ranks of his citizens, (£4, £3, £2 and £1 men, as they reckoned, or much about £12, £9, £6 and £3, according to one account. *(Brerewood, 1614)*) Out of each rank, 90 were to be chosen as Senators and Aldermen and half of them would be assigned by lottery to govern the city for that year. Also 60 sheriffs, five out of every twelfth part of the city, were to govern the territory. They were also divided into 12 parts. It was to be settled yearly by lottery which part of the city should send rulers into this or that part of the countryside. Besides these allocations, Plato required that of six elected by most votes out of the first rank, three were to be set apart (by lottery) as surveyors of the houses, edifices, high-ways and water-courses in and about the city. Of those so elected out of the first and second ranks, five were to be clerks of the market. Again, one of 12 was chosen out of the whole company of competitors to be Master of the Revels and the three out of 12 with the most votes were to be Umpires and Disposers of prizes in solemn games. Courts were to be set up in each ward of the city. In private legal cases for the prevention of corruption, judges would be appointed by lottery as the occasion required. Similar arrangements were to made for the public trials. The election of priests and those who have charge of holy things should be left to god himself, for him to dispose as he pleased by lottery. In all these examples it was necessary that the parties on whom the lottery had alighted had to pass some form of trial afterwards to see if they were qualified. Only then would they be accepted or disallowed.

Actual use of lottery by the Greeks: But let us leave this theoretical framework and move on to actual uses of the lottery. There are many famous states among the Greeks who have tried it, especially the Athenians. I will pass over Sparta where I find little was done using this kind by lottery, except that the order in which the candidates for any office were scrutinised was decided by lottery; they then had to pass before the Suffrages of the Assembly, who had the power to choose or refuse them. *(Plutarch)* At Athens many of the offices and employments, both civil and sacred were disposed of by lottery. Some offices were wholly elective, such as Areopagites [judges] who sat at Mars' hill on matters of greatest consequence, such as wilful murder and the like. They were chosen from those that had, without blame, born office before elsewhere and who continued in that authority so long as they lived *(Demosthenes.)*

Athens: The legislature: Most offices, though, were designated yearly by lottery, as for example their sacred Senators or Legates who were sent year by year to the common Council at Delphos. The ordinary Senators, or the Council of 500, which formed the government and judicature of the ordinary affairs were all drawn from the commoners. They were chosen *(Sigon)*, it seems, by putting together the names of all those of each ward that were capable of that dignity. Their names were noted on little tablets or tokens of brass and put into one vessel. An equivalent number of black and white beans, all but 50 black, were put into another vessel. As each man's token was drawn out of the one, a bean was drawn out of the other. So he passed to further trial if he were approved, or he was rejected for that year if his bean proved white or black. *(Demosthenes)*. And so fifty men were extracted out of each of the ten Wards. (They cannot really be termed tribes, because a tribe is, as the word suggests, only a third part of one of them). Thus the whole number was made up for the Council of 500. *(Aristotle)*.

Out of those who were thus dignified by benefit of the bean, nine were advanced by the same means to a further place of authority and named as Rulers or Regents. Of these there were six Masters of the Ordinances, the Master of their Ceremonies, the Mayor for the year and the Marshal. *(Demosthenes)* After the 500 were thus designated and the nine Regents drawn out, the lottery was again cast or drawn to decide which of the ten Wards should rule first. The leadership of each of them lasted little more then a month, to wit, the tenth part of their year. Which one ruled next and so on to the year's end was also decided by a lottery. *(Thucydides)* All these princes, as they were styled, for the Ward that had the white bean for the principality then took over and drew again for the ten Presidents that would rule for the seven first days and then ten more for the seven next and so on till the 35 days were covered, which was the full time of their whole principality. From the same ten the post of Commander or Provost was drawn out by lottery. His governing lasted for one day of the seven. None of the ten were allowed to have it more than once or more than one day at a time, because the keys of the castle at Athens were in his keeping. And so of the seven who were favoured by the white bean, of necessity three of them were debarred from it. *(Pollux)*

Athens: The judiciary: When cases were to be heard and tried, the Masters of the Ordinance used a register to call together those that had power of judicature into one place. *(Aristotle)* There were ten courts that heard the pleas of several kinds of suits. They were marked with several letters, set in several colours (so it seems) over the several court gates. The lottery assigned a competent number of persons according to the quality of the suits to be heard to each court *(Lucian)* by the drawing of beans or sometimes acorns (acorns are also reported to have been used in this business *(Aristophanes)*) with the letters on them that belonged to those courts. Each of the persons so allotted first received a rod from the Clerk which had the name of the Court written on it, or was of the same colour as the letter over the court gate. He went with the rod and his bean or acorn to that court that had the letter of the same colour and was admitted there as the judge. *(Demosthenes)*.

Besides these ordinary judges there were also certain Arbitrators or Umpires (other than those chosen by mutual consent of both sides) who were assigned for the hearing and ending of lighter matters; they were likewise divided among them by a lottery. *(Pollux)* They too were assisted by certain clerks of the pleas, also designated by lottery, from whose sentence, if it was not liked, appeal might be made to the judges.

Both for the Senators and the nine Regents, it was constantly observed that if someone who had been drawn was either rejected upon trial or had died during the time of his service, others might immediately be found to replace them in a second lottery. *(Plato)* There was a great penalty for anyone who intruded himself into a court or council who had not been duly assigned to do so by the lottery. *(Demosthenes)*

Athens: Other offices: I have found further offices appointed at Athens by the lottery. Ten Treasurers taken out of those of the best rank; Ten Controllers or Auditors, to whom most of the other Officers were to give account of their government within a certain number of days after their time expired, with free liberty granted to any man that would stand up to accuse them of, or charge them, while they were in office, with anything which was done when it ought not to be. There were also Ten Surveyors or Scavengers; ten Wardens of the Ports; ten Clarks of the Market. There was also the Office of the Eleven, where ten were Sheriffs or Bailiffs and had charge of the common jail, executions and arrests within his own Ward and the eleventh was a scribe or registrar joined on to them to make writs and enter actions; and there were officers also for each Principality previously mentioned who chose one of their number by lottery to attend on them for the keeping of their writs and decrees and for the entering up of their orders. *(Demosthenes)*.

Now of the officers thus elected by lottery some had sacred as well as civil employment. *(Pollux)* It was not only the king or master of the mysteries and holy rites who dealt most in such sacred matters, but also the mayor for the year and the marshal had several employments in their superstitious services. Also designated by lottery were the 10 priests who had to procure prodigies and perform certain superstitions every fifth year. There were also priests for their many gods, such as Jove, Vulcan, etcetera. (*Lacon*) Many others also followed this practice, both in other parts of Greece and elsewhere as at Syracuse in Sicily, where, of three chosen by votes out of three Families, one was yearly designated by lottery as priest for Jove. *(Cicero)* Again those on whom the lottery lighted had to pass some trial afterwards and only then were allowed or disallowed insofar as they were then found to be qualified.

§5. Distribution of offices: The Romans

We pass over from Greece to Italy, from "Athens, the Eye of a great part of the whole known world to Rome the Head of it". *(Pliny)* It is reported at Rome that Romulus would not allow priests to be appointed by lottery, but by election only. *(Dionysius)*. Yet it was by lottery that the Vestal Virgins were thus designated there in succeeding ages, when places became void by decease or default. One of them was thus taken from the twenty picked out by the chief Priest. *(Gellius)* For civil offices the Romans are said to have imitated the Athenians, but in truth they took their own course. *(Delrio, 1618)* Not many of the offices themselves were divided out by lottery; they went mostly by election and votes. It was the employments or tasks within those offices which were divided out by a lottery. It is in this regard that the tragedians compare the business of their state to dice-playing, when it prefers not the worthiest but those that have had the best luck.

At first, after the death of Romulus, the 200 Gentry were divided into tens and cast lots for the ruling of the state, taking turns among themselves. Each ten had their 50 days and each of the ten his five and then the next ten after, until they had all taken their turns. But they soon grew weary of that course and on the election of Numaes it expired.

After the ejection of the Tarquins and the end of kings, rule was by the two Consuls or Mayors. When some extraordinary business came up to be done by them, but could only conveniently be done by one of them, such as the dedication of a temple, the nomination of a dictator or Sovereign General, the keeping of courts for the creation of some new officers or the like, Brutus settled the issue by ordering that a lottery be used to decide who should have the honour of it. *(Livy)* It was quite ordinary and usual to use this manner of decision when choosing who should stay at home, who went abroad, or both to go abroad when the waging of war in several places was considered, or when the governing of several Provinces was needed. This was "a course not unusual in other states also". *(Conon).*

When officers were both together in the same service with equal authority, they sometimes used the lottery to take their turns daily. *(Livy)* Similarly they would decide who should stay and who should return for a time, when some state business required the presence of one of them at home. Only one Praetor was at first ordained for civil jurisdiction at home, because the Consuls were often called abroad by the occasion of war. As law suits grew, because of access of foreigners to the City and as the number of provinces increased, two Praetors were then needed. At first they shared the city jurisdiction between the two of them by lottery, one to take cases between citizen and citizen, the other to take cases between citizens and foreigners. Later, they, together with the vice-consuls and vice-praetors all cast lots together in common for the two jurisdictions at home and for the sundry provinces abroad*. Exceptionally these commissions continued in authority after their year had expired, or it might be by special favour under the Emperors that they had such authority conferred upon them. *(Livy)* As well as judicial employment, the lottery also decided who should have charge and oversight of public stage plays and solemn sights; this was highly esteemed employment. It was felt to be a major disgrace if anyone of rank or degree was to be excluded from the lottery process for these employments, although we find that it was done sometimes. *(Suetonius).*

---

* The processes of election of Cicero as one of the Praetors and the allocation of his tasks by a lottery are graphically described in Robert Harris's 2006 novel *Imperium.*

As the state expanded, others offices were added as well those of Praetor. The Questors [Treasurers] likewise had their employments assigned them by a lottery. From the ranks of those who had been Treasurers, Tribunes were sometime designated by lottery if none of them had offered themselves to stand for the office. From their numbers too, some were assigned by lottery to go abroad to settle new colonies. *(Plutarch)* The Aediles [Surveyors] were also designated by lottery. This happened when a number of candidates had an equal number of votes and it was uncertain therefore which of them should be chosen. This might also be used in other offices. (*Cicero)*

Solemn assemblies which enacted laws and elected the greater or lesser magistrates came in three stages. *(Gellius)* In ancient times, things that were done by the courts which Romulus had established and ended in the time of Cicero. In the middle times, before the Empire, either the main body of the people, sorted and ranked according to degrees either of wealth or birth, were each again divided into hundreds or centuries. Or the same people were divided into tribes (without any distinction of degree) according to their place of abode and again subdivided into hundreds or centuries. In the first and oldest times the courts were all called out in random order to give their votes. So scrupulous and superstitious were they, that if by chance the court that came first was deemed to be ominous, then the assembly was dissolved forthwith to be re-convened on another day. In the early middle period, when the chief officers were chosen, the lottery was only used to decide which hundred should first be called upon to vote and so (as it were) give a leading voice to the rest, the rest being called in order, without a lottery. In the later middle period each one of the tribes in the assembly was called upon to vote, the order being determined by lot for all of them. This procedure is what Gracchus thought would be best for the common good. *(Livy)*

For warlike employment both Consuls and Praetors had their Legions and Armies allotted to them by this means also. Tribes were sometimes assigned by lottery as to who should offer soldiers for service and also to decide which persons of each Tribe should serve. *(Livy)* In this respect it is worth remembering the fraudulent act of the Consul M. Curius, who, when a sudden muster was to be made and no young men appeared, cast a lottery on all the Tribes. The lottery of that Tribe which came next to hand was cited by him as being the first-drawn. But it appeared that this was not the case, so they confiscated his goods and sold him for a slave. *(Cicero)*

In the civil jurisdiction, cases were handed around among the magistrates by lottery, at first sparingly but in latter times more ordinarily. Some magistrates would have to try cases of treason, some of murder, some of extortion and the like. These magistrates would, using a lottery, also extract from the whole company of those who had power of judgement in such cases a sufficient number as the law required to assist them in judgement. This is what the ancient writers called the 'Sorting of Suits'. It was not, as some have thought, the ordering of cases, but the assigning of judges by lottery for the hearing of each case to prevent corruption and packing. *(Cicero)*. In any case it was lawful for either the defendant or plaintiff, upon just ground, to challenge any of the judges allotted to him. This was something which was allowed in the hearing of cases of monetary fraud by the more moderate emperors. Another judge would then be drawn by a lottery in his room. Sometimes counsel was assigned by lottery to the parties contending the case, at the discretion of the court.

Augustus is reported *(Suetonius)* to have randomly chosen a certain number of Senators to consult with at set times about matters which were to be moved in an open hearing afterwards. This might be to dispatch businesses without any hearing, yet to make it seem that the whole assembly had some hand in it. Augustus also used the lottery to assign some to attend the assembly during the harvest-time, to ensure a fair number attended while giving the rest the liberty of absence. It was by lottery that the city was parted into certain regions or wards, with the yearly officers appointed to share those wards and to take charge of them. This practice continued for a long time afterwards. *(Tacitus)* It was by lottery that Augustus required that two of those that had formerly been Praetors would be chosen yearly for the custody of the Treasury. But because of evil-doings this did not last long. Using the lottery he attempted to reform the whole body of the Senate. Augustus first chose a certain number and after an oath was administered to them, gave each of them power to name five persons that they thought were fittest for government, none of whom was their own kindred. From each of the five he drew out one. But this device of his had no great good effect and was soon given up again.

In Tiberius's reign the lottery was used to clear laws that in some cases were then questionable. And in Vespasian's time it was either Mucianus or Vespasian himself, or both of them, as some suppose, severally and at several times, assigned by lottery who to see to make restitution for the wrongs done during the recent civil war. And in an extraordinary move, the lottery was used to rid the courts of a multitude of suits that delay in justice had then clogged with. And during Domitian's sons' time a new college was established out of which Masters of the Revels were chosen by lottery for his imperial disports. The Senate also tried to curry favour with Domitian by decreeing that some of the Roman knights, selected by lottery should attend on him fully attired. *(Suetonius)*.

Lastly we find that legates or lieutenants, some of whom had special powers, were occasionally designated by lottery. The use of the lottery in this matter is sometimes questioned. Although some were opposed to it, yet the greater part went with it and would have still retained it as a sovereign preservative against ambition and corruption and a singular remedy for the preventing both of enmity and envy. In this regard they esteemed it as a kind of divine ordinance which was carried out without fraud and conspiracy, as it ought to be. *(Tacitus)*.

§6. Distribution of offices: Italy today

Venice: The practice of civil lottery in matters of offices and employment is still usual to this day in Italy and in some other states that are generally renowned for their wisdom and policies. Among these is the state of Venice which many *(Dartes, n/k)* take to be the very mirror of policy, with some supposing it to be a model of Plato's old platform. The whole body of the Venetian gentry are, as of right, admitted into their General Council at 25 years of age but not ordinarily any earlier. They may apply for it at the age of 20 and if the lottery favours them, they then obtain it. For this purpose they meet once a year on the 4th of December. Then those seeking it, having formally made proof of their gentry status, have all their names cast into a pot. It is brought up to the Doge, before whom stands another pot with an equal number of balls in it, one-fifth gilt, the rest silver. He draws a name out of the one and then a ball out of the other. If it proves to be golden he is thereupon admitted; if it is a only a silver one then he is held back at least a year longer. Again, in their choice for the office of electors (but not so much for main offices) they are decided in part by a lottery in a manner somewhat like that which Augustus once used, as explained above.

For the designation of their Doge, first there is a lottery about the lottery, with lot-use and voting in a prolix and intricate manner interchangeably mixing the one with the other. When the vacancy for Doge arises, either because he has been deposed or as is more usually by his death, all their gentry of 30 years of age or upward (for none younger are admitted) are assembled together. They come up in order of the place where they sit (lotteries having been first cast to decide which side of them shall come up first) to the lottery pot. This has as many balls in it as there are of them, but only 30 are gilt. A child then draws out balls until 30 gilt ones are found. For these 30 the child draws again a second time from another pot that has only nine gilt balls. The nine thus drawn withdraw themselves into a conclave, where among themselves they name 40 so that each of them has at least six votes. Out of the 40 so named, 12 are again selected by lot. This 12 chooses a further 25, each gaining at least eight votes. From these 25, nine are again set apart by lot. These nine nominate a further 45 as before and those 45 being again reduced to 11 by lot. These 11 choose 41 of the chief senators, which at last has the power to elect a Doge. These 41 are then subjected to an oath sworn by them and some other solemnities are performed. They choose whom they judge to be the worthiest by each writing his name on a scroll. The scrolls are mingled together and then drawn out as they come. The fitness of the person first drawn is discussed. If he has 25 votes with him he was wont anciently to carry it without further ado. But in later times they go on and he who has the most votes above that number, whether he came first or last to hand, has the place. If none of them has enough votes, they begin again and continue until someone was nominated that had. *(Contareno, 1599)*

Again in their yearly assemblies for the choice of other officers, all their gentry have a vote in the Council (no-one is excluded). They draw first for 60 gilt balls out of two pots by a single lottery, half out of the one and the other half out of the other. Then the 60 chosen draw for 36 places by gilt balls out of another pot in a second lottery. The 36 that have thus been drawn and having alighted on the golden balls twice, will have the power to nominate candidates to whatever offices that are then to be chosen. They do it like this: going apart into conclaves by nine and nine in four companies, where they all, in order of years in each company, draw balls out of a lot-pot. These have marks on them for the various offices and according to whichever ball that each of them has drawn he can nominate whatever citizen he wishes for that office. If he gets six votes out of those nine then the choice holds; if not then another must be nominated by him, until someone is approved. By this means among those four companies there are four competitors nominated for each of their Offices. One of them is chosen by most votes of the whole Assembly, with the electors and the families of the parties nominated being excluded.

Tuscany: In a somewhat similar manner it is reported *(Grimston, 1611)* that in the Tuscan state [Florence] they choose, not their electors, but their officers. Those that are capable of office are divided into three ranks and accordingly cast into three boxes. Out of the first they draw the magistrates of the top rank, the middle sort out of the second and the lowest out of the third. By drawing out five names for each office, it is awarded to he who has the most votes in the Council. But their election stands only if it pleases the Duke to confirm it.

§7. Lotteries for sharing various tasks

Generally speaking there have been many places and sorts of people who have often shared employments using the lottery. In wartime, garrisons, sieges, fighting fields and set camps were often managed thus. Those that serve together could have had their times, places and courses assigned to them by lottery. This also applied equally both to the watch and the ward, to assault and defence, or any such employment as their lottery place should require.

Even though Emperor Theodosius was a great commander, it is not a vulgar commendation to say that he was content to take his turn by lottery among the rest just like the common soldiers did in their military services. *(Virgil)* In single combats, a champion was sometime singled out by a lottery. According to the poet *Homer* it was the lottery which determined which of the two combatants should strike first. In jeopardous exploits, or where a mass of troops might cause confusion, hindering rather than helping, the lottery was called in to order and marshal the matter. It is said that the lottery decided who should be enclosed in the wooden horse's womb at the taking of Troy. When Timoleon needed to cross a river with his army in the face of the enemy, he took the rings from his section leaders, intending to make a draw among them to decide in what order they should cross. But when a ring that had a trophy engraved on it came first to hand, they ceased all further lot-drawing and with all speed they crossed over and so defeated the forces that stood on the other side to prevent their passage. When Pericles, found he could hardly restrain his inconsiderate and over-eager people, he divided them into two parts, assigning them by a lottery. Some were to skirmish and some to rest and make merry. *(Plutarch)* The merry-makers were those that had drawn the white bean: and this is the origin, said a Greek author, of the by-word applied to those that live at ease: "That they have a white day of it", an allusion to the white bean. In the case of desperate military situations, when the combatants were resolved to die rather than fall into the hands of the enemy and to be at his mercy, it was sometimes decided by lottery who should slay either other. This was how *Josephus* the Jewish historiographer escaped, with his lottery coming out with the last man's, whom he persuaded to surrender himself with him to the Romans. Deciding who should be the common executioners to all was a dilemma for the Jews who were besieged at Masada. At Eleazar's instigation, they chose ten by lottery among them to be the common butchers to the rest. Each of them first presented their wives and children and then himself to be slain. This being done, one of those ten was again singled out by lottery to dispatch the other nine and in the last place himself. At other times too, some were designated by lottery to be the slaughters and some were assigned by lottery to bury the slain.

At Syracuse *(Plutarch)* the order of delivery of advice at the court was set by lottery, a practice continued into Cicero's time in some cases. Dionysius is famous for one of his acts when in a lottery based on letters of the alphabet (as was used in the Olympics), he drew the letter M. When one jester him said he should play the mome or the fool, he answered that he would prove to be not a mome, but a monarch. And he made good on his word because this chosen general turned into a tyrant. This grew into a proverb: "M. is his lot" *(Zenodotus)* meaning that he is either a fool, or of a fellow of no worth. A similar story is told of the assemblies in Rhodes where both rich and poor were at liberty to speak their minds freely in all matters, the order of their speaking chosen by lottery. *(Sallust)*

On voyages *(Virgil)* some were chosen by lottery to be put ashore to explore, especially where it was suspected to be difficult and dangerous. And at sea they sometimes used a lottery to see who should row and who be otherwise employed. Those whose lot it was to tug at the oars took their places by a lottery. Both in public works as at the building of Tyre and in private labours as at Vulcan's forge, as in mutual combinations as at assault on the Cyclops, each man often had his task or standing assigned to him by a lottery. Nor should the great pride of the Egyptian tyrant be forgotten when he compelled tributary kings to take turns by a lottery to act like horses in his chariot when it pleased him once a year to ride in state. *(Pliny)*

In solemn entertainments too, the order of appearance was sometimes agreed by a lottery. When it fell to young Pompey (by lottery) to entertain Augustus and Anthony on his galley, he said that with a cut of his sword he could become master, not just of Sicily, but of Italy too. But he held back, he said, because of his oath or was it because he feared for his own security, or maybe he was not ready for such greatness. Another case is that of Miyas's daughters who it is said, in a mad fit, cast a lottery to decide which one of them would give their children up to be eaten at a feast. *(Plutarch)*. This was an echo of the choice of the women of Samaria during a siege of that city. *(1 King 6:78)*

In a word, so frequent was the use of a lottery in this way that some Grammarians *(Eustacius, ~1150)* have mistakenly thought that lotteries were so common among the Greeks that this is the origin of its name because it was by this means that men were usually called to this or that work. But this is just an example of ordinary speech, though a figurative use, when men are said to have this or that office allotted to them. *(Act 1:7)* This is not because a lottery selected them, but that it was by election or otherwise. In this way our Saviour was truly said to have been anointed a prince, a priest and a prophet *(Hebr 1:9)*, though no prophets had ever been anointed nor was any such material as oil ever put on His head. By not noticing this some have supposed a lottery there where indeed there was no lottery at all. *(Bodin, 1580)*

§8. Distributing land by lottery: An example from scripture*

We have seen how frequently the lottery was used among all sorts for distribution of civil and sacred offices and services. Its use has been no less frequent in the division of inheritances, lands and possessions, goods and chattels and the like. Rewards as well pains and penalties, honours and dignities have also often been dispensed by lottery. At the first entrance of God's people to the promised land the whole of the land was divided up, generally by a lottery, which was by God's own appointment among the 12 Tribes. Concerning this partition there is some dispute among the learned arising from the words of God's edict as recorded by Moses: "Unto these (that is the 12 tribes, though Levi be left out, because Joseph in Manasses and Ephraim make two) shall the land be divided to inherit according to the number of their names, (that is, of their persons, as the word name is also elsewhere used). To many you shall give a large inheritance and to fewer a less. To each one shall inheritance be given according to his number. Notwithstanding, the land shall be divided by lot and according to the names of the Tribes of their Fathers shall they inherit. According to the lottery shall the possession of it be divided between many and few". *(Num 26: 23; Act 1:15)*

The question is: why the greater number should have a larger portion and the fewer a less, when each part was to have its portion assigned it by lot? For the solution some would say *(Lyra, ~1300; Baronius)* that it was to fall out by God's special providence by miraculously directing the lotteries, that the greater amount

* This section is concerned with a single biblical example, which is examined in minute and extensive detail. The payoff for Gataker is to show that this is not a special 'extraordinary' example, just an ordinary lottery for dividing the lands of Israel.

of ground should fall to the greater number of men and the less to the fewer. But that is not likely, for had it been so meant, God would have said: "To many I will give a larger portion and to fewer a lesser. Divide thou as equally and exactly as thou art able to do by lot. And I will cause it to fall out so that the more men shall have more land and fewer men less." or "Do thou divide it into unequal parts; and I will make it fall equally to fit every Tribe's turn." This would mean that the casting of the lottery should be Joshua's work only, but the fixing up of more and fewer with larger or scanter possessions and portions would be for God's own immediate disposition. But this is an idle conceit because the outcome itself was controlled by the lottery and we find that some of them did indeed receive scant portions and complained about it. Others had more bestowed on them and then they were well able not only to people their own lands but were also willing to admit others on with them. *(Josh 17:14)*

Others *(Masius, ~1570)* think that the 12 men assigned to the office of dividing the land by lottery had their powers conferred upon them by virtue of that Edict. After the lottery was performed according to the partition made by others who were employed by them, they enlarged or straightened the boundaries of several portions as they saw fit. By virtue of which power they were able to adjust each portion to the number of the people that were of that Tribe and to whom the same lot had fallen. This is indeed more probable than the former and we often find that some alterations and changes of this kind are made after the distribution of possessions are settled by a lottery.

But the soundest explanation that some others *(Lyra, ~1300)* have conceived is that the Edict mentions a two-fold partition and both of them are necessary. The former is a general division of the whole land (taking this side of the Jordan to be held by the Reubenites, Gadites and half the Tribe of Manasses) into 12. Shires or cantons which were equally divided, were then to be distributed by a lottery. In the latter process a particular subdivision of each canton or shire was divided unequally among those of the Tribe on whom the same lottery had fallen if their families or kindred were more populous or penurious. *(Numb 16:55)*

Now as God ordered, so Joshua accordingly did. He divided the whole land among them by lottery. He began the work as soon as the land was at any rest and afterward went on with it until he had made an end of it. He was assisted by God's appointment of Eleazar, the High-priest and the 12 Heads of the 12 tribes. Their several lotteries and in what order they came is left on the record by the Holy Ghost. At the first session or solemn meeting for the performance of that business, the first draw fell to Judas and the second to Joseph in Ephraim and Manasses. At the second assembly the seven other tribes, to wit, Benjamin, Simeon, Zabulon, Isachaar, Asher, Nephthalim and Dan, (which was the order they were drawn) had their portions allotted them. The rest of the land, not previously assigned, was divided into seven parts, not by ten men, as Josephus said, but by 36 rather, or 21 at the least, (three-a-piece out of each tribe, either of the whole 12, or of those seven whose turns then were to be served) employed specially to that purpose. *(Josh 14:1)*

Concerning the manner of lottery used in that action there is some diversity of opinion. Some *(Schindler, 1612)* think that the names of the land parcels were put into one pot and the names of the tribes into another and that one chosen person, to wit Eleazar drew for them all. Others *(Josephus)* imagine that there was only one pot of tickets containing the names of the portions, out of which one of each tribe drew for his own tribe. Others *(Masius, ~1570)* lastly suppose that the tribes' names only were put into the lot-pot and that each tribe, as it was drawn, had the choice of which piece of land to select. This first opinion seems the most probable, both because one drawing so might well end it all, so there would not be a second. So the question might be who should draw first and who should ask for a new lottery? And again, because it is not said in the story whether such-and-such a Tribe drew or was drawn first or second simply, but that the lottery came out first or second for such a tribe, which did not agreed with the third.

There was indeed a special hand of God in this lottery, (as there is often in others) since it was done by special appointment from Him. *(Chytraeus, ~1580)* Because of this, it may seem to some worthies *(no ref)* to be ranked as an extraordinary lot, especially considering how aptly it fits with Jacob's prophetical prediction in his last will and testament. But I take this lottery to be properly included in the list of ordinary lotteries, because however much there may have been a special providence of God in it, so that it thereby fulfils the prophecy of the holy patriarch, the main matter that it was applied to and aimed at by those who used it is likely to have been seen as nothing more than an ordinary partition of possessions which conquest and God's gift had given to them, without any expectation of a special direction of them or of the tribes they were drawn for to specific parts and seats.

Just as the whole land was generally divided by lot, so were the cities assigned to the Levites by dividing them among themselves by lottery according to their families. God had commanded that 48 cities in all should be assigned to them, more from those that had more and fewer from those that had less. The Levites were divided into three Families according to Levi's three sons, Kehath, Gershon and Merari. The Kehathites were subdivided again into two ranks, to wit, the Aaronites or the issue of Aaron, Kehath's nephew by his son Amram, which alone had the Priesthood and the rest of that house which came not of Aaron. There were lotteries cast by them by their several families to decide what tribes should be assigned to which cities. The Princes set down how many cities each tribe should be afforded according to the quantity of their possessions and the number of their cities; also which cities in each tribe should be given to them as most convenient for their abode, who were then to be dispersed among all parts of God's people. When this was settled by them, the four families drew to decide which of them should have which of the cities which were set apart for each tribe. And so the Aaronites had 13 in Juda, Simeon and Benjamin. The other Kehathites had 10 in Ephraim, Dan and half of Manasses. The Gershonites had 13 in Issachar, Asher, Nephthali and the other half of Manasses. The Merarites had 12 in Reuben, Gad and Zebulon, making up the whole 48 in all.

Just as at their first coming into the promised land, the possession of it was divided by lottery, so at their return again unto it from the Chaldean captivity, a colony was drawn out by lottery for the peopling of Jerusalem. One was taken from each of ten and so a tenth of the whole company was found for the restoring of the City, besides those who had voluntarily offered themselves. The remnant was left to replenish other places and to take possession of the residue of the country round about. Indeed the whole city was shared out by lottery into three parts by the three seditious commanders during the time of the Roman siege (if we might believe the counterfeit *Ben-Gorion (~1100),* or at least his abridger, for the true *Josephus* said otherwise).

§9. Distributing goods and chattels: Biblical examples

Just as lotteries were used for the partition of lands, so too have they been used for moveable goods and chattels. The lottery was used in some cases for setting tithes. "God said: every tenth one of thy bullocks and of thy flocks, or lesser cattle, goats and sheep, as they pass under the rod, shall be holy to the Lord. There shall no regard be had of good or bad, nor any exchange be made of it". *(Levit 27:32)* It was a tenth or rather that which fell precisely in the tenth place which was strictly due to the priests. But where great herds of bullocks or flocks of sheep were involved, knowing which was tenth was not easy. So God decreed that every tenth one should be touched and taken by the tithing-man's rod as they came out of their stalls or their folds and so were set apart for the priest. This is what God alluded to when he told His people that through the prophet, "He would cause them to pass under the rod and bring them into the bond of His covenant". This is a metaphor taken from the way that shepherds count their sheep using a rod or a sheep-hook. God would search through His people and sort them, just as the shepherd does with his sheep, choosing the better sort of them, rejecting and excluding the rest, taking them into His fold to be in league with Him and under His charge.

Other examples can be found in the division of booty, prey and spoils taken in war. Lotteries are said to have been cast when Jerusalem was sacked by the Chaldees. Her people were enslaved and shared out by lottery among the conquerors. The nobles of Nineveh were similarly treated when that city was sacked, whether by the Medians or by the Scythians, who attacked it several times. *(Herodotus)*

This also applied to goods which were ill-gotten by pillage or stealth; as when David complained that his enemies had divided up his garments among them by a lottery. *(Psalm 22:19)* This is something which good writers *(Calvin, 1584)* have reasonably supposed was first practised upon David, at a time when he was forced to flee for fear of his life. His house was rifled by his foes and his goods right down to the very garments he wore were seized. It is likely that a lottery was used to shared them out. But there can be no question (the Holy Ghost has testified to it *(Matt)*) that the soldiers that executed our Saviour shared out his garments between them. One garment was the coat without seam; there are some that say that garments woven or wrought in this way are wont to unravel if they are torn. To save this garment from being quartered *(Suarez, 1613)*, they cast lots for it. For the rest of the garments or for just the other two (for it is not likely that there were more than three in all, a shirt, an inner and an upper coat) they were cut into four quarters (which many did not see and yet *Mark* evidently said) and were likewise shared by lottery with each of the four soldiers gaining a fourth part. What form of lottery was used by them is not apparent and is not greatly material. The popish tradition says *(Becon, 1560)* it was done by casting dice, which they say to this day were three in number. They may believe that, but there is one at Triers and two other at Saint Saviour's in Spain, as well as some others would quote *Nonnus* when he speaks of Christ's passion, though others again *(Falkenberg, 1569)* with better reason understand that he suggested that it was done by finger-matching. This involves divining or guessing how many fingers the other person will hold up, which the same author has also described in more detail elsewhere. It is a kind of lottery anciently much used in serious businesses, as well as in sport and pastime. It seems that Nonnus might well mean that it cannot be practised well except when two only do it at once. Poets such as Homer who is one of the best, often took liberty with the precise truth of a story and the ordinary use of those things they deal with. So it would be no marvel therefore if Nonnus should fail somewhat in this regard being esteemed one of the lower rank of such poets.

We will leave out the doubtful uses of lotteries, such as the one that Solomon alluded unto. *(Proverbs 1:4)* He brought in some thieves, not so much inviting them to join in his adventure (for there they had nothing to ventured lightly but limb and life), as promising them that 'he shall cast in his lot with them', that is, they shall have an equal share in whatsoever they get. This is similar to the way in which legitimate dealers in joint stock are wont to trade together. *(Junius, ~1590)*

Under this heading we may add using a lottery to designate or pick out persons some of whom are to be saved and some to be slain. There are those *(Chald, ~n/k)* who explain that this is what happened when David judged the Moabites. Two cowards were to be destroyed, but with one coward to be saved alive. Most commentators *(Lyra, ~1300)* turn it another way. Mostly they understand by God's speech, where he bids the prophet to "pull the flesh piece by piece, every piece of it out of the pot or cauldron and not to cast lots about it", as signifying that the people should not all be destroyed with some saved, but that they should all utterly be destroyed without distinction or difference. There are some of late who understand this otherwise. But it was evidently this use for a lottery that was cast for one of the two goats *(Levit 16:1)*, whereby the one was taken for the scapegoat to be saved and sent out alive and the other was left to be slain and to be a sin-sacrifice to God on behalf of His people. This was only a divisory, not a divinatory lottery to tell which was fitter for the service, both being equally fit. And these are all the examples that I find of this use of lottery in holy writ.

§10 Various profane (non-biblical) uses of ordinary yet serious lotteries

Among profane [non-religious especially classical] writers there is almost nothing more rife then the use of lottery of these kinds. Inheritances among coheirs were often divided by lot. *(Dionysius)* There is the poet's fiction of Saturn's three sons who wanted to share out the heavens, the sea and hell, which we will not dwell on. *(Lactantius)* There are also the Grammarians with their groundless conceit of the derivation of place-names like Claros, Lacedaemon and various other places. *(Eustathius, ~1560)* Thus, I would say, we find in the Peloponnese area that the right of possession by joint conquest when it was recovered was shared out between Cresphontes, Temenus and the Sons of Aristodemus, though there was some trick used in it, as we shall show later. Thus also the dour sons of Lotharius, namely Charibert, Gunthram, Chilperis and Sigebert divided the realm of France between them after their Father's decease. *(Gregory of Tours)* So too did Frederick the second king of Denmark and Adolph Duke of Holst divide the territory of the elder John of Holst between them when he died without issue. *(Chytreaus, ~1580)*. "And this", said the Orator, "is what Oedipus's two sons should have done rather than engage in mutual war and strife as they did at length, working to achieve each others' overthrow". *(Dionysius)*. And yet in part it is said they did take turns, with either of them having their year, with the lottery at first ordering it.

The Civil Law decrees that for the goods and chattels of every courtier who has deceased, that a fourth part is to come to the court. It is to be divided by the heir or his executor into four parts and then a lottery be cast for which of the three parts he shall receive and which fourth part goes to the court. There are many good reasons rendered for this course. As it is said: "That which is held in common is commonly neglected. Men think they have nothing at all, if they have it not apart from others"; and, "That out of an envious disposition (like the wronged mother in Scripture) they allow things often to be spoiled rather than that another should have any good of them". *(1 King)*

The same is likely to be done where there is a choice of some chattel that is bequeathed to many. Or it may be that the one that it was bequeathed to, in dying, leaves various executors, if they cannot otherwise agree. In our common law too, among other means of partition of land between partners or female coheirs, it allows the following: the land is divided up into parcels as equal as may be and then wrapping up scrolls with names of each parcel on as many waxen balls, they are to be drawn by the partners, in order of years, out of the bonnet of some otherwise indifferent party. (*Littleton, 1480*)

In newly built cities, for the first settling or altering of estates and also upon the enfranchising of some that were foreigners or not free beforehand, each one often had his house or portion of land or the tribe he should belong to assigned him by lot. This was the sort of thing expected of the poorer sort at Solon's hand in the alteration of the Athenian state. This was carried out by Lycurgus, though not without much ado in the Spartan Commonwealth and also by Romulus at the first founding of the Roman state. *(Dionysius)*. In Egypt it is reported that it was usual to assign by lot what land each man or each kindred should till. *(Aristophanes)*.

After the conquest of some country, it was usual both with the Greeks, Romans and others, to divide the conquered land by lot, either among those that had done service, or among others also of their own people. Nor should we omit that sometimes they were too premature in this procedure (like the hunter that sold the bear's skin before he had killed or caught her), by dividing more among themselves than they either had presently in possession, or indeed could ever attain to. *(Thucydides)*. When a country was overpopulated, or unable to maintain her own people because of a long famine, it was common to decide by lottery who should stay at home and who should go to seek their fortunes abroad. *(Livy)* If during a war a course of action could not be agreed on, as happened in the Palestine expedition, commonly called the holy war, when either Tyre or Askalon should first be assaulted, it was a lottery that was used to end the strife. This procedure is still in common use in the common-wealth of Venice. *(Salmuth, 1607)* When prey was taken in the field, or during the sacking of some city, it was usual divide the proceeds by lottery whether it was goods, jewels and garments, or heads of cattle, or men in person. A story worth retelling is that of Probus, the Roman Emperor. When a horse that was captured on the field of battle was presented to him and it was reported the horse could travel a hundred miles a day, it was thought he would keep it for himself. But he said it was a beast fitter for a flier then a fighter and had it put to hazard in a lottery with the rest of the booty. When the draw was complete, Probus was one of four men who were to share the prize. Contention grew among them as to who had right to it, whereupon it was once or twice again put into the lot-pot. When Probus's name still came out it was then agreed by all that the Emperor himself should have it. *(Vopiscus)*

In distribution of gifts, rewards or alms, where everyone's turn could not be served and when many have an equal interest in it, then it cannot be easily divided out. A lottery was used to decide which way or to whom they should go. Danaus is reported to have disposed of his daughters by lottery among the sons of Aegyptus. *(Appolodorus)* It was by a lottery that the two Tarquins, Titus and Aruns are said to have decided who should kiss their mother first, after the Oracle had told them that whoever gave his mother the first kiss should reign. But Brutus their cousin is reported to have got in front of them both by kissing his grandmother in the ground. Others say that they agreed both to kiss her at once. (*Livy)*

When naming infants lotteries have also been used. Paris and Helen are said to have decided the controversy between them about the naming of a daughter that he had had by her in this way. The argument was whether it should bear his name or hers. *Chrysostom* also fondly tells of a superstitious practice for naming a child: candles are set up and given names. They are then lit and the candle that lasts longest decides the child's name. Both the Messenians and Campians are said to have agreed by lottery to be called by the common name of Mammerites, after the name of one of their gods. *(Alsius)* Superstitious papists too, are wont to choose the name of their patron saint by the device of a lottery. *(Serarius, 1609; Bonfinus, 1568)*.

In some cases in civil law it can be uncertain which party is the plaintiff and which is the defendant. As both commence their suit they may put that doubt to the decision of a lot, at once, one against the other, but not in the main business of the suit itself, as some mistake it. *(Ulpian)* This is similar to the civil law practice where the custody of cautions or evidence is spread among those that are equally coheirs. At the election of a Pope, the cardinals in the conclave have their cells assigned to them by lot. *(Synod Basiliensis, 1431)*.

At solemn sacred or public feasts in ancient times each one had his portion of meat assigned to him by lot. We observe that among God's people [the Hebrews], a tenth part of their cattle was set apart by lottery for a tithe. Among the heathens too, a solemn vow is made to hand over a tenth of the increase either of their fruits of the earth, or of their cattle, to their Idols. The Arabians are reported in olden times to have yearly given over a third part of their cinnamon, selected by lot. This was offered to the Sun and the Sun, as their fable puts it, should set fire that one-third part itself. *(Plutarch)* It was in their festival lottery that the heathens would hold that the first portion which was drawn was held to be holy and accounted as the share for one of their gods, usually Mercury, whom they deemed President of Lottery. I take this is what is termed 'Mercury's Lot', rather than that which others say of an olive leaf, but without any good ground. So too in the division of lands as mentioned before when settling new colonies or states, some part of it was usually first set apart by lottery for sacred uses.

In markets when the buyer and seller could not agree, they often used to draw cuts, or cast cross-and-pile, or settle it by another kind of lottery like the finger-matching formerly spoken of, to decide whether one or other's price should hold. This was a custom that was sometimes prohibited in some cases. *(Homer)*

§11. Punishment by lottery

A kind of lottery was sometimes employed when imposing fines when there are too many offenders who were all to be punished. Augustus fined those who did not turn up at the Senate as often as they should by enforcing an absence fine on each fifth man that the lottery alighted on, remitting it for the rest. In some life-and-death cases there have been very important uses of the lottery. *(Dionysius)* We mention in passing the fable, fondly fathered upon Athanasius, that when he was about to sacrifice one of his sons, Melchi Melchisedeck's father thought that he should first cast a lottery with his wife, to decide which of them should choose the son to be exempt from that hazard. After the lottery, it was the wife who chose to have Melchisedeck saved from having do the choosing. In another fable the Virgin of Messenia was demanded as sacrifice by the Oracle for the murder of Tisis. A lottery chose which Lesbian maid was fated to be thrown into the sea as sacrifice; but she was saved, it is said, by certain dolphins who carried her safely to the shore. Others such as Arion have been saved in the same way, if these stories are to be believed.

Poets say that such a lottery fell on Hesione, the daughter of the king of Troy and it was her fate to be exposed to the sea monster. The seven young men and an equal number of maidens were required each year by the Minoans from Athens to pay for the death of Androgeus. *(Plutarch)* The children of the Spartans used to be sacrificed to Diana, until Lycurgus finally altered that inhumane practice. *(Panson)* Nor shall we stay with the stories of the Persian King who tithed out [decimated] his magicians when he discovered their frauds (as is reported in our ecclesiastical stories), nor the misery of the army of Cambises on its Ethiopian expedition, when for want of victuals they selected a tenth part of themselves by a lottery so that the rest could eat meat. A mere glance will be sufficient at the memorable and lamentable fate of the father and son called Flori; they were commanded by Augustus to cast a lottery for one of their lives, whereat one of them offered himself to be slain without using the lot. Once he had been slain, the other one thereupon slew himself. *(Turnebus, 1580)*

Nor to make too a long story of it, the tithing out [decimation] of enemies can be found in many references when they have been taken by surprise and captured either by trickery or in wartime. A French bishop reports that the Saxon pirates have just such a savage practice. They choose, by lottery, one-tenth of those taken at sea to be sacrificed to their gods. *(Sidonius)* Earl Godwin's cruelty was notorious. When 600 Normans came over, claiming the right to Alfred's crown, he slew nine out of ten of his enemies, the tenth being chosen by lottery. Then the remaining tenth were again picked by lottery and put to the slaughter. *(Camden, 1594)*

The most famous and frequent use was the Roman practice of this kind [decimation], termed by them as their Ancient Law or their Country Custom. *(Plutarch)* If a troop of their soldiers in the field or at camp had deserted their colours, left their stations, or had carried themselves with cowardice in fighting, or were otherwise disorderly, they were to be punished thus: in order to frighten them all and yet to save of some of them, a lottery drew out usually a tenth of the number that were at fault, sometimes more, sometimes less. By an ignominious kind of execution they were made an example of to others. The rest of them were only punished with some other kind of disgrace. Although we find this tithing of delinquents was ineffectively attempted once by Caligula, it was indeed practised and put in execution at several sundry times, by Appius, Julius Caesar, Augustus, Anthony, Apronius, Crassus, Galba and by Julian the Apostate. It was also used by Macrinus, who sometimes seemed to be mild (which in truth he was not) in that he would only draw out one in a hundred for execution in that kind. Others would sometimes take out twenty apiece from each Legion that had fled and three out of each hundred for those that had given way to the enemy for execution in that kind. (*Tacitus)* Neither is this manner of military discipline altogether unusual with the martial men among us even to this day. Soldiers who have been condemned as a group are permitted now and then to cast the dice for their lives upon the drum-head, so that some are executed and some are saved.

§12. Lottery as a figure of speech

Using the word 'lot' in the general sense often springs from figurative speeches and phrases, where it is taken to mean whatsoever a man has or holds, or howsoever he come by it. But that in itself does not mean that a lottery was used. It was neither by lottery or by chance that a man obtained such things, but by counsel and advice, or by gift, purchase, descent, or otherwise and that is what is signified as his lot and is said to be allotted to him. *(Horace)*

Among the Greeks an inheritance is most usually and universally termed 'a lot', though this ordinary significance of the word is missed by some. It was such a reference in the Epiphanius *(Demosthenes)* which led to the mistaken belief that the Virgin Mary was married to Joseph by a lottery. *(Casaubon, 1589)* It is a way of referring to God when it is said to be the portion of those that serve Him and they are said to be His inheritance. *(Deut 18:2)* So the right to glory and an eternal life is said to be their lot. *(Coloss 3:12)* This is not, as some of the ancients have thought, a matter of free choice, having regard to the general nature of a lottery. It has no regard for the party on whom it favourably falls, nor is it directed or determined at all in its motion by him. This form of lot is one which comes by way of inheritance, with an eye had to the particular use of it which might be specified in the settling of such estates. *(Chrysostom)*. Hence it is also found that in holy writ 'to cast a lot' is put for 'to inherit'. God is said to have cast a lot to set up some places for wild beasts and to have divided lands and countries out for them. This alludes to the process used in dividing the land by lottery amongst those that were appointed to people and to possess it. *(Micha 2:5)*. And in a word, whatsoever betides men, be it good or be it evil is said to be their lot and their allowance. In a way this is an allusion to a divisory lot, whereby lands and goods, either of inheritance, purchase, or prey and parts or portions of diet and rewards good and bad, have from time to time usually been divided out among many.

Appendix to Chapter 4: Does the use of lottery *always* imply divine intervention?

[This section is new in the second edition. As stated in Gataker's Introduction to his second edition this is his main response to his critics, such as Balmford. Although four arguments are put forward, they seem to be just the same one in different guises. God knows everything, including the outcome of every lot; therefore any use of lottery invokes God's judgement and is unlawful, or as we might say sinful and therefore prohibited. No, says Gataker, some lotteries are not sinful, but for reasons other than God's omniscience. I feel that Gataker may have been trying to wear down his opponents with acres of flannel. What follows is little changed from the exact words that Gataker used.]

But here we are required to make some stand a while, for there are many that question the truth of something which is affirmed here, to wit, that: in these ordinary lotteries nothing is expected or required but that which is in the natural power of the person using it and being used by it. Now howsoever they deny it, or refuse at least to defend their case that: an extraordinary providence is present and working in all lotteries, there are others who join in with some controversies about the use of lotteries. They peremptorily avow and so stiffly maintain that: some such matter is to be expected and required even though it is not in the intentions and minds of the parties that use them, yet it is in regard of the proper scope and nature of the action itself. That which by these arguments they endevour to evince.

Argument 1: It is a senseless thing to refer a doubt for resolution to that that is most doubtful. But such is mere uncertainty: for in judging, it follows no rule, nor regards truth and right any more than falsehood and wrong. The doubt therefore in a lottery is not referred to mere uncertainty but to some higher power ruling it.

Answer 1. To omit the word 'doubtful' would have been very ambiguous in this Argument and few peradventure would have understood the Author's meaning therein had he not explained himself thus. *[Gataker gives no reference to this mysterious Author, but presumably it is Balmford]* I answer briefly (with all other exceptions excepted): It is not senseless to refer a doubt wherein no such matter of truth or falsehood, right or wrong is questioned to that which has no regard at all of either. But such are the matters that are referred to these ordinary lotteries, as the following discourse evidently shows. And I would gladly accept either from this disputant or any other, what matter of truth or falsehood, right or wrong may be tried by lottery. It is not senseless therefore to refer such doubts to mere uncertainty, though it be such as it is here said to be.

Argument 2: That the chance that is in every lottery is a means of resolving a doubt as it is subject to the direction of some principal agent. This principal agent must of necessity be a man or some higher power, because nothing can be a principal agent in the resolving of any doubt unless he has some knowledge and appreciation of that doubt. But this cannot be man, because he does not rule over uncertainties. And nothing inferior to man has such knowledge of these doubts that a lottery is conversant about. It must needs be some superior power therefore that in a lottery is appealed unto.

Answer 2. It might well be wished that the Author of these arguments had explained his meaning here (to prevent strife about words) as he did in the former. As it is now propounded, I deny the proposition produced for the proof of his definition; that anything which has knowledge or apprehension of the doubt yet may be principal agent (by such power as he that makes use of it may impart it) in the deciding of such doubts and questions, as are by ordinary lottery generally decided.

For example: I may make the track a beast or the falling of a staff be the decider of my question, depending on which way it shall go, without any special reference to an extraordinary presence or a higher or superior power. Anyone who says that this is a wrong thing to do might as well say that there are no doubts which can ever be decided in this way. Despite refusing to accept this as a way of deciding doubts, there are those who recognize that such methods are widely used. There are several assertions joined together here and this is what they imply: either uncertain events or a special preference of a superior power must of necessity decide in lotteries; but in some lotteries there is no certainty of any special preference. Yet by such lotteries some doubts are decided. Some doubts may therefore be decided by an uncertain event; but the uncertain event can have no notice of the doubt decided by it.

The thing which decides the doubt may therefore have no notice of it. In other cases the fact that doubts may be decided by those things that have no notice of the doubt is a point so evident and in practice so frequent that nothing can be so apparent or more usual. By stirring up, a beast may decide my doubt; even if he is dead or asleep, although he might be neither, nor is it aware of it. A test or touchstone may resolve my doubts over some ore or some coins of which I have my suspicions. Not to add that the doubts by these ordinary lotteries which decide things either not concerning what is or is not or what should or what should not be, but what shall be done. Such kinds of doubts require no such notice at all of the doubt in that which the party in whose it is to dispose of his own actions shall please refer such doubts unto.

Argument 3: Man in the use of a lottery being a cause by counsel cannot by reason wittingly or willingly subject his action to fortune. For then the acts by fortune should be according to the intentions of him for whom it is fortune. That is contrary to the nature of this kind of working. Then fortune should be the instrument of counsel. Then also by the same reason a man may willingly and wittingly submit his action to necessity and be willingly constrained. There must therefore be a higher power which man's counsel in this business subjects itself to.

Since this is a somewhat complex argument, an enthymeme [probabilistic argument] even, I will reduce it to a syllogism [three parts, two premises and a conclusion]: In a lottery a man is necessarily subjected either to fortune or some higher power. But he cannot subject his action to fortune in a lot, therefore it must be to some higher power. The assumption is thus proved. Man, where he knows by counsel what course to take cannot by witting or willing reasons subject his action to fortune. But in a lottery man takes a course by counsel and therefore cannot subject his action to fortune.

Answer 3. Man, where he is caused by counsel, or (to speak of common capacities) where he works by advice, cannot subject that particular action wherein he so works to fortune or to chance. Or to speak more plainly: man cannot work with uncertainty in so far as he works advisedly. But in the use of a lottery man does not do all that is done there by counsel, in subjecting only and in referring himself to the decision and determination of fortune (or of the uncertain event rather, because the former term is strictly speaking too narrow to comprehend the whole matter of lotteries) not in directing or settling the uncertain event, which he refers himself unto. If this author's meaning when he says that a man working by counsel cannot subject his action to fortune; that he cannot subject to fortune that particular action of his wherein he so works. The proposition of the first syllogism is unsound, there is no necessity that a man in the use of lottery should subject his action in that manner to fortune at all. But if his meaning is that man working by counsel cannot subject some other act of his to actual events or refer himself therein for some other act of his to be ordered by uncertainty, then the proposition of the prosyllogism may well be denied. A man may by counsel resolve to shoot at random, or to fling blind-folded at a mark. Neither is this to say that a man may wittingly or willingly work unwittingly or unwillingly, but that he may wittingly or willingly refer himself to that which in its work is guided neither by his wit or his will. Nor is it to say that counsel may work by fortune, but that by counsel a man may cast for himself using an uncertain event. In which sense it may also be said that fortune or uncertainty may be the instrument of counsel. That is, by counsel a man may make use of an uncertain event, by referring himself to it. And I suppose that very few lot-casters will be easily induced into believing that they cannot do that which they often do. Or others either that that cannot be which they see often done. Nor will all the inferences heaped upon it prove to the contrary that which they cannot willing and wittingly refer themselves to an uncertain event. For this argument does indeed tend to prove the utter impossibility of all lotteries, or of referring any question to them.

Argument 4: It is the natural order of things that when men have no means in their own power likely to put their desires into effect and yet they desire and seek to have them effected, they seek out their desires from a higher power. But so it is in a lot, for there is no likely or probable means of getting such a resolution as a man desires, therefore men look for some higher power in a lot. The nature of the lottery implies as much.

Answer 4. Not to repeat myself too much: the dimness, perhaps, of my own bad eyesight maybe the fault, but not to meddle with the conclusion and the exploitation of it, I answer: neither of the premises are generally true and if not, then neither can the conclusion be true. Not the proposition, for a man may well without breach of the natural order often seek resolution of his doubts from someone inferior to himself. In less ordinary controversies, he may delight in so doing. Thus two noblemen contending over some matter of husbandry may refer to a mean peasant for the resolution of their tiff. If planning their route, whether by the high or the low way, when one likes the high, the other pleads for the low, they may refer the decision to a servant, or anyone they randomly meet.

The reply could be that they have some such means in their power then, those inferiors, whoever they may be. This may be deemed an insufficient exception, because the party appealed to should, it seems, in reason be ignored since they may want to use all means, until they light on him. Then they have some, so it helped to answer the assumption for the same reason that it may be said that in a lottery men have means in their power likely to effect their desires. With the uncertain event that they make use of for a lottery they therefore need not seek any higher power in regard of such a defect.

And so I pass to the assumption that affirms that in a lottery there is no likely means of getting such a resolution as a man may desire. I am not sure how to take these words. They may have a double meaning, but neither is true. If the meaning is as they themselves directly propose, that in or by a lottery there is no likely means of getting such a resolution. There is nothing less true, especially when lotteries are cast by joint liking. Even if it was true the conclusion which is inferred here it would not hold. Rather it is a case of the natural order being to leave the lottery alone and to seek some superior power instead. Or if peradventure the meaning is that in such matters as are referred to the lot there is no likely means of procuring a result. That is not true either. We pass over the previous exception which the author in his reply gives just grounds to insist on. No doubts or controversies are decided or resolved by any lawful lottery, except those things which men can resolve and decide otherwise. In the selection of officers which some do by lottery, others by majority voting. In common bargains and law-suits, the lottery can be used, but it can also be settled by a third party or by arbiters chosen by both sides. In gambling nothing can be decided without a lottery. Apart from this gambling example, I would like to see one other case which is decided by lottery only, which cannot be settled by other means. When a lottery is used, despite other means being available, the assumption is unfounded. Nor when lotteries are employed in such matters is there anything averred in this argument which says in respect of its action that it is the work of some higher power.

That is enough to briefly answer these arguments. The first did not touch the use of lotteries in controversies where no matter of right or wrong, truth or falsehood was questioned. The last, that no lottery is used on controversies which can be resolved by other means. Lotteries for gambling come within the scope of neither. The second and third do not hold for any lottery at all, unless it is declared impossible for a man to refer to an uncertain event to decide any difference. No man would acknowledge this to be true. Although these arguments do not undermine that which I am affirming here, I still thought it worthwhile to spend a few words examining them, because that author deems that they touch on the very life and soul of the controversy when considering the use of ordinary lotteries for serious purposes. Now with these rubs removed I return to mine own project.

[In the original 2nd edition, Gataker now continues with examples of ordinary lotteries for serious uses]

Chapter 5

The lawfulness of ordinary lotteries and precautions in their use

§1. False arguments in favour of the use of ordinary lotteries

This kind of lottery is lawful when used with due precaution. Most divines acknowledge this, but the arguments that some of them bring forward are not as sound as many of them would wish. The precautions that most of them propose are either unsound or superfluous, as a view and survey of some of them will now show. In the arguments made for the use of lotteries, the general error of most authors is to confuse the ordinary and the extraordinary lotteries with each other and so draw unreasonable conclusions from the one to the other. (This muddle can also cause much mistakenness elsewhere.) This is like the false reasoning that because of Ehud's slaying of Eglon *(Judg 3:21)* that the Jesuits and Romanists would justify the murdering of Princes in the present day, because they suppose that they are heretics and enemies of God's church. *(Patrus. Consist., ~1550)* Or it could be from Phineas's killing of Zimrie and Cozbi, *(Numb 25:7)* that some would nowadays justify the same kind of execution of delinquents if they were surprised by someone in a similar [sexual] act. Or comparing the Hebrews' invasion of the land of Canaan and the rooting out the Canaanites with God's special permission *(Deut 7:1)*, to the Spaniards' dis-peopling of the West Indies, as they term them, in those places they had seized, justifying seizure in any other part of the world and seeking to subdue or destroy its inhabitants in the same manner*. *(Vitoria, 1593)* Let the arguments of one *(Aret.)* who has heaped up the most serve for the rest, to show how confused men have been in dealing with this argument:

Firstly, said he, "lotteries are guided and governed by God to a good purpose". True; but men's sins are also guided to good purposes by God by drawing light out of darkness, *(2 Cor 4:6)* and turning evil to good, using man's evil will to work towards and effect His own holy will. For He disposed and ordered all things, even the wickedest and the worst things and being infinitely good would not allow any evil. He knows how to do good even with evil. *(Augustine)*

---

* This is an example of the 'black legend' which demonised the Spanish Inquisition and colonial exploits of the conquisadores.

Secondly, "lotteries have their origin from God, who commanded lots to be cast upon the two goats and elsewhere decreed the division of the Land of Canaan by lot". But these examples and their like, taken on their own warrant no use of the lottery beyond the particular cases mentioned, any more than the commandment given to Moses to make a brazen serpent (a type of the Messiah) would otherwise warrant the regular making of images for religious use. *(Numb 21:8)*

Thirdly, "God approved the lottery as practised by Joshua and Samuel and for the discovery of Achan and the election of Saul". *(Josh 7:16)* This is true. God approves whatsoever He commands. But God's approbation of what He commands gives no warrant for what he does not command. This is well-known to the author *(Aret.)* as is shown by his writing that: "The examples of the Saints are not to be imitated randomly". And again, what Joshua did, he was enjoined to it by God, so no man may take this as an excuse to do likewise, unless he has the same commandment from God to do so. *(1 Sam 14:41)*. And what he said of Joshua may be said also of Samuel.

Fourthly, "In other cases, godly men have also laudably used lotteries; as in the ministry of Zachariah in the choice of Matthias, or in the discovery of Jonathan. Nor was the lottery that the sailors cast on Jonah disallowed". In some of these examples, such as that of Matthias there were extraordinary [supernatural] actions done by special warrant. In others such as those of Saul and the action of the sailors on Jonah and Jonathan, though they were not expressly condemned, nor were they yet allowed, so neither of them can be well justified. And lastly the others, such as that of Zachariah are a point in question and must be proved warrantable by some other ground.

Fifthly, "They make for God's glory, because recourse to them brings in the judgement of God". Using this argument might make a falsehood be for God's glory, but it is not therefore allowable. *(Job 13:4)* Indeed, simply by offering to have recourse to God's immediate judgement without special warrant is itself unwarrantable.

Sixthly, "They end great strife and inexplicable law suits". The use of the lottery is profitable and commendable if it is allowable and warrantable. But that is the point to be proved. Evil may not be done with the aim of good coming from it. *(Rom 3:8)* The smallest moral evil may not be admitted even if it prevents or avoids any great natural evil or if it achieves the greatest political good. *(Augustine)*

§2. Good reasons for using ordinary lotteries for serious purposes

We turn now from the arguments of this nature that are usually brought forward to confirm the truth in this point. Because of their invalidity and insufficiency we will leave the various authors to make good with them as they may. We will attempt to give some sounder grounds. For the moment we repeat the testimony of Solomon, who when speaking of such kinds of lottery as these said that "The lot causeth contentions to cease and parteth between the mighty". *(Proverbs 18:18 KJV)*

These words show that the Holy Ghost manifestly not only allowed and approved the use of the lottery in such cases, but also recommended it to us as a wise and discrete course for the taking away of controversies and questions of this kind and the preventing of law-suits or other quarrels that might otherwise arise. The reference is pregnant and the proof express, considering by whom it is spoken. Neither shall I need to spend many words at present to urge or enforce the case, nor need I support it with other arguments. This is partly because most divines generally agree with me in approving them, though many of their proofs are not pertinent. One obvious argument would be sufficient in a non-controversial matter. It is also partly because my point will receive further strength from the arguments that will be produced later for the next types of lotteries: those used for gambling, which are more questionable than these. I refer the reader to the later chapters for fuller satisfaction. We will next proceed to the consideration of the precautions which must of necessity be observed in the use of such lotteries.

§3. Eight irrelevant precautions when using lottery

Just because such lotteries are said to be lawful, do not think that this justifies every particular instance whenever it was, or has ever been practised. Particular circumstances often alter the nature of actions and make things unlawful that otherwise are not. The use of the lottery is only approved in those cases where the circumstances do not cause corruption or change. *(Cicero)* In this regard it is justifiably said by those that deal in this argument and allow the use of such lotteries that there are certain precautions or rules which direct and limit their use. But they fail not a little here, since most of their proofs are either insufficient or not pertinent. As a result many of their precautions are either unsound or superfluous because they do not deal with the nature of these lotteries or with the ordinary use of them. We will first briefly consider these precautions and then set down some other, more appropriate precautions for the use of ordinary serious lotteries.

The first irrelevant precaution that is usually given is that: "Men should only use lotteries, as with the use of the law or of arms, in cases of necessity when they have tried all other courses, where all others fail and when nothing else will serve to produce the effect that we would have. Otherwise, to use lottery would be a tempting of God". *(Aquinas, 1270)* But it is not necessary to require any such necessity, since the thing that is put to the lottery in this way ought to be a matter of mere indifference, as will be explained later and its outcome is just the same. So even if there are many diverse ways or courses to end a controversy, a choice may be made among them, so that each one is as fit and equal as any of the rest. The lawsuits mentioned above by Solomon, which were alleged to be determinable by lottery could have also have been settled by many other means such arbitration and compromise or by the concession of one party yielding to the choice of the other. *(Gen 13:8)* So it is not simply a matter that either of them enforces or warrants the use of a lottery nor is there any tempting of God in such cases. There is neither the need nor the expectation of any extraordinary work of God. On the other hand if a lottery was either required or expected, then God would indeed be tempted, whatever was the necessity of enforcing a lottery.

The second irrelevant precaution is that: "A lottery should be undertaken reverently and religiously with a solemn prayer to God, just as was once done when choosing Matthias". *(Act 1:24)* It is true indeed that nothing ought to be done irreligiously or irreverently. But there is a great difference in the religious and reverent usage of things which have to be performed and are limited by the amount of work involved. It may be that there is no lack of due reverence in some actions even when no solemnities are observed. It is true that we should pray continually and that all our actions, even the least and lightest of them, even our sports and pastimes as well as the more serious civil affairs, should be sanctified by prayer. *(Thess 15:7)* But how or in what manner? Man is not bound at every act, at every bargain he makes, or every penny-worth of ware that he sells, to fall down on his knees and conceive a set prayer. There is no more need to say a new grace for each course that is brought to the table, or for each dish that is carved at the board, or for every other bit of meat that he puts into his mouth. The prayer conceived at the beginning of the meal is sufficient for all. The morning sacrifice sanctifies the whole of an ordinary day's work, though ejaculations, as they are termed, may be used in their season, as the occasion shall require. (*Psal 55:17)* So here with the lottery no other sanctification is usually required any more than is common to other civil affairs. There may be some cases when a prayer might be used. This could be when the matter is more weighty and the outcome is of some consequence, as in the choice of a magistrate or of a combatant, or in the division of land where some special cause is to effect one part before another and the like. Otherwise solemn prayer is no more necessary during the use of a lottery than it is in any other ordinary business whatsoever. Nor can I see what good ground or warrant can be given that some kind of prayer is required in lottery-use because this way God will discover what He himself has secretly decreed. *(Zanchius, ~1580)* This would be an instance of a sacred and extraordinary lot. It is not a sound course to reason from the extraordinary to the ordinary, nor from sacred to civil, or from the particular to the general.

A third irrelevant precaution is "that no superstition or curiosity may be mixed in with the use of the lottery, but that the outcome be religiously expected from God". Superstition indeed alters the nature of a lottery and turns it from a mere divisory into a divinatory lot. As we shall see later, some care is needed to distinguish between them. In a divinatory lottery we expect the outcome of the event to come by ordinary means from God, as is common in all actions. But to expect an immediate and extraordinary result by a lottery is no more lawful here then elsewhere and is indeed mere superstition as we shall show later.

The fourth and fifth irrelevant precautions are that: "We should not enquire by lottery into unlawful things such as what has become of stolen or lost goods", or "to foretell the future". That is to turn a lottery into sorcery. *(Josh 7:16)* Lotteries such as these are merely divinatory, not divisory.

A sixth irrelevant precaution is that: "We should use no texts from scripture in our lotteries". *(Augustine)* It is true in general that holy things should not be applied to profane uses, but the abuse touched on here is that of the use divinatory lotteries which are simply unlawful whether such sacred things be used in them or not.

A seventh irrelevant precaution is that: "They are not to be used in ecclesiastical elections although they may be used in temporal dignities or offices". So why not in the one as well as in the other? If the people that have power to choose are divided in their choice and the competitors for the place are generally held equally fit why not choose for both using a lottery? There are other writers of good note who grant this point including many popish ones (except the Pope who has prohibited them). *(Cajetan, 1525)*

The eighth and last irrelevant precaution is that: "No hidden or crafty connivance be used in them". This happened when Temo the Priest decided a controversy between Cresphontes and Aristodemus. *(Pausianias)* The story here is reported variously by many authors and they are mistaken in some particulars. Later we shall explain this. Meanwhile it may suffice to say that whatever is said here, crafty procedures are unjust and consequently unlawful, especially where both parties have an interest in what is to be shared. I would not dare condemn Caesar's trick when punishing of his mutinous troops. When it was in his power to choose who to slay or to save, he carried out the matter so cunningly that the lottery fell on those that had been faultiest and most forward in that business*. *(Dionysius)*. Nevertheless I say that such injurious and cheating devices are unwarrantable. Even so this precaution seems to be needless because the very nature of a lottery excludes all such courses. Therefore to give such a precaution concerning a lottery, is like saying that a lottery must indeed be a lottery or else it cannot be a lawful lottery. If the outcome is settled by such counsels or courses there is no uncertainty there and consequently no lottery. The question here is how a man may lawfully use a lottery, not whether he may use some other course instead while pretending it was a lottery.

§4. The implications of indifferency or What is meant when the matter of the lottery is 'indifferent'?

These have been the most common precautions given, but because most of them are immaterial I shall instead propound some other precautions that would limit the use of this kind of lottery more precisely and head off the most usual abuses which are met in such lotteries. These precautions may be referred to under two

* This incident happened in the Roman Civil Wars, and is recorded by *Suetonius*.

heads; they concern either the **matter** that they are used for, or the **manner** of using them.

Concerning those matters or businesses where a lottery may lawfully be used the general precaution is that lotteries are only to be used when things are indifferent one way or another. To better understand this precaution, a word or two of explanation of the word 'indifferent' is called for. There are those that suppose that there is no act which can be totally indifferent and so according to their judgement if lotteries may only be used for indifferent things, they may not be used at all. It is true that in the Schools there are two received axioms that may seem to contradict one another, to wit: "Every action is indifferent"; and "No action is indifferent". *(Gersonides, ~1320)* They try to save this seeming contradiction with a distinction such that of naked and clothed: that every naked or bare action simply conceived is indifferent, but no clad action is indifferent in its particular circumstances. For example, say they, to strike is indifferent, but to strike an innocent, or to strike without authority, or to strike in this or that case, or this or that person, that is not indifferent.

But back to the task in hand. The word 'indifferent' may be taken in two ways: either it puts good and evil as opposites (more especially to such actions of virtue and vice that deserve more special praise or reproof); or as it puts into opposition those necessary good duties such as things that must needs be done against evils that are simply forbidden because they may in no-wise be done. In the former sense it is said to be indifferent when it is neither good nor bad, neither lawful nor unlawful. In this sense there are many natural actions which are not the result of reason and which therefore do not come within the scope the moral law. If a man talks or walks in his sleep and the like, his actions are regarded as merely indifferent, there being no law about it which may be observed or transgressed in them. *(Cicero)* In general there are many actions that are said to be indifferent because they are either simply good, but they may be tainted and corrupted so that they become evil by some particular circumstances. Or they may not yet so absolutely evil that sometimes, in some cases and in some qualified circumstances they may not only become good but prove to be necessary duties.

Nevertheless it is indeed true that any particular moral action or inaction of the reasonable person which proceeds from reason can possibly be indifferent in this way. Of necessity it must be either conformable to the rules of God's holy word or not conforming with it. Indeed according to accepted norms in common speech the word 'indifferent' is taken with some latitude of signification when it is attributed to actions, which though good and warrantable or even necessary, are yet not greatly praise-worthy because there is no special matter of goodness in them. For a man to eat when he is hungry, to drink when he is thirsty, to provide carefully for his own family, to love those that love him and the like, in strict truth according to the accepted meaning are not things which are absolutely indifferent. *(Bernard, ~1120)*

In the latter sense a thing is said to be indifferent if it is good and lawful that it be done, but not because it is a necessary duty that may either be committed or omitted, done or left undone, without sin. This is how many particular actions are indifferent. The ground for this is that the law of God, though it binds humans to be guided by reason to do nothing but good and to do good at all times, yet it does not bind them to do all good at once or at all times. So that there are many good things that may at sometime or other be done; and a man may make a choice whether he will do any of them. But he is not necessarily tied or enjoined to any one of them. For example: A student having various books about him in his study it is indifferent whether to choose this one or that, refusing to pick on the other books for the present, there being no special occasion to urge the use of one book more than of another. Or for a man that carries a pair of knives about him, he may be indifferent as to which one to draw and use when the occasion requires. *(Plutarch)* This is the nature of this precaution when it says that by putting the issue to a lottery, it should be such that a man may lawfully either choose or refuse to do it or to leave it undone.

§5. Use choice not a lottery when something is known

This precaution divides itself into two distinct branches according to the quality of those things that are against or support its indifference.

The former (against indifference) is that lottery may not be used for anything that is evidently unlawful or evil in itself, either by the omission of a necessary good duty or by yielding to something wicked, ungodly or unjust. So consequently in this case it is evidently apparent on other grounds what a man ought to choose to do or to refuse. As we have seen, the outcome of a lottery is uncertain and to make a necessary act depend on an uncertain event cannot be without sin, because it makes that which is necessary in God's law both uncertain and contingent. Therefore in such cases a man should follow and be led by the grounds and rules of religion and reason and should not put to hazard something that he might do or not, if he already sees and knows good grounds why he should or should not do it. (*Deut 5:32)* When a man sees evident grounds against doing a thing, then he may not do it. And what he may not lawfully do, he may not put to hazard to see whether he shall do it or not. And on the other side, what a man sees necessary grounds for, he is necessarily bound to do. What he is necessarily bound by, he may not refuse or forbear to do. And what he may not refuse, he may not put to the hazard of refusing. *(Bernard, ~1120)*

To illustrate this by some instances.

Offices by lot: Many may stand for an office either in the church or the commonwealth. Some may be fit for the office, some are altogether unfit, or some fitter and some less fit with very obvious differences. In this case for those persons who have the power to call and admit them to these offices, they would be utterly outside the law to decide which of them shall have it by using a lottery. This would hazard themselves into a bind and do that which they ought not to do.

It might result in accepting someone who was wholly unfit. This happened when the high-priesthood was once so put to the lot, with the lottery lighting on a silly rude clown. That simpleton hardly knew what the high-priesthood meant and therefore became the object of scorn to all sorts. *(Josephus)* Or the not-so-fit could be picked by lottery when a better choice might have been be had, as happened in some of the offices at Rome. *(Tacitus)* The lottery makes no distinction between good or bad, nor takes any notice of the fitness or unfitness, or the worth or unworthiness of those that are put together in it. In this regard, there are many who worthily condemn such promiscuous lotteries and justly prefer for the most part the alternative course of election rather than lottery. *(Aristotle)* It is generally accounted to be a greater credit for a man to be elected then to be allotted randomly to any place of employment.

But where the various competitors are judged equally fit or are all fit with some good competencies though with some small inequality, then however the lottery falls, it cannot alight on an unfit competitor. As was said "though a man should be blindfolded and throw stones at them, he could not miss hitting a good man". *(Xenophon)* So it is not unlawful to dispose of civil or sacred places or offices by lottery among such near-equals, especially when there might be much labouring and contending for them by the sundry persons engaged on either side. By this means they may all be quieted and someone picked out and pitched upon without disgrace to any of his competitors or discontentment to his friends. It is for this reason that in most states where offices are disposed by lottery, if elections had been used prior to the lottery, then the lottery would only be used among those of sufficient worth. Again after the lottery there would be a public trial of the winners to inquire into their courses and abilities. If they were found insufficient or faulty they might be rejected and others taken in their stead. Apart from that, where offices required some special kind of skill, be it military, musical or the like, they were either wholly exempted from the lottery, or the lottery was cast only on those that were found, after trial, to be expert in that particular field. *(Plato)* It is understandable that men would be loath to take on a physician by lottery when they are sick, or a pilot when they go to sea, whose skill they have not already tested or had some assurance otherwise. So it would be much less fitting if it were only by a lottery and without any further enquiry, that committed a man to the helm of the state and the life of many hundreds into the hands of any man that the lottery might light upon.

Mercy killing by lottery: It would be unlawful for private men in some danger and distress and wary for their lives, to decide who shall slay either other by casting lotteries, as they sometimes did, because that would be a plain breach of God's precept. *(Josephus)*

Reprieve by lottery: Where two malefactors are condemned to death but one is to be spared because it is a special occasion, it would be unfit for the public magistrate to put it to hazard who to spare and who to punish in this case. This happened among the Jews *(Matt 27:15)* where some offender was given to them to grace their feast. (I pause now to discuss the lawfulness of that course, but take it for granted that there are good grounds for sparing someone.) In this case, if the two parties are unlike, one a debauched rogue that has often been before in similar villainies, the other but a novice newly fallen to the trade and this his first known offence *(Josephus)*; or if one was an obstinate and desperate wretch, the other penitent and likely to prove an honest man afterwards. To decide by lottery is wrong.

Decimation (punishment by lottery): In war, though, consider again when a whole band had offended but where executing all of them would be too great an injury to the whole army and not punishing anyone would set an evil example. With little time available to consider the particulars of who may best be spared, who the worthiest to be punished and all alike deserving death and it being in the power of the General to put all to death, it is lawful for him to tithe them, as we said they sometimes did and decide by lottery who shall be saved and who slain, as an example to the rest. *(Tacitus)*.

Charity by lottery: It would be an abuse of the lottery if in matters of alms and liberality a man was to make beggars draw cuts for his money, making play and sport out of his alms and his prodigality (if that is the right word for it). The mad Antiochus sometimes did this and, as *Bernard (~1120)* wrote, so does the Pope with his. This abuse of the lottery amounts to an inconsiderate casting away of something which ought to be disposed of advisedly.

Sharing by lottery: Two persons in want seek relief from a man who can only help one of them. It is apparent that the one has far more need than the other and is nearer to the party in whose gift is the relief sought. For him to make them draw cuts for it in this case is not warrantable because he can clearly see here who should better be relieved and may not therefore put it to the hazard of a lottery. But for those in office who hear the clamour of many of the poor pleading for some pension, it would be right to cast lottery among them to decide who has it first and who can expect it later. If a man can spare a tool of some trade which two poor men of that trade are seeking and there are no grounds for him to satisfy one rather than the other, here likewise it would be neither unlawful nor unfit to determine by lottery which of the two shall have the tool.

Medical treatment by lottery: It would not be completely unlawful for a physician having many patients asking for advice, to draw cuts as to which of them he saw first. This is similar to what happens in the Netherlands where waggoners cast dice to see who should be employed first and water-taxi-men decide who should have the first fare. *(no ref given)*. But if, as is reported, the physician were to put sundry prescriptions into a pot and to draw out each one in turn to give to the next patient, that would be a gross and fearful abuse. It clearly tends to put not just the health but the life of the patients at risk and would make the physician guilty of wilful murder. This is putting to chance and uncertainty something which ought to be managed by skill and counsel. *(Aristotle)*

§6. Convenience and expediency

So far we have considered warnings against using the lottery in distributing necessary duties or in the things that are evil in themselves and appear to be so. We now consider the use of lotteries for things that are not in themselves evil, but the consequence of their use may in all likelihood prove inconvenient or inexpedient. The reason is that things which are indifferent and are good and lawful in themselves can become unlawful to us when they grow inconvenient or inexpedient when used. (*1 Cor 6:12*)

So in matters of indifference, things that are not be in themselves evil, may, in some circumstances easily become evil. Great regard is needed about their convenience and expediency. Under the head of inconvenience I include all such things that may tend towards any outward evil. Under the head of inexpedience I refer all those things that may bring a man within the danger of some spiritual evil.

On the point of convenience and inconvenience the rule is that some things are in themselves lawful and warrantable and may seem convenient in some respects, inconvenient in others. When therefore the conveniences and the inconveniences are balanced out in an equal and indifferent judgement, the action is then to be deemed either convenient or inconvenient, as one side or the other appears to weigh it down. If the conveniences are the greater or the weightier that can make the thing in question convenient; if it is the inconveniences that are more and weightier that may justly be deemed inconvenient.

So in the use of a lottery about a matter which is not in itself evil, if the conveniences on the one side outweigh whatever inconveniences that may be produced on the other side then the action is convenient and the lottery is therefore lawful. But, contrariwise, where the inconveniences that shall, either of necessity or in all probability appear to accompany the thing questioned, or ensue when it is done and are so great that the conveniences that stand on the other side shall not be able to countervail, then this action is rightly disallowed as inconvenient and the lottery is consequently unlawful.

Examples of reasonable lotteries with inconvenient consequences:

Public affairs: A few private men may be content to make use of a lottery although to admit to it may in all likelihood prove prejudicial to the public. This is an unwise course and is unwarrantable because the public interest outweighs the private and makes the action inconvenient. It is worth observing that among the Romans when settling the ordinary employments of their Officers and in many other affairs, they were often arranged by lot. But when any extraordinary event happened or there was especially important business to be dispatched, they either completely ceased their use of the lottery *(Livy)*, or limited their use of it. After things quietened and settled down they returned again to the use of the lottery. Some in office craved the suspension of the lottery, urging and instantly calling for this. This happened when they were condemned by the lottery to failure, being balked and rejected, where others in the state-service were preferred before them. But the regard for the common good prevailed and they would not agree with those that accepted the hazard of the lot, except where the outcome might prove inconvenient which in other circumstances they ordinarily did.

It is not true therefore, as *Edmunds (1600),* one of our writers has said, "that Rome directed the main course of her government by the fortune of this mock-destiny". (This has been described as putting the helm into the charge of one who is stark-blind.) The officers themselves were not ordinarily chosen by lottery, nor did they retain the use of it in matters of special weight or difficulty. The only consistent use of it was in dividing out provinces and jurisdictions, in a similar way to our judges who cast a lottery for their circuits and for which of the two in each circuit should hear private suits and which hear the public pleas. This is a course of action that is broken when employments were of more special importance. So, if by using the lot the result was not beneficial for the state, they might well over-ride the lottery and dispose things otherwise.

It may be lawful for many to join together in a sweepstake-lottery (as well as in a free contribution, which Job's friends sometime did *(Job 42:11)*) to raise up an honest man who has been crossed or suffered uncertainties and hence fallen on hard times. For the state to give way to public spending of that kind in order to raise up and enrich some decayed bankrupt seems unwarrantable. It will probably damage if not impoverish many others and in this way, out of hope of great gain. may wrong both themselves and their families by this. This course is scarcely warrantable considering the hindrance to the many that is procured by the helping of one*.

Goods held in common: Men may be contentious and ready to take their discontents even into the smallest details. Commonly in these cases they are wont to think that what they hand over is better though it may not be not so and think the worst of that which comes to them even though it is better. So when a division has been made with as much equality as can be, or with such inequality as they shall agree upon, then it would not only be lawful and convenient but laudable and commendable even, for their mutual satisfaction to assign each one his share by a lottery. *(Plato)* However when a man's goods are shared with another and are completely mixed up, then it is not unlawful for a man to put his whole right to them to the hazard of a lottery. This will procure and purchase his peace of mind, which could not be had otherwise, to ensure that someone who he would not wish by any means to be at odds with, if it lay in his power to do so. Yet it would not be lawful for a man to enter the hazard of a lottery which he may not win and which he cannot afford to lose or which might in other ways prejudice him and his family, just because the damage that might thereby accrue would be

* As mentioned in my Preface, Gataker seems to be unaware of the state-sponsored lotteries which were organised in England in his time, for example to help the American colonies.

greater than anything which could free such an action from imputation of evident inconvenience. *(Livy)*

§7. Sin and expedience

From the point of expedience and inexpedience the general rule then is that if a thing is not a necessary duty and is otherwise a matter of indifference, it may not be done where there is strong presumption upon good grounds that it spiritually endangers the man using the lottery or others when it creates the occasion of sin unto the one or the other. I would exempt necessary duties because they must not be omitted even though they may be an occasion of sin for others even if we ourselves cannot do them without some sin. The sin of others does not exempt us either, for there is no duty so holy but that many may and will take as an occasion of evil thereby. Even amongst the ministry of the word, because some few have turned to evil should not as result mean that duties are to be neglected or omitted, because man's corruption cannot free anyone from the employment that God enjoined him to do.

Nor for the sake of ourselves and our own sins are such duties to be left undone. For then no good work at all would be done by us because we can do nothing without some sin sticking to us by doing it. A diseased person therefore should not give up eating and by fasting to starve himself (as Pomponius Atticus and Corelius Rufus once absurdly did), because in feeding his body he shall at the same time feed his disease. *(Wootton, 1605)* Nor should a melancholy man pine himself to death just because of where he is, a place where he can only come by melancholic food that does not suit a man of his constitution. He should use what he can get to preserve his life if no other can be had. Sometimes men give up hearing the word, praying, participating in holy things and the like just because they cannot hear so attentively, pray so devoutly or receive so reverently and religiously as they would and should. They should still endeavour to do all the duties that God requires of them as well as they can, leaving the results of their effort as a matter for the good providence of God in regard of others and to His gracious acceptance in regard of themselves. (*2 Chron 30:18)*

But when things are indifferent and are not necessary duties then if a man was to do something which in all likelihood would spiritually endanger another, that would make him guilty of soul murder. To do something that spiritually endangers himself is to make himself guilty of self-murder. *(Gersonides, ~1320)* And surely if it is unlawful and a tempting of God for a man needlessly to plunge himself into danger of death in regard of his body then it is no less unlawful, yet a far greater sin, for a man to do the same in regard of his soul. Remember that God's commandments not only forbid sin, but even what may be a means and an occasion of sin, although it may not be sinful in itself.

Therefore needless and unnecessary lotteries, even though they concern things which are otherwise lawful, when they are likely to cause or from experience are found to occasion much sin, are absolutely unwarrantable and because of that are inexpedient. However it is not unwarrantable, if, in a matter of common or public benefit, such as the repair of a bridge, the rebuilding of a hospital, the erecting of a school and the like, for a group of men of good ability to agree among themselves to put to hazard by a lottery whatever sums of money each of them shall disburse or dispend toward the discharge or support of these schemes and if the sums involved are no greater than the estate of any of them may well bear and when they cannot readily agree upon a distribution rate in other ways.

It is also worthwhile for the better encouragement of this kind of activity when a group agree in common (their minds and states probably known to each other) to contribute equally towards the price of a jewel, with one of them chosen by lottery being conferred with this commodity. I see here no reason why this should be unlawful. But it would not be so if a man in this kind of lottery has put to hazard something which he knows or probably suspects that he cannot or is unwilling to part with because the loss of it may either disenable him from doing other necessary duties, or enrage him and so make him guilty of sin in God's sight. If he was to needlessly join in with others in such an act, to try to draw them in and incite them, not knowing but presuming them to be both able and willing, by this means he may be causing them an occasion of sin, especially if in such an action he can see it would carry on to many abuses and be an occasion of much evil. I cannot see how a man could be free from sin in doing this, nor can I conceive with what comfort of conscience a man can receive or retain what a lottery in such a case shall cast upon him, coming in all likelihood in part out of the purses of those that either are altogether unable to afford such sums, or have strained themselves out of a greedy desire and hope of lucre and gain and being unwilling to lose and to part with what they put in, wretchedly cursing and blaspheming God's name for the loss of it. When such occasions of evil can be seen or foreseen it makes all such lotteries unlawful to everyone who takes part in them, considering the inconveniency and inexpedience that is in them. Therefore the more able and willing a man may be to sustain a loss which befalls through a lottery, the more lawful is that lot. *(Bernard, ~1120)* And the better known they are to be able to sustain such a loss the more warrantable is the lot, especially where the occasion is voluntary rather than neccssary,.

To conclude briefly the grounds of this twofold precaution. The lottery involves uncertainty, but it is necessary to do God's will by avoiding things which are evil either in themselves or consequentially and therefore not a fit matter to be put to the uncertain outcome of a lottery. The use of a lottery should be to determine some question or doubt. But no question ought to be made or doubt be moved when it involves the committing of any moral evil or the omitting of any necessary good duty or of doing what God forbids or of not doing what he enjoins. *(Pliny)* No lottery may therefore be used lawfully in this case. Lastly, what a man may not do even though a lottery determines it, that is to put in vain the determination of the matter by a lottery. Under oath, if it is observed, a man may not do evil. Much less so for a lottery when such evil things may not therefore be put to it.

All moral actions are of three kinds in relation to God's law. Some are simply enjoined as necessary duties; some simply inhibited as moral evils; and some freely permitted and left to our choice as are all actions described as indifferent. The rule here is that a lottery has its lawful use in indifferent things only, things which may without either offence or inconvenience be done or left undone. In this regard the greater the indifference in the outcome of the event the more lawful is the lottery. And so, contrary to that which is commonly delivered and almost generally received, the less weighty the matter for which a lottery is used the more lawful that lottery would be.

§8. The manner of using a lottery

There are two other precautions concerning the manner in which lotteries are to be used. Whereas previously I advised that a man should always be willing to forgo and part with whatever he puts to the hazard by a lottery, and as for the matter of the lottery itself, that he should be willing to part with it. (Although a man may sometimes be willing to part with something that by law he should not part with.) The party to such a lottery should be so disposed that he is willing to sustain some loss, including whatever loss as might befall him by the lot, if that is what happens. The reason for this is evident: if a man does something unadvisedly and is discontented afterwards, then that action is an occasion of sin for him. Anything that is put to the hazard of a lottery is in a sense already forgone as soon as it is put thereunto. Therefore a man ought to be willing to forgo whatever the lottery might take from him. If he is content with that then cast the lot.

But here some might say: is a man then bound to be willing to give up his known right just because he might, in some cases, commit it to such hazard? Or is it such that in this case he may not lawfully desire to obtain it? I answer: A man is bound not absolutely but conditionally to depart from is his right when a greater evil might follow from his exercise of it by whatever means he chooses to do so, though he may lawfully desire to obtain it in other ways. *(1 Cor 6:7)* So in this case, where a man, rather than losing it, willingly seeks it in other ways and would be as willing to put it to the hazard of a lottery as he would to lose it, otherwise it would be folly for him to risk it this way. He ought to be no less willing, having yielded thus far, to part with it when it shall be played out. What he might lawfully desire, he might lawfully retain if it might be had with convenience. The rule here is that no man should put anything to the hazard of a lottery except that which he could willingly forgo.

§9. No advice from God in ordinary lotteries

The last precaution is: We should not expect any special or immediate decision or extraordinary work from God when directing a lottery on a certain course, nor should anything be concluded as a result. *(Delrio, 1618)* Expecting any such thing is to presume more than God has promised. Since He has nowhere promised any special providence in these cases, then men must look instead to they way the lottery acts on the equity of their cause when they seek to justify their quarrels. They must not seek to interpose God or His providence in such courses, except insofar as they would work on any of our actions, be they uncertain, contingent or necessary. So putting anything out to the hazard of a lottery with expectation of an act of God's providence is to presume that which God has not promised and to make trial of it to tempt God. That is where many of the heathens' lotteries are at fault. What I mean is that they involve the putting of something to the hazard of a lottery to thereby see if God will interpose Himself in a special manner for their benefit, recovering what is their right or for the clearing of a cause. That is in effect an attempt to see if He will work in an extraordinary way for us as we will it. It makes prior presumptions and expectations without good ground and is hardly religious. So any conclusion drawn with that purpose (invoking God's judgement) from the result or outcome of a lottery is undoubtedly superstitious.

Therefore in a lottery of this nature the thing hazarded must be put wholly to the chance or uncertain outcome of the lottery in regard of the act of the person. This does not exclude the providence of God from the action, any more than it does from other civil affairs which are managed by counsel and advice. A person may also, if the thing is of some weight, use prayer to interpose but only in so far as he shall see fit. But do not expect any extraordinary or immediate effect of the hand of God in carrying it through, as to how it would be right for it to go, or for what is best that it should go. *(Malderus, ~1610)* This is because we neither know how far ahead God sees fit to interpose His providence on us, nor has He left us any promise in His words, either general or special that He will immediately at any time or on any occasion interpose in that manner.

In the division of lands, which should be made as equal as may be convenient, there will still be some apparent inequality because things cannot always be well divided up. A man may, in equity, have a right to the best part because he is the eldest in an inheritance that is intended to go equally among all. But to expect an extraordinary hand of God to dispose it according to whatever rights that equity might ordain is unwarrantable. It is also no less unwarrantable to conclude that when two stand for an office and one of them is fitter and more sufficient for it than the other and because the question between them is put to a lottery, just because the lottery alighted on one of them, then God has given His approval on that one's side.

§10. Conclusion

The rules then are

Firstly: a lottery determines no rights and consequently lotteries are only to be used for matters of fact and not for matters of right. 'Fact' relates not to facts past but future facts only. A lottery should not decide who has the best right to the biggest share or who is fittest for an office. They should only determine who shall have the prize and enjoy it or take it away. Otherwise it makes an ordinary lottery into an extraordinary one, a mere divisory one into a divinatory lottery, not a lottery for division alone. Later we will show that lotteries for divination to be utterly unlawful. *(Chytraeus, ~1580)* Civil lawyers seem to say the contrary, when they claim that lotteries are to be used not only in questions of fact but in questions of right too. *(Salmuth, 1607)* Yet in a sense they are in accord with what we say: lawyers simply mean that lotteries are not to be used in questions of fact that have passed when it is a question of whether a thing was done or not done. For no ordinary lottery is able to decide that. But if the question is who has a right to a thing, then in that case the lottery would not be used to determine who in truth has a right to it. Rather, for the sake of peace and quietness it decides who shall enjoy it because the right to it cannot be easily settled. So a lottery decides who shall have possession of it. Until then the right is undetermined. It is an example of failure, therefore, when the judiciary undertakes to determine a matter of truth or right by lottery, a course that is reported as usual among the Russians. *(Hackluyt, 1560)*

Secondly: no indication of right or wrong can be grounded on lotteries. Since no extraordinary power or providence is to be expected from a lottery, so nothing of that sort can be concluded from the outcome of it. It does not indicate what ought to have been or ought to have gone so, nor does it show that it was God's will in approving that it should be so because that is how it fell out. But does not the work itself, some may say, manifest God's will? I answer: there is a twofold will of God, a disposing will and a directing will; a will informing and a will over-ruling; a will prescribing what should be and a will preordaining what shall be. When something therefore has fallen out in a good or bad way it is apparent indeed that it was God's will either to perform it or to permit it. For nothing can possibly come to pass either without or against His will. But that does not mean we can conclude that by rights it ought to have been so. Otherwise we would have to conclude that the Jews ought to have crucified Christ, because God allowed them to do so, maybe even that He preordained it. *(Act 2:23)* In a case where the matter is put to a lottery by those in who have the power to do so, it may be truly said that it was God's will, specifically his disposing will, that the lottery should go as it had gone. But it does not consequently follow therefore, that according to God's directing or informing will it was right that it had gone the way it had.

Chapter 6

Ordinary lotteries used in gambling and their lawfulness

Gambling: So far we have considered those ordinary lotteries which were termed 'serious' because they were used in deciding more serious affairs. We now proceed to the less serious sort. These are variously called 'sporting lotteries' *(Perkins, 1596)*, 'ludicrous lotteries' *(Estey, ~1603)*, 'lusurious lotteries'. *(Serarius, 1609)* Whenever lotteries are used in games, sports or pastimes for recreation and delight it amounts to gambling*. Within their scope I make so bold as to include those solemn games, if we may so term them, but as they are commonly so styled. These are the exercises of valour, strength and activity, or trials of art and skill and dexterity in some faculty which were so famous and frequent in ancient times both in Greece and Italy but especially among the Greeks. *(Aristotle)*

§1. Deciding the starting order of games and revelry

The kinds and courses of lottery used in gambling are many. A lottery could be said to be used in a game either at the beginning or the end when the result is put, either in whole or in part, to some uncertain event. Sometimes only the joining or beginning of a game or sport is put to a lottery; as when it is determined who shall play and who stay out or who shall join one side. This is usually done by the shuffling of arrows together behind some one's back and then casting them aside, half one way and half the other. Another method is used the game of bowls, where the number of bowls belonging to each man are cast out together by one of them and those whose bowls meet nearest together are paired up. Or at the gaming tables which of two sides shall lead and begin is commonly decided by the casting of most points [on dice]. In chess it is done by turning a pawn on the board according to the colour of the square or quarter that it stayed or rested upon, or by one person guessing at two pawns hidden in the other's two hands. At

* Gataker does not use the word 'gambling', which would not be invented for another century or more; his description is that of 'lusurious lots'. One might quibble at including the 'solemn games' of the ancient Greeks (Olympics) under the heading of 'gambling', but Gataker clearly does so here. It could be argued that although mainly about skill and effort, luck (chance) plays a part; also although money is not directly competed for, the reward for the winner is a significant prize. I will continue, with Gataker, by including all such games under the general heading of gambling or gambling lotteries.

those famous Olympic games, the wrestlers and combatants were paired off as the runners and riders by fours or more, as they drew out letters and took their turns according to the order of those letters, with the odd man, if any were, taking on whoever had the better of the pair that fought last. *(Lucian)* There as elsewhere, in chariot-driving and horse-races, running or rowing for wagers and the like, the contenders had their stations or standings assigned to them likewise by a lottery. It is even thought that the combatants had their weapons allocated by lottery. Also in shooting, singing or playing competitions, where two could not show their skill at the same time, they had their turns and courses settled by lot. *(Pausanias)* The Masters of the Revels at Athens shared the minstrels of the city amongst themselves by lot. If it was ambiguous in any of these exercises who had done best or who had indeed won the wager, with two maybe coming home to the goal at once, then it seemed to be within the power of the Tryers to decide which of the two of them should have the prize due to the Victor either by sharing it between them or putting it to a lottery.

Lotteries in revelry: In lesser and lighter matters, when folk were disposed to be merry in private together, they sometimes drew for whoever should tell his tale first; *(Chaucer, 1476:* "now draweth cuts, or ye the further twin; the which that hath the shortest wins") or who should first read the riddle or tackle some question which had been propounded, with a reward for the one who could read it right, or who was to argue with some others in some school-question or the like. In merry meetings it is common to draw for someone in the company to be Master or Moderator of their mirth. This is not altogether unlike the custom in many countries at some special times of choosing a festival King and Queen, except that they usually do it with dice or the like, or with a bean and a pea, as was formerly used in their choice magistrates. *(Serarius, 1609)* So the younger sort have sport in choosing a 'King' by lottery who then told the rest of them whatever he chose and they had to do whatever he told them. It was in this kind of sport that Cyrus, while still a child discovered the kingly spirit and courage within him. And so it was also for Athanasius, who by acting as a 'bishop' among boys like himself, is reported to have taken the part of a grave bishop very well, which held out the good hope that he would indeed prove so to be. He afterwards succeeded in his see. *(Aldhelm)*

§2. Games of chance

Now in the foregoing cases, a lottery, although used about the game, is still outside of it than in it, only making the beginning and entrance to it. But at other times the lottery is used for directing the game itself and deciding its result, either in part or in whole.

A lottery is only used in part when art and industry are required to further manage that which has been allotted. In many games of cards at the gaming tables a lottery procedure is used to distribute of the cards amongst the gamesters. This thereby assigns each of them their chances, dealing them something to be further worked on. But whatever uncertainty has dealt to them, art and skill has to be employed as well if they are to manage and work on their game. These kinds of games were known by, or not so unusual among the ancients. There is evidence that they often compared a man's life to such games, where a man cannot make any choice over his own chances, but can by art and skill make the best use of that which randomly befalls him *(Plutarch)*.

If the whole game is settled absolutely by chance then it would be like the various games of dice and cards which depend solely the fall of the dice, either who throws the most or whose chance comes first by the goodness or the fitness, as it is called, of the chance of the cards. There are other sports too which were also known to the ancients. There is the finger-matching game we spoke of before which is still much used in Italy. *(Falkenberg, 1569)* In other sports as well, such as the various childish pastimes like cockle*, even-and-odd, heads-and-points, cross-and-pile and the like, we find most of them were used by the ancients either wholly in the same way or very nearly the same.

There is one kind of lot-sport or lot-game which I leave to last, although I am not sure whether I should call it lot-sport or not. In Russia it is said that at marriage the bridegroom puts money into one of his boots. If the bride should happen on this boot first when she comes to pull them off, she not only keeps the money that she finds there but she is freed forever from pulling his boots off again (unless it please her to do it of her own wishes). But if she misses it, she not only loses the money, but is tied ever after to the performance of that duty. (*Hackluyt, 1560*)

To this we may add banquet-lotteries where there are two sorts of prizes, some containing a free gift, others a matter of charge and expense, or it maybe a mixed matter of either. *(Lampridius)* So we read that at some festivals and other times Augustus used a lottery to distribute certain gifts among his guests, some of worth and value, such as gold, silver and garments, coins of all sorts; foreign, ancient and others; and some other prizes were mere toys and trifles, such as hair-cloth, sponges, pincers, scissors and the like, with merry poems on them of doubtful and double meaning, which seemed to glance at and nip them to whom that lottery had befallen. It was that monster of men Heliogabalus, a second Nero, who used to impose a mixed lottery on whom he pleased both in public and private. Sometimes it was a matter of gifts, sometimes a matter of charges of such extreme inequality that some people were not hurt nor impaired at all by them, only mocked. But some were utterly undone by them, because according to what they drew they had to pay in and lay down either a pound of beef, a dead dog, ten flies, ten fleas, ten bears or ten camels; or it was to be so many pounds of lead, silver or gold, etc.

---

* 'Hot cockles' was a popular game at Christmas in medieval times. It was a game in which the other players took turns striking the blindfolded player, who had to guess the name of the person delivering each blow. Hot cockles was still a Christmas pastime until the Victorian era

Others received as their lottery a result which made many rich that were poor before and others as poor that were rich before. This monster delighted in nothing more than in mischief and miseries of the many. *(Suetonius)*. These forfeits were sometimes either written or painted on their spoons, just as we nowadays commonly have painted emblems and poesies on fruit-trenchers. Sometimes we make use of these to make sport in a similar manner.

Sometimes a lottery such as this was put on sale as a joke. Augustus used to do this sometimes in his games by showing the back side of pictures only. In merriment he proposed to those that were at the table with him, that to join in the game they had to put up a price to draw a picture, with he who bid most having it. This is like our raffles and lotteries, where a certain number who venture their money are admitted to cast dice or to draw for some prize or prizes. Concerning these kind of lotteries our civil lawyers and others are divided in judgement. Some refer to them as serious divisory lotteries which contain a twofold virtual contract: the bargain and sale between all the adventurers being undertaken jointly and the owner or owners of the prize or prizes that they are to draw for, so making it a sale for such a sum as all their adventures put together amounts to *(Delrio, 1618);* or it could be seen as a society or fellowship which has been formed between the adventurers themselves, agreeing to draw lottery or cast dice for that which they have bought in common; or it could be, as they term them, a running or unlimited lottery, with only a single contract of bargain and sale between the owner and the adventurers. An example would be the fisherman's draught, the fowler's fortune or the merchant's venture at sea where men buy the bare hope of a share in the result rather than an actual amount. *(Pomponius)* There are other writers *(Perkins, 1608)* who bring within their ambit all kinds of unlawful games, but for all I that can see, these games are no better than ways to help relieve either base spendthrifts or beggarly bankrupts, who are the least deserving of relief. And so we have seen the various ways that lotteries have been, or may be used in and about games.

§3. Are such games unbecoming to Christians?

There is much questioning and disputation among the learned concerning when a lottery is used these 'games of hazard', as they are termed. *(Erasmus, 1515)* Various reverend and religious men pass a peremptory sentence on them as being altogether unlawful and unbecoming for good Christians. Yet among those that impugn and oppose them there is also a diversity of opinion. Some of them allow those games that are carried partly by chance and partly by skill which they suppose do not come within the ambit of a lottery. They only condemn those games that depend wholly upon uncertain events. For example, *Babington (1583)* says "Dice I utterly disallow, cards and table I condemn not"; *Perkins (1592)* says "For mixed plays at cards and gaming tables, consisting partly of hazard, partly of wit; as they are not to be commended, so they are not to be condemned". Others of them *(Fenner, 1587; Balmford, 1593)* utterly and absolutely reject all games that have any spice of lottery or uncertain outcome at all in them. *Estey (~1603):* "Ludicrous lots are not beseeming Christians". Others again may glance at these games in general, but it is uncertain whether they agree with either view. There are even some *(Calvin, 1584)* who may not agree at all with either on different grounds from theirs, disallowing some of these games but not all of them, or not all of the manner in which they are used, as will be explained later.

It is clear that there are some *(Balmford, 1593)* that by producing reasons for disallowing one kind of game, must, if their grounds be admitted, condemn both kinds. For if one is evil and not allowable because it depends upon a lottery and on chance then the other must likewise be evil and unwarrantable insofar as they depend in part on it. And on the other side, if those authors will avow and justify one sort of game they cannot but (secretly) give approval also for the other, since they both stand on the same grounds and both are built on one foundation.

There are some *(Perkins, 1592)* who would say "mixed games are no lotteries", that by distinguishing the nature of these games, that one is a lottery but the other is not, or that there is a lottery in one, but not in the other. This would be true, as some do, if we defined a lottery to be a kind of consulting with God *(Aret.; Zanchius, ~1580)* and a method of seeking to be informed and directed by Him. But there is no lottery at all in this case. If we define 'lottery' in the proper and ordinary signification of it then there is a lottery just as much and as well in both cases. The only difference is that there is a mere lottery in the one and a mixed lottery in the other but a true lottery in both.

The argument that a reverend writer *(Perkins, 1592)* brings to try to prove the contrary is that because in a lottery there are two things required: first a chance or uncertain act; and secondly an applying of that chance act to the determination of some particular and uncertain event. The dealing of cards is an act involving uncertainty, but the determination of victory in mixed games derives not merely from this uncertainty but as much or more from the wit, skill and will of the players. Therefore the dealing of the cards is no more of a lottery than when the Prince's Almoner doles out alms by putting his hand into his pocket, giving one man six-pence, another twelve-pence, another two-pence or whatever comes forth. This argument, I say, is not sound, because it reasons from the particular to the general. The dealing of the cards does not determine this uncertain event, namely, the outcome of the game or its victory. Therefore it is not applied to the settling of any uncertain outcome at all. This is an unsound consequence and is also untrue. For it is manifest that the dealing of the cards is applied to the settling of this uncertain outcome, fixing the cards or casts so that each one shall have to exercise his skill with them. Hence even by his own description it is a lottery. So too is the dealing out of alms in that way, if it is done to try to see what will randomly fall to each one's share in this way. It could equally well be done by the drawing of rushes or cuts, things which are commonly taken to be lotteries.

I hold that these gambling lotteries and games which consist of such are not evil or unwarrantable in themselves, nor that lotteries used in games are unlawful.

In this assertion I am dissenting from the views of some others of religion and learning, whom in other ways I worthily respect and embrace. I only desire to have my grounds duly viewed and examined to see if they prove firm and sound. If so, then the frame built on them may stand; if weak and unsound it may fall before the truth, as Dagon did before God's Ark. *(Sam 5:4)* If I am wrong I myself promise to lend a hand in the overturning and razing of what I now raise up, if it can be shown to me to be anything other than what is warrantable by God's word.

Reasons why gambling lotteries are not evil in themselves

Having laid the grounds concerning the nature of lotteries in general, I now proceed to deduce the reasons why gambling lotteries of this kind are not evil in themselves:

§4. First reason why lotteries are not evil: If sanctioned for use in civil affairs, why not gambling also: Anything which may ordinarily be used in civil affairs whether of greater or lesser weight may also be used for matters of recreation and delight. That a lottery may be ordinarily used in other civil affairs is given the express authority of God's spirit when speaking through Solomon who said it was for the ending of contentions in matters of suits or strife, whether weightier or of less weight. The words in this text are indefinite, but there is nothing to restrict the ordinary use of lottery either there or elsewhere. The word used there originally related to law-suits but in its ordinary use extends to contentions of all kinds. *(Proverbs 6:14)* And the practice of God's people as recorded in Scripture shows that even mean matters could usually be decided and settled by lottery. In the matter of tithes it did not matter how many lambs the Levite [priest] took, whether he had one of ten, two of twenty, etcetera, it was decided by a lottery. It was a matter of no great weight what gate of the Temple such-or-such Levites should wait at. *(Levit 27:32)* I say it was not important despite the fact that it was a mean matter to be a porter in God's house, (though it seem to be mentioned as one of the meanest places of employment there), only that it was fixed who should wait at this gate and who at that other gate (as who should stand at the North door of the Church and who at the South, to receive peoples' benevolence on the occasion of some collection). It was not a matter of great moment and yet was that also decided by lottery. *(Luk 1:9)* Neither was it greatly material which of the priests offered incense or which dressed the lamps, etcetera, yet that also went by lottery. (The offices themselves were not allocated by lot, only the distribution of particular duties or stations among those of the same office. *(Sam c10)*) Since a lottery may therefore be lawfully used in other ordinary affairs with God's word warranting it and nothing elsewhere restricting it and given that it was the practice of the godly to carry it over even into mean matters, I do not see why they should be banished out of our sports, any more than out of other our more serious civil affairs.

§5. Second reason why lotteries are not evil: Only used for less weighty matters: If we consider the nature of a lottery correctly and the great uncertainty in it, we find that it is fittest for matters which are of least moment and it is not fit to be used in any weighty affair. Anyone making use of it for serious matters is usually more cautious. By disposing things beforehand, it then becomes less important which way the lottery falls, or that as little as possible may be left to chance. When it is a material matter of some consequence which might go one way or another there will be no wise men who would willingly put such weighty matters to the uncertain hazard of a lottery. (I will not comment on what the iniquity of others may force a man into, when a lesser inconvenience is allowable in order to avoid a greater one.) So the things which are naturally best sorted using a lottery are those in which a lottery may most lawfully be used. The lightest matters are best sorted thus because of the nature of lotteries and therefore a lottery may most lawfully be used for things of that nature.

§6. Third reason why lotteries are not evil: Indifference in the outcome: If we consider the nature of the things that are wont to be put, and may lawfully so be put to lottery according to the rules and precautions previously delivered, we find that a lottery is no more unfit or unlawful for gambling than it is fit for or lawful in any other ordinary employment. Actions freely undertaken and which are indifferent and which may be done or not done are, as was formerly shown, fit subjects for which a lottery may be lawfully employed. This is my reasoning: matters of mere indifference are things which a man may lawfully either do or not do and it is immaterial whether he does them or omits them. These are such where a man may lawfully decide, either by the will of another or by the hazard of an uncertain outcome whether he shall do them or not. Why should not a man let some doubtful event decide something when he is free to do it or not do it? It is not so much the seriousness of the business but his own freeness in this regard that makes it a fit matter for the lottery to work on. But using a lottery in gaming (or using it in any business, be it serious or gambling, with the qualifications and cautions as before) is only letting a matter of mere indifference be put to the hazard of an uncertain event. Examples of this would be: who shall join in or stand out of a game, who shall lead or follow, who shall overcome or yield to the other side etcetera. These are merely indifferent matters and which may, without sin, be done or not done or done one way or another. Therefore the use of a lottery in such cases and the putting of such matters to the hazard of a lottery is not simply in itself evil.

§7. Fourth reason why lotteries are not evil: No lottery is either holy or profane: If gambling was evil in itself then it must be a sin either against Piety in the first Table or against Charity in the second. For every moral evil must be a breach of God's Law, the whole sum and substance of which are summed up by those ten commandments in those two tables. *(Exod 31:18)* Every breach must necessarily be brought within the scope of one of those two and consequently be a breach either of impiety against the one, or of iniquity against the other.

But the use of a lottery in games is not in or of itself a sin either against Piety or Charity. It would be both superfluous and ridiculous to spend time and ink proving that the use of a lottery in game is not against Charity and that it is no breach of Charity for men to draw cuts or cast arrows to decide who shall bowl or shoot first. Superfluous, because it would only prove what no man denies. Ridiculous, because it would only contradict what no wise man avows. To charge gambling with impiety has as little ground as the other.

To prove this, consider that all forms of impiety may be referred to under two heads: profaning hallowed things, or hallowing things that are profane. *(Ezek 21:4)* It cannot be imagined how any impiety could be committed unless it is by denying holy things their due respect or by giving the same where it is not due. But gambling lotteries are not of themselves guilty in either of these ways. Of the latter kind, even their greatest adversaries *(Yates, 1622)* will clear them, there being no taint which charges them with hallowing anything which is not otherwise holy. And in the former kind they may be cleared also on grounds of God's Law from profaning anything that is holy. ("Those on the other side offend by placing nature and inferior causes in God's place and deifying instead of vilifying slight occurrences of small moment" Gataker comments in a note.) That is because the thing used in them is a lottery and nothing can be profaned by it except what is used in it. (By lottery I mean simply in so far as they are lotteries. If a lottery is made of holy things, such as parcels of Scripture or of the elements consecrated in the sacrament, etcetera, that is not anything concerning the nature of a lottery, but an abuse which clamped on to it by some men's particular practice of it. Therefore it is no part of our discourse and is to be severed from it.) A lottery is not a holy thing, either of itself or in its own nature or by virtue of any divine ceremony. All holy things are of two sorts, either things which are holy of themselves and in their own nature as is God himself and as are His titles and attributes, or else they become holy, not from their own nature but by means of some special divine ceremony sanctifying and reserving them to some holy use. This happened to the Ark, the Tabernacle, the Temple, the seventh day of the world before Christ and the first day of the week since Christ. *(Gen 2:3)* Now in neither of these respects can any lottery be said to be holy, not of itself or its own nature, for it is nothing else but an uncertain event applied to the settling or deciding of some doubt. The essence of it, a mere uncertain event, insofar as it is an uncertain event has no holiness in itself at all (otherwise all uncertainties would also be such), nor can it gain or procure any holiness to itself just by someone's application of it to any purpose whatsoever, much less by the applying of it to a profane or common purpose, whether more or less weighty.

Nor can a lottery be holy through any divine ceremony, since every such ceremony must have warrant from some sacred words and no-one can produce any word of any ceremony whereby lotteries are specially sanctified and set apart for uses which would bring them within the scope of holy and sacred things. Just because some particular lottery has sometimes been used in this way, that can no more impart holiness to all lotteries in general than that the religious use of water in Baptism even in the Baptism of our saviour. Nor does the sacred use of bread and wine in the Lord's supper make all water or all bread and wine in general to be holy and so consequently barred from ordinary and common use by men in cases of necessity or for their lawful delight.

Those writers are in the wrong who would allow lotteries to be used in gambling, yet add the caution that great reverence and religiousness must be used because in regard of holy things they must be done in a holy manner. If indeed the lotteries that are used in general civil matters as well as in sacred uses are to be holy things then they may never, even with caution, be made a matter of sport and pastime or of gamesome recreation. *(Perkins, 1592.)* Nor can the light use of them ever be corrected and qualified because it will always have that deadly poison in the heart and pith of it, not merely adhering or cleaving onto the bark or outside of it. But civil lotteries are not like this and therefore the gambling use of them does not profane any holy thing. And if it is neither the un-hallowing of something hallowed nor the hallowing of any thing unhallowed, then it cannot be brought within the scope of impiety or sin against the first Table. And if it be cleared from all sin against the first Table and is not charged with any sin against the second Table, it must remain discharged of all sin in general and consequently be justified as being agreeable to God's word.

§8. A fifth reason why lotteries are not evil: Nothing un-natural is being used: It may be taken from the benefit of Christian liberty that every Christian man has the free use of all of God's good creatures and may employ them for such purposes as they are enabled to by any natural power (within the bounds mentioned above). *(Calvin, 1584)* But in these ordinary civil and divisory lotteries, whether they be serious or for gambling, the thing is used for no other purpose or use except what it has a natural power so to do. I understand 'natural' not so much a work which a thing does through its natural instinct or inclination, but such as it has a natural capacity for and which is neither done by the will of the person that makes use of it on his own, or through the mutual consent and agreement of those that jointly make use of it, that it may be enabled to be effected. *(Krackewitz, ~1610)* This is something, I suppose, that no man can deny in the use and work of a lottery either for gambling or in serious affairs. For it is in its nature to move or to be moved diversely and be uncertain in regard of those that make use of it. It is also within the power of the users, by mutual agreement, to decide whatever matters are ordinarily to be settled thereby. Therefore, so long as the use of lottery is kept free from superstition, impiety, injustice and dishonesty, it should no more to be excluded from a Christian man's recreations than any of the other things or ordinances whatsoever which have any natural power to delight and give contentment of that kind.

§9. A sixth reason why lotteries are not evil: Innocent games also involve chance: It may be taken from the fact that since the lottery is generally agreed to be based uncertain events which would also include sporting activities, so they should not be debarred from lottery use either. Tell me now, who would be so excessively austere or extremely superstitious to deny men the opportunity to enjoy sport with whatever uncertain outcomes occur naturally? May one not take pleasure at a man shooting or catching although he is blindfolded? Or may we not delight ourselves as we sit by the seaside observing the waves when a fresh gale drives them to leeward and they come wallowing one over the another onto the shore? *(Pollux)* Or is it utterly unlawful to laugh at our pranks when either ourselves or others trip up (in a way when no hurt ensues from it), or when someone treads unawares in some unclean thing? Or would it be less warrantable to give chase to a hare that we come across by chance rather than the one we intentionally sought to find? If we may lawfully amuse ourselves with these and other similar uncertainties, may we not as well (I would dearly love to know of any reasonable person who thinks otherwise) do the same with the shuffling of arrows, the drawing of tickets, the dealing of cards or the roll of a die? If men sitting by the seaside may delight themselves by observing waves making for the shore, why should we quibble at the thought that they might well lay a light wager with each other on how many waves will beat on the beach in some stretch of time? Or to resolve that some light and trifling difference could be decided by using whatever number of waves that either of them guesses would come in within such-and-such a time? What difference does it make if a man refers such light controversy to such a chance outcome? It is the use of the bare name 'lottery' which seems to be the bugbear here and this name breeds such a superstitious conceit of the uncertain event used in this way. But it cannot reasonably be denied that this is indeed a lottery according to the true and strict nature of it.

§10. A seventh reason why lotteries are not evil: A lottery is an indifferent thing: This may even be drawn from the grounds and grants of those that oppose on this point. It may be framed like this: anything that is indifferent is a lawful matter of recreation; but a lottery is an indifferent thing, therefore a lottery can be a lawful matter of sport. This proposition is confirmed by the definition some give of recreation, namely "Christian recreation is the exercise of something indifferent for the necessary refreshing of body or mind". *(Fenner, 1587)*

The assumption, namely that a lottery is by its own nature indifferent is thus proved from this definition of such things that are indifferent in their nature. 'Indifferent in nature' describes that which has been left free and we are neither commanded or forbidden to use it, but is such that we may, in Christian wisdom find it either beneficial or hurtful for us. *(Fenner, 1587)* A lottery, or the use of lottery is such a thing; not simply commanded nor again anywhere forbidden or condemned as evil in itself, so by the former definition therefore consequently it is indifferent and thus a lawful matter of Christian recreation and delight. (Note that Solomon's proverb ("A lottery stinteth strife") is a permission rather than a precept not so much a commandment as advice and counsel, commending to us a wise and prudent course, not enjoining or imposing it as a duty necessary to be done, but seeing that other courses may without sin be used as well in such controversies and things often are effected by means other than a lot, which Solomon would also allow)

§11. And lastly (eighthly) reason why lotteries are not evil: No specific ban or approval for them: The use of lotteries in gambling is not against God's word, but is given sufficient warrant by it, as will be shown. Where the wisdom of God's words have not been determined on any matter or manner, or other circumstances of a thing show it to be lawful in itself, such things are left to man's discretion and wisdom. *(Fenner, 1587; Perkins, 1592)* Otherwise we would hang in perpetual suspense having no rule at all to direct us by. And where things are left to man's discretion and wisdom there is sufficient warrant under the circumstances for any choice a man shall make (as when magistrates publicly enjoin, or private persons seek to practise) so long as it shall not be against the general rules of God's word concerning it. *(Calvin, 1584)*

To aid understanding of this point, consider that in order to do any act and to do it in this or that manner, if natural reason itself will not provide sufficient direction then there must be warrant for it found in God's word. And a man must know that he has such warrant for it because "Anything that is not done in faith is sin". *(Rom 14:23)* I would add that where natural reason does not of itself afford sufficient direction then the answer comes from the words given to us in moral matters. These correct the defects which were caused by the fall from grace of our first parents. But it does not cut us off from the help we get from the use of God's words for direction in such actions, but adds a further and fuller help thereunto.

First then, in general, for the act itself: if it is good and lawful and allowable by God's Law and there is either precept or permission in God's word for the doing of it which is either directly and expressly stated, or it is inferred as a just consequence, then: if it is a precept, it is necessary and must be done; or if a permission only, it is indifferent and may be done or not done, as shall seem good to the party whom it concerns.

Secondly as for the subject matter, the manner of it and other such circumstances: if they are determined by God's word then they are lawful as the word of God had enjoined. Where they are not determined then they are all lawful in so far as the same word does not forbid them. In the former, the rule is that; "he who is not with me, is against me". In the latter the other rule, "he that is not against me, is with me". *(Luk 9:50)* When deciding what to sacrifice and where, it was lawful to do it in any place because no specific place was designated, but afterwards it was fixed that the place could be nowhere else than that which God had expressly assigned for it. So for the Passover and other offerings and the time and season of either, the ordinary sacrifices (I mean the voluntary or freewill offerings) might be offered at any time, *(Deut 12:5)* because no time was determined for them, but the Passover might be celebrated only at one time because the time of it was determined.

This is how I would answer some of the frivolous objections made by some Separatists*: "What warrant", say they, "have you to use this or that form of prayer, or to pray upon a book?" I answer: it is sufficient warrant that we are enjoined to use prayers in such kind, confession of sin and supplication for pardon, etcetera, with no set form of them being laid down. Therefore any fit form is warrantable and any unfit form that we might use would not be so. And let a man demand of one of them, if and when he prays, what warrant he has to use the form that he then uses, he can only answer that he can do no other. So it is for a book, that the means of help are not determined, one amongst others, so this therefore is not unwarrantable. And if anyone is asked how he proves that it is warrantable to use a printed book to read from in church, he can only answer as before. Neither precept nor practice can be found in the word for the use of a thing that was not known in those times when the word of God was written.

§12. Conclusion

But to apply this to our present task:

First, it is granted by all that recreation has, in general, good warrant from God's word *(Eccles 3:4)* as a thing allowed by permission and enjoined by precept. If that has not been expressed directly then it is at least justified as a consequence and I will therefore not need to prove it.

Secondly, as for the matter and manner of doing it, or the things we may recreate ourselves with, nothing is specified. Therefore any means of recreation that is not against the general rules of comeliness and decency, convenience and expedience, religion and piety and the like, is allowed by the word of God and thus have sufficient warrant from that.

For example if the question is whether bowls or chess is lawful or not, what more can be said in justification of them than that, in general, recreation is allowed by God's word. The matter of it in particular is not determined, so these games are not prohibited and are therefore lawful and allowable. The very same may be said of lotteries and gambling. In general, gaming is allowed. No particular matter or manner of it prescribed and any of these games is therefore lawful and not against the general rules of God's word. A gambling lottery is one such and therefore allowable.

If anyone says that the particular matter or manner of a recreation has been settled, he must show where. Or if anyone can say that a particular form of lottery is against the general rules of God's word, he too must show which and how. Oth-

* Separatists were English protestants who wished to split with the established church, unlike the Puritans who sought reform within it. Gataker gives no reference for these 'seperatists'.

erwise there is almost no civil action that could be justifiable, such as: going out in doublet and hose, wearing band and cuffs, carrying a man's purse in your pocket, sitting on a stool at table, crossing the water by boat when one may go across by the bridge, the eating of pork, blooding or anything strangled and the like. It may be deemed enough to make an action unwarrantable because there is no particular precept or precedent for it in Scripture, or because it is questioned or condemned by some without any reason or sufficient cause being rendered as to why it should be questioned and condemned in that way.

And so I conclude and leave with this last reason taken from the common grounds that other ordinary recreations are not questioned which means that all will either stand or fall on the selfsame grounds. Since something in particular is not prohibited nor is against the general rules of God's word, so it must be of good standing until the contrary can be proved.

Chapter 7

Answers to the principal objections made against gambling

§1. Classification of arguments

There are some of the former authors who object, saying that they can show how this kind of sport or recreation by lottery and the use of gambling is against the general rules of God's word. So I will examine the several objections that are brought by several men against gambling. I will deal with them as frankly and as even-handedly as I am able, propounding all of their arguments as I find them, not picking out the weakest and passing by the pithiest, or setting out one part or piece of them and concealing the rest. Insofar as I can, I will gather all I can find from those writers that I understand to have dealt in this argument and express them as far as they themselves would do to their best advantage. To do this in a more orderly way I shall expound their arguments under two heads: principal arguments; and minor arguments of lesser weight. The principal arguments tend to prove that gambling is simply unlawful and so evil in itself. The minor arguments (which will be dealt with in the next Chapter) tend to prove that gambling in all its forms is either inconvenient and inexpedient and as such has been generally disallowed and condemned by the best or the most people.

The former (principal arguments) may again be sorted into two ranks according to the terms of the thing in question, namely: a lottery used in recreation, or recreations by gambling. Both are taken from lotteries and their nature or their proper use and purpose; or it takes it from the nature of the recreation and its use and purpose.

§2. First objection: A lottery comes from divine providence

The first main argument comes from the nature of the lottery. It is claimed to be a work of God's special and immediate providence, a sacred oracle, a divine judgement or sentence. Making light use of a lottery is therefore an abuse of God's name and so a sin against the third Commandment. *(Daneau, 1586; Perkins, 1590)* This argument is derived by various authors in diverse ways:

First they reason that God's special and immediate providence is not to be vainly or lightly used, but in every lottery there is an especial and immediate providence of God, therefore no lottery is to be lightly or vainly used. The proposition of this syllogism (such as it is) is further confirmed by an argument which is taken from the tenor of the third Commandment. "God's name is not to be lightly or vainly used". But God's providence is God's name; therefore God's providence is not to be lightly or vainly used. *(Perkins, 1590)*

This assumption is confirmed by two testimonies: one divine, one human. The divine testimony is from that sentence of Solomon "The lottery is cast into the lap, but the whole disposition of it is of the Lord". *(Proverbs 16:33)* So although the nature of a lottery lies wholly in the things that are of us, yet the disposition of it is wholly of God. That is: here God does not use our means of cunning, practice, strength, steadiness of hand or such like, but takes it wholly unto Himself. *(Fenner, 1587)* The human testimony is a saying of *Jerome,* who said that "a lottery is a hidden and incomprehensible predestination, ruled by God". Who would dare play with this then?

Firstly, I say that the principal syllogism is in itself unsound. There are four 'terms', as they say, in it. I show this by a similar paralogism [false reasoning] which is built of the same frame and set upon the same ground. God's providence being His name is not to be used lightly or as recreation or sport. But in all things, or in every action that is, there is a providence of God. Therefore there is nothing nor any action that may be used for sport, and all recreations should be utterly cut off. This and that are both of one making, but neither of them can both be sound. The conclusion therefore does not follow, albeit the premises were both true.

Secondly, the assumption is not sound. It is not true that in every lottery there is a special and immediate providence of God. To discovery why, remember two grounds which were formerly laid out:

The act of the Creator and the act of creatures should be distinguished in these cases. The uncertain outcome in regard of the creature is one thing, and God's providence directing and ruling or over-ruling it as all other actions, is another thing altogether. A man may therefore play with the one but not with the other. This is what we do in acts which are not done randomly, but are carried out and managed by our own art and industry. Even so they are accompanied with God's providence.

It is not the uncertainty in an outcome that would make it God's work of immediate providence. Many things are uncertain and are not works of God's immediate providence nor do they imply His special presence. If a lottery based on an uncertainty was to be a work of God's immediate providence and in that regard implied His special and extraordinary presence, then all uncertain outcomes should be as such. For when a thing is such-or-such, then necessarily all similar things are also such. But if a bird flies up before a man going on his way, or if a dog crosses a man's bowling ball while it is in play when it is unlikely to do otherwise; that does not imply special or immediate Providence. Nor does it with a lottery.

§3. The real meaning of Proverb 16:33

But let us examine the proofs that are brought to strengthen this part. First, as for that saying of Solomon, there are many good authors *(Krakewitz, ~1610; Peucer, 1572)* that explain it as relating to singular and extraordinary and miraculous lotteries only; such as, to use the words of one of our adversaries *(Estey, ~1603)*, "as are used immediately to find out God's will". We dispute this and say they are no such and neither is it now lawful to use any lottery at all for that purpose.

But these words seem to be more general. In the original the words are: "The lot, it is cast into the lap; but every judgement or disposition of it (for there is no article there answering our English 'the') is of God". *(Proverbs 16:33)* As Solomon said elsewhere in Proverbs: "Many seek the ruler's face or favour; but each man's judgement is from God". *(Proverbs 29:26)* And, "The horse is prepared for the day of fight, but salvation is of God, (or belonged to God), is God's". *(Proverbs 21:31)* In these words the only importance is that there is a providence of God in all things, even in the least, in the most random of things and among all the rest which are named as lotteries. And so is there no more said of lotteries there than is spoken of elsewhere, not only of lotteries alone or uncertain things only, but of all men's thoughts and purposes, words and works, counsels and courses (as we have previously shown). As well as what is alleged by some authors, who urge this saying as proof of their point, they confess elsewhere against themselves when they say, that "The disposing of the chance is secret that it may be chance indeed and wholly of God, who directs all things". *(Balmford, 1593)*

I will make this a little more clear, because this reference is the main pillar and buttress that supports and upholds those on the other side. But first, suppose there is only the ordinary providence of God in lotteries, just as it is in ordinary civil actions and affairs. Might it not yet be truly said of them: "The lottery indeed is cast into the lap; but every judgement or sentence of it is of God"? If that is so, as no doubt it well might be, then nothing more can be concluded from it, apart from the implication that it is the providence of God as was spoken about before. We could take out the word 'lottery' and substitute 'issue of war', 'law-suits', 'judgements of God by casualties of fire' *(various Proverbs & Psal)* or similar events, all of which are known to be produced by ordinary providence and known secondary causes. You might as well say that "Horse and man, sword and shield are prepared for the field, but all victory is God's", or "However it is that some using friends, some using bribes seek to curry favour with the judge, and that judges themselves are sometimes led by sinister respects, yet they sometimes proceed according to the right apprehension even though every man's sentence and every doom they give is God's", or "Although fires and falling edifices often happen through man's negligence, even so there is no evil but God's". And would not the sentence be true of these too? If it was (and none will deny a divine hand in the disposition of all such events) then anything said about a lottery may truly be said about all such events, neither inferring or enforcing any extraordinary or immediate act of God in it.

But to take these words as they are usually read, "The lottery is cast into the lap, but the whole disposition, **or** the whole disposing thereof, is of the Lord". *(The Kings Edit KJV*)* It may just as truthfully be said with good warrant that in a great many other references in scripture besides those produced by my adversaries, that the whole issue or outcome and disposing of all things great and weighty, or less and lighter is 'of the Lord'. This does not exclude the means that God works by or with in most of them, nor does it imply an immediate providence universally in them. What it does truly show is that it is wholly in God's hands to dispose of the outcome and issue of all things and to cross them or give way to them as He shall see fit. A man might as well and with equally good grounds exclude everything else whatsoever from gambling as well as lotteries, if we are to believe all these other men's speeches and actions which they allege (together with others, who are yet more general and of larger extent) in regard of anything that can be picked out of this saying.

§4. Estey's error: God's immediate providence in every lottery:
The objection can be made that there is an immediate providence of God always in the one (lotteries) but not usually in any other. As *Estey (~1603)* said: "It ruleth in all, but in the most by means; in a lottery it is immediate, which therefore to dally with is dangerous". I answer, that yes indeed it can be presumed that in every lottery there is an immediate providence of God. But that is not yet proved, although it is more than is required of me. He that said it should make that proof. It may be disproved as follows:

First, if in every lottery there is necessarily an immediate work and providence of God, then is it in the natural power of man to make God work immediately at his pleasure. It is naturally in any man's power to cast a lottery at his pleasure. As *Yates (1622)* puts it: "Such false dice must be barred because it would counterfeit every cast with an immediate hand of God" But to say that it is naturally in a man's power to set God to work immediately at his pleasure is absurd. When the wind drives the waves to the shore or shakes down the decayed leaves it would be senseless to say that because a man observed them or laid a light wager with another about how many would come in or fall down within some set time, that either of them could draw in the hand of God to alter natural courses and currents and make the one come in, the other fall down, fewer or faster than they would do of themselves. Would it not be absurd to say that men settling some difference by reference to the return of the floodtide could cause God to work to immediately to bring back the tide? Hence we can say that there is not an immediate work and providence necessarily in every lot.

Again, who cannot see that the outcome of a lottery in this or that manner ordinarily comes immediately from the act of a person? *(Plutarch; Cicero)* For ex-

---

* So Gataker was aware of the KJV Bible translation, but, apart from this one instance chooses to use his own version or translation. Curious!

ample: In the mixing of scrolls or tickets together, the motion of the vessel wherein they are mixed (regardless of the purpose for which it is done) causes some to lie this way and some to lie that way, (every new shaking causing a new sorting) and so some will lie higher and nearer at hand so more likely to be drawn next, some lower and further off not likely to be drawn so soon, unless you dive deeper. Neither can any man say certainly that there is ordinarily any special hand of God in the shuffling and sorting of them, changing the course of nature or the natural motion of the person or thing and so causing some to lie higher and so nearer at hand than otherwise and some to lie lower and so further from hand. In the shuffling of cards, it is the hands of he who shuffles them that arranges the cards and it is his choice whether to stop or to continue that act of his. In the casting of dice it is the violence of the caster which causes the things cast to move, until either that force runs out or some opposite body hinders them when they will cease to move further. That is what determines the chance of the outcome.

Yet suppose two men agree to settle a doubt without further ado, using cards, taking them as they lie, left by those that last used them. The position of the cards is as they find them which had been caused by whoever had left them there. The cards may be all over the place or it may well be following some special occasion and hence otherwise, but yet is it uncertain and so it is a lottery to them. It would be against reason and sense if a man imagines that some immediate providence of God was procured to place the cards in the way that they are lying, still unstirred at the moment when the doubt or uncertainty was referred unto them.

Or lastly to take the example of another sort of lottery commonly used by children in games. When they play at even-and-odd, or at heads-and-points, is there any such immediate providence as these men dream of? If there is, it cannot be exercised in arranging any bodily motion of the insensible things (for the lottery, be it by stones or pins has already been disposed by him who holds them), nor could it be by directing the hand of another in choosing or in placing his pin (for his own will is led by guess and conjecture). It can only be by inclining the will of the child guiding his conjecture; which shows how senseless it is to say such a thing, as any reasonable man would judge. The same may be said of those serious lotteries *(Dionysius)* where a child is employed to choose and pick what he likes and by his choice the controversy or question is decided. Also there is the case where the parties to a lottery-decision each choose for himself one of the lottery options openly exhibited but distinguished by some difference which is secret and unseen to them.

Yes, but was it not *Jerome* who said that a lottery is divine predestination (according to *Estey (~1603))* and who would then dare dally with it? Where Jerome said so, I cannot find. I can only find that where he was supposed to have said (as cited before) that there was a secret hand of God directing the lottery that lighted on Jonah, although he added no general rules for ordinary lotteries that can be gathered from it. But did not *Augustine* say that Zanchie said that predestination may be termed a lot? True, Augustine did indeed say something to that effect, as I previously alleged (in Chapter 4), to wit, that God's saving grace is called 'our lot' because there is no choice in it but God's will alone and so our salvation depends on God's free favour and good pleasure only, not on man's merit. But that is but a trope [metaphorical speech], comparing the freeness of God's choice to the indifference of a lottery and does not relate to any matter of men's worth or desert and so is in no way of concern to this present business. It gives no force to any proof that a lottery is the same as that which it is figuratively compared to.

It may be granted that a lottery which is cast by God's special appointment to discover which person God has assigned to some place may in some sense (though very improperly) be termed 'God's predestination', because it is a sign of, or a means to discover God's will and is usually seen as the sign of His will. *(Aquinas, 1270)* But that has nothing to do with the lotteries that we now treat with. It is unsound reasoning to jump from extraordinary to ordinary actions. And so much for the first form.

§5. Balmford's blunder 1: Gambling as an abusing of God's name

On the same grounds they reason thus: whatsoever directly or of itself or in a special manner tends to advance God's name is to be used religiously and not to be used in sport, just as we may not pray or swear in sport. But the use of lottery directly or of itself and in a special manner tends to the advancing of the name of God by attributing to it His special providence in the whole and immediate disposing of the lottery and the expectation from the outcome. Therefore the use of lottery is not to be allowed in sports or gambling. *(Balmford, 1593).*

I answer: the assumption is not true if it is understood universally nor does it conclude anything on the question if it is taken in the particular. The proof attached above hardly makes good sense. Maybe it is the printer who is at fault. But if the meaning of the author, as I conceive it, (for I must go in part by guess) is that the disposition of every lottery is wholly attributed to, and the outcome to be wholly expected from the special and immediate providence of God, then I deny this and none of the references produced prove it. The former of them, concerning the ordinary lottery or lotteries in general was examined and answered sufficiently before.

The latter part of Balmford's argument relates to an example of an extraordinary lottery (choosing a replacement Apostle *(Act 1:24)*), where there was indeed an immediate and special providence. But extraordinary examples make no general rules. Neither is it a good course of argument to reason from a special or singular event to the general and universal, much less from one extraordinary act or event to all ordinary courses of the same kind. This is what makes the difference between them, between the extraordinary lottery where there is an immediate hand of God for a special purpose and the ordinary lot where there is not. One of them had to fall with certainty no matter how often it was cast, as in the lottery that was used for the discovery of Achan *(Josh 7:16),* and Jonah and in the election of Saul and Matthias *(Act 1:23)* and the like. But the other sort could be cast again and again in the same case, as for partition of goods and chattels which descend by inheritance or are bought in common, by those who do not wish to constantly and certainly fall out over the share-out.

§6. Balmford's blunder 2: Lotteries tempt God to produce a special work

Moving on from the argument that using a lottery in gambling is an abuse of God's name because it plays with the work of His immediate providence, my adversaries further charge is that it tempts God to produce both a special work and immediate sentence to decide vain doubts. At first they argue in this manner: "We are not to tempt the Almighty by a vain desire of a manifestation of His power and special providence. But by using lottery in sport we do so, therefore we may not use lottery in sport." *(Balmford, 1593)*

They seem to prove their assumption in this way: it is tempting, nay mocking to call on God to sit in judgement where there is no necessity to do so, or for the settling of trifles. But by using lottery in sport, God is called on to sit in judgement to decide on trifling matters where there is no necessity. By the use of lottery in sport we therefore tempt and dishonour God. *(Daneau, 1586)* This proposition is confirmed by its resemblance to the advice that is given, namely that we would dishonour our King and Council by whose government all live, if children were to be called upon to determine their sports. *(Estey, ~1603)*

The assumption is 'proved' by comparing a lottery with an oath: a lottery by its nature necessarily supposes the providence and determining presence of God, just as an oath by its nature supposes the testifying presence of God. Both in oaths and lotteries prayers are expressed or understood. Just as in an oath, so a lottery is an act of religion in which we refer the settling of weighty matters that cannot otherwise be determined to God. *(Perkins, 1592)* Therefore the use of it is ever enfolded and sometimes also expressed both as a confession that God is a sovereign Judge to determine such things and as a supplication to Him that by the lottery, when it is cast, He will be pleased to do so. So neither a lottery nor an oath is to be used except in cases of necessity and extremity. Being a solemn act of religion it may not be applied to gambling. We might as well jest with the sacred word, the sacraments and with oaths, as with lotteries.

There might be several arguments framed in these allegations; but because they are all built on one ground and stand on one bottom, I have thought best to put them together in the following manner so that the same common answer might serve them all.

Firstly, using a lottery in sage and serious matters or for sport and delight does not in itself show any desire for the manifestation of God's special power and providence in an immediate disposition. That is the case, and would be so unless men were to offend against the caution given before and in doing it by trying to see whether God would vouchsafe to work immediately and extraordinarily or not. But that would not be because of the nature of the thing itself, and is not necessarily implied in the ordinary use of it. Nor is there any such calling in of God to decide doubts in a game when the matter in question is put to an uncertain event. *(Lyra, ~1300)* There was no solemn calling on God to determine the tithe *(Levit 27:37)*, in the example before alleged out of the Law. And therefore as a consequence there is no such tempting of God, as is here charged, in the use of a lottery whether it was used in a case of necessity or otherwise.

Indeed, if the lottery is such as they say it is then it should not to be used in any business at all upon any occasion whatsoever. For "It is not lawful to tempt God in any case whatsoever". *(Deut 6:16)* But, they say, to use lottery in any case whatsoever is to tempt God. It is not lawful therefore to use lottery in any case whatsoever. This assumption is evidently proved by the former grounds and grants: to require a work of God's immediate power and providence in this or that kind is to tempt God. But the use of a lottery in any case requires a work of God's immediate power and providence (for in every lottery, say they, it is such). Therefore to use a lottery in any case whatsoever is unlawful. But this conclusion is untrue because a lottery may lawfully be used in some cases. The former ground therefore is false.

It would indeed be unlawful and a tempting of God to use a lottery as they *(Delrio, 1618)* would have it used, as only requiring and expecting an extraordinary work of God in every case or occasion whatsoever, even when there is no express appointment of it from God and although all means should fail otherwise. To have recourse to extraordinary means when the ordinary fail is to tempt God by refusing to depend and wait upon Him, as our Saviour implied, when despite the Devil's temptation he refused to speak to his Father to have stones turned into bread, least by so doing he should tempt God even though this was a case of extremity. *(Matt 4:3)* That was at times the sin of the Israelites when in the wilderness, the extraordinary lotteries that they contemplated would never be allowable. And to speak the truth, by the course and force of their discourse, every use of a lottery is thus disallowed and condemned as unlawful and unwarrantable. For them it would not have been any more lawful to desire through an oracle that God is called upon by lottery to discover His hidden will when they cannot have it in other ways (as *Augustine* yet would have men do), than to require a manifestation of it by special revelation when priests are not sure what to decide in some doubtful cases.

Secondly, an oath and a lottery are not alike and therefore the comparison laid between them will not hold. There is nothing in an ordinary lottery which puts the special providence or the immediate and extraordinary work of God to work. In an oath the truth of the thing testified is put to His testimony. There is no such solemn invocation of God in any lottery. But in any oath which calls on God expressly or by implication to witness the truth of what we avow or to the truth of our intention to perform whatever we promise, there is such solemn invocation.

The definition of each thing is contained in the whole nature of the thing defined. Now a lottery may be defined without this, but an oath cannot. Yet there are some of the adverse party (*Balmford, 1593*) who define a lottery from the writings of *Lyra (~1300)* to be "the use of the variable event of some sensible thing to determine some doubtful or uncertain matter". This definition of a lottery contains nothing about what is supposed to be the very nature and essence of it, nor does it say that it is of the same essence as an oath, which therefore cannot be defined without it. Nor do the references produced prove it. They only prove that prayer was sometimes used *(1 Sam 14:41)* (but a faithless prayer by one of them without any word or warrant) before an extraordinary lottery which called on an extraordinary power and providence to direct the event. The thing intended meant that the lottery involved no natural power, either of the man using it or what was used in it. This kind of prayer has no place and is not lawful for ordinary or mere divisory lotteries.

For example: In assigning and setting tithes, it was not lawful, much less necessary to pray to God to give a right lot, so that every lamb or kid that in course of time was the tenth might certainly or constantly come to hand that way. But they do not prove that a prayer as part of a lottery as it would be part of an oath or included in an oath, as the usual definition of an oath appears to indicate. In election to sacred or civil offices, prayer is used or at least ought to be used. But it does not follow therefore that prayer is a part of the choice, or that therefore that it is in the nature of elections to necessarily suppose a special providence and determining presence of God. Indeed prayer may be used both before gambling and during gambling, just as both before and at mealtimes but that does not therefore determine the nature of a game nor does it pre-suppose a special providence of God and a determining presence in it.

Lastly, a lottery is not a religious act or holy thing in itself, as has been suggested earlier. There is a great difference between a lottery on the one hand, and the word of God, the sacraments and oaths on the other. There are things that are holy of themselves and in their own nature, as the very definitions of them will soon show and therefore can only be holy. But a lottery is not by its nature or in its definition holy and therefore is not always and necessarily sacred. There are things that are holy, as ever, in our ordinary use, whereas no lottery that we can use nowadays is holy. Nor indeed was it ever so, except in extraordinary circumstances. Because God has taken something from ordinary use to apply it to something holy and extraordinary does not exempt this kind of use in general. The thing itself is only so used in a special form, detached from civil, light or ordinary usage and only so long as it is set apart. For example: The use of water in baptism does not prevent a man from playing with water *(Yates, 1622)*, even with the very water that may afterwards be used in the sacrament of baptism, or once was so used but is not now. In like manner when a lottery is extraordinarily used for a special sign of God's immediate election and choice, anyone who holds the result of that lottery in contempt or treats it lightly shall be guilty of abusing a holy thing and God's name in so doing. But this does not apply to someone who uses a lottery for sport or gambling even though that lottery had been used in a sacred business before. There remains no more holiness in it after its use is over than there was in the bush that burned but did not waste, when God manifested himself to Moses, after that manifestation was once ended.

§7. Fenner's folly 1: A lottery is God's sentence

Again some argue like this: God's oracles (being his name) may not be used for recreation. But lotteries are God's oracles; therefore a lottery may not be used for recreation or sport. *(Fenner, 1587)* The assumption is said to be proved thus: Solomon called a lottery a judgement when he said "The judgement of it is of God". He showed that God Himself sits in judgement by it, and that the lottery is as God's deputy who is Judge of the world, whereby He himself determined the things that were doubtful and such as no art or wit of man is able to discover. *(Proverbs 16:33 et al)* It is not only scripture that makes a lottery the sentence of God, as it is in most weighty matters of God and man, life and death; it is the very oracle and determination of God's will wherein a man must accept without any contradiction or motion to the contrary. Even the Gentiles themselves also knew it to be God's oracle. *(Fenner, 1587)*

These proofs of the assumption are unsound and insufficient. Firstly, in the testimony of Solomon, though the word he used in his native sense and origin signifies 'judgement' and is therefore one of the necessary attendants of a lawful oath, as the learned well observe. But a lottery is not termed a judgement; though the word that naturally signifies it is applied to it and might be properly used of some of the special kinds of it. Nor does the ordinary use of the word signify it, but is used more generally for any custom, manner, course or carriage whatsoever, be it light or weighty, just or unjust. An example of where it was used relates to the profane and preposterous behaviour of Eli's sons towards God's people when it was used by Samuel. *(1 Sam 2:13)* He described, said one of the ancients, "not a courteous king but a self-willed tyrant". It has also been applied to the superstitious and savage demeanour of Baal's priests toward them and this is how the best and most of the interpreters take it. The word which was used there is therefore too weak to bear such weight as is placed upon it here. As for God's immediate sitting and sentencing in lotteries, (of which further anon) the conceits of it breeds a superstitious use of them (and they must therefore be abhorred). A taint of this can be found in a speech of an author *(Cartwright, 1617)* which he cannot be freed from when he said, that "lotteries are available for the finding out of the most hidden things and they have often been used for that purpose"; and also that "by them (lotteries) doubtful things may be determined when no wit or skill of man could otherwise be able to decide". But what hidden truth can be discovered by any lottery? Or what can be decided or settled by a lottery that might not also be settled by any third party or even by a child or an idiot just as well as by a lottery if it should so please the parties contending it to refer themselves to it?

§8. Fenner's folly 2: Lotteries were once God's oracles

For the instances alleged they reason like this: that lotteries were once used as God's oracles in various cases therefore they are all so. Or, since lotteries were once an extraordinary oracle of God in some cases when they were specially assigned by God for that purpose, therefore they are always so. Both the consequence is unsound and the consequent untrue. For the first, it does not follow that if it is sometimes extraordinary then it is always so. For example: The noise that David heard over his head in the mulberry trees was God's oracle to him. *(2 Sam 5:24)* Should every similar rustling that we may chance to hear in trees over our heads be therefore a divine oracle to us? If the Philistine's speech to Jonathan and his armour-bearer was an oracle of God to them *(1 Sam 14:8)*, shall the same therefore be said of it now? Or does it always have to be like this? To reason along these lines, as some of the ancients *(Jerome)* do, is to go from dreams to lotteries. Just as it does not follow that all dreams are divine oracles just because God sometimes, even often, delivered his oracles by dreams, so it no more follows that all lotteries become such, just because God at some time used a lottery in this way.

Again that fact that lotteries are not always, especially not now, God's oracles or any such divine sentence is evident for the following reasons:

Firstly, God's oracles and sentences are certain and constant, for His word and sentence is "yea and amen". Those lotteries whereby God sometimes gave sentence, such as that by which Achan was discovered *(Josh 7:16),* even if they had been cast over and over again, or cast by different persons of God's appointing would have still constantly lighted on no other tribe but Juda's, no kindred but the Zarchites, no household but Zabdie's and no person but Achan. But in an ordinary lottery there is nothing more certain than that every new shaking of the lot-pot may give out a new sentence. Suppose that we select one minister of religion by lottery from a whole hundred in our city who should visit the pestilence-house. If the lottery was to be drawn four or five times in this case, each time with great solemnity, would it light certainly and constantly always on the same man? Or suppose four or five of several companies in several places should, after their business was solemnly commended to God by prayer, cast lots for the same employment among the same parties. Would it be certain or at least probable that they should all light upon the same person? (Gataker adds in a footnote that it is the practice to use repeated drawings in lotteries for offices in Venice and Tuscany, as described in Chapter 4.) Would it not be frivolous, impious even, to say that with every second shaking or drawing, God alters His sentence and so accuse Him of inconstancy? Or that to several companies he gives a different sentence and so to charge Him with contradiction and contrariety? This is an argument that the heathen man has used *(Ovid)* quite rightly against those that dived for divine oracles into the bellies of brute beasts, so it is of equal force against those that would fasten a divine sentence on every lottery wherever it is cast and however it is disposed.

Secondly God's oracles always accord with justice and equity, but the sentence of a lottery is certainly not such. Suppose a matter of right, wherein he that ought to yield will not yield, is, by mutual consent put to a lottery. Does any man dare say with certainty that it will go with he who has right on his side? Or in war-time, (for decimation) suppose a whole troop is put to a lottery for their lives because among them there are many that are in no way faulty. Dare anyone say that the death-lottery would not light on any but those that indeed deserved to die? In Achan's case a man might well say with confidence that it would surely light on the delinquent and on no other, and by such means God had then given warrant to search for him. But not in any ordinary lottery which cannot distinguish right from wrong any more than guiltless from guilty, because a lottery is ready to go indifferently for or against either. *(Serarius, 1609)* It is not therefore God's sentence.

Thirdly, there cannot be an oracle of God which contradicts his revealed word. But a lottery may do so and often does, so it may free the guilty and condemn the guiltless. *(Deut 25:1)* It may give to one what is another man's right. It may assign things to be done which are evil and impious and has often done so. It has assigned some to the priesthood who are wholly unfit for it, and destined some to be butchers and murderers of their brothers. No man, I suppose, would be so witless and senseless as to justify as warrantable or agreeable to God's will whatever sentence or judgement is given by a lot. All this must be denied if lotteries are to be considered as divine oracles.

Fourthly, if a lottery is God's sentence, what need would men have to be curious about examining and trying the fitness or unfitness of those that they admit to a lottery for the bearing of any office either in Church or the Commonwealth? *(Aristides)* (I spare to ask those of the Popish sort *(Aquinas, 1270)*, why they then forbear to select their ecclesiastical officers by lottery, if a lottery is God's sentence, because such things, they say, must be done by the inspiration of God's spirit. As if God's spirit and his sentence were not sure to concur!) It was an idle suggestion by Plato, that having left the designation of priests to god's own appointment through lottery, he would then allow trial of them afterwards, as if it was uncertain whether they had been fit or not when the gods themselves had made a choice of it. For is God not as well able to judge their fitness or unfitness as any man could? Or do they distrust God and fear that he will be partial in his sentence when His constant commendation is that He is no respecter of persons? This evidently shows that the general advice for all those that use the lottery in any weighty affair is. Do not imagine a lottery to be a verdict of God's oracle, but rather a sentence so uncertain, so inconsiderate, so heedless that it might well run them into a whirl-pool, drawing church and state after it unless they use human caution to manage it more warily. Do we think that there was any such fear in the lottery that Samuel cast to decide who should be king *(1 Sam 10:2)*, or was there any need of caution to be observed in it?

§9. Fenner's folly 3: Lottery outcomes are binding

If a lottery was a divine sentence then it would be unalterable and unchangeable, the sort that men were bound forever to rest in and abide by, as is peremptorily claimed by *Fenner (1587)*. It is then a matter of danger of sin and disobedience to forecast anything worse or better without further inquiry, consultation, consideration or attempt. Man's sentence is sometime held as such and God's ever so much more. So it was in those ancient lotteries when God extraordinarily gave sentence to Saul and Matthias. *(Acts 1:25)* Ordinary lotteries are quite different.

Firstly, in private affairs no man is bound to stand by the result of any lottery which he never consented to. I say, in private affairs, because the law in some cases enables magistrates to compel the contending parties, willy-nilly, that they abide by it, which they may not be permitted to do in other cases, as is expressed in the letter of the law. When selecting a bride, it would be an idle thing for a young man to tell his parents, that of two maidens suggested to him for marriage there was one of those two which they did not like. Yet, their son might have said, they ought to give their consent because, after invoking God's name in that business and having cast a lottery for direction, the lottery had lighted upon her. (This tale comes from a learned man *Bucer (1541),* and concerned a nobleman's son). It would be much more idle for him if he was to propose to one of the maidens that she ought, in conscience, to have him and none other but him and that she might, without guilt of sin or disobedience, not refuse him because God had given such a sentence in a lottery which he had cast. Truly if it was a lot and God's oracle then it would be binding, without expecting any man's confidentiality or consent for it. If it is God's oracle then it would necessarily so bind, as in Saul's case. He was unwilling at first, but was forced in some way to accept that which the lottery had imposed upon him.

Secondly men may by mutual consent alter or change their lottery result with each other, as Levinus and Marcellus once did. (*Valerius Maximus*) This was at the request of the Senate after a plea by the Sicilians because they greatly feared Marcellus and wished for someone else. But may anyone alter God's sentence by mutual agreement, such as a wife her husband and in breaking her covenant with God, just because her husband is content to agree to it? Or could those whose lottery was a divine oracle, like Saul, have elected to surrender this right to another, despite the people's willingness to have yielded to it? Or might Matthias have resigned his place to Barsabas, if Barsabas had, by mutual consent taken it from him? What if in the choice of a priest to visit the pest-house the lottery should light on someone who was so fearful that he immediately sank down in a swoon and someone else more hardy than he had then offered himself voluntarily to that office? Would it be lawful for him to accept or wise to refuse and insist that he had to do it even though unfit? Another tale along these lines can be found in the counterfeit fables of *Prochorus*, when John saw from a lottery that he was to go over sea into Asia.

Lastly, in some cases it could be a sin for a man to retain something won in a lottery. May a man with a good conscience retain a thing which was his brother's by right, which the iniquity of the lottery had, for quietness sake, yielded to another? Is justice served by saying it is God's sentence? And may not the wronged party lawfully endeavour and argue that in conscience a wrong has been done against him, and that if he can, he may try to recover what is rightfully his? Matthias would have sinned if he had renounced his Apostleship. So did not that silly idiot Phannias sin as well by accepting the High-priestship, even though it was assigned to him by lot? *(Josephus)* In all these men's positions the lottery result should also be God's sentence and it was His choice for an immediate call to that office. It is a senseless conceit to suppose that any man should sin by following God's call or by doing it after God's sentence.

§10. Were heathen lotteries religious?

It is observed that among the heathens they believed their lotteries to be of the most religious kind and inviolable, but in truth this was not always so. *(Cicero)* They indeed held that it was a very prudent and politic method to prevent various inconveniences. In some ways it was also religious, as some superstitious rites would often be used in their public affairs and in all other public or private solemn yet civil employments. It was held to be a heinous offence for any private man to alter the course of any business which the state had thereby established.

There were some *(Demosthenes)* however that did not reckon the lottery to be such a sacred and peremptory sentence; and that a man might be rejected when chosen if it was already known that he was unfit for the office or that it was found to be so by some further trial. Indeed they might and even usually set aside the result, sometimes of necessity, when the winner was too disabled to do that which by lottery he was selected to do. Sometimes for religious reasons the winner was restrained from taking up whatever the lottery had assigned to him. This could happen after the lottery was cast at the request of the parties themselves, sometimes by the earnest entreaty of others, sometimes due to one consideration, sometimes upon another; when and upon better advice they doubted that if their course was not altered it might prove prejudicial to the public.

By doing this they are to be deservedly approved and commended and so to be preferred before the superstitious Jews *(Josephus)*, who rather than break the order of the priestly employment set at first by the lottery, allowed the service of God to be wholly neglected for some space of time during the siege of their city because all the priests that ought at that time to have done the service had by then been killed. It is true that in civil law all appeal is ordinarily denied from the sentence of a lot. But that does not mean (as some of them *(Scacchus, 1635)* fondly say), it is because the sentence of a lottery is the sentence of fortune, or of God who has no superior in this world. Rather, it is as others (*Gregoire, 1582*) say, with a better colour of reason, that this course is taken for the more speedy dispatch of the business and that departing from it in some cases would hinder others from ever coming to a result. That is because a lottery is the most equal and indifferent course that can be and no corruption or partiality can be charged against it. It is usual for matters to be put to the lottery by mutual consent, so in this case their own act justly concludes either side. *Plato* agrees, and his model state blocked all appeal from those judges that the parties themselves had chosen by mutual consent. In the Athenian state, though they might appeal to the main judges, the arbiters or umpires were assigned to them by lot. Yet since they had mutually agreed to have themselves referred to them, it is apparent that they could have no appeal.

Let me add one further thing: in some cases of civil law no remedy would ordinarily be granted in a division made by lottery over some inequality, just because the hazard of receiving the lesser part and so sustaining a loss was the same for both. Even so, the opinion of good lawyers is that if the inequality was too great the magistrate might lawfully interpose his authority for the redressing of the wrong.

To draw all this to a head and so end this argument. Let any man possessed of ordinary reason judge how a lottery could be said to be a sacred oracle or a divine sentence and yet one that neither absolutely ties any man in matters of fact nor determines with certainty any question of right. It would be one that never spoke with certainty and would often speak unadvisedly unless it was constrained by human caution as to what it should say.

I add only a conclusion: that if all lotteries are said to be God's oracles then it is in the power of man to make God give out oracles at his pleasure, which is an absurd thing to say. Again I say, it is not in any man's power to make God work miracles when he likes.

§11. The proper use of lotteries

We proceed from arguments about the nature of lotteries to those concerning the proper uses and purposes of them. It is here that some people reason from the affirmative, some from the negative.

From the affirmative: whatever God has sanctified for a proper purpose is not to be perverted to a worse end. But God has sanctified lotteries for proper purposes, namely the ending of controversies. Therefore man is not to pervert them in a worse use, namely for play and by gambling, to get away with other men's money, which had uncontroversally been his own before. *(Balmford, 1593)* The argument conceived like this is faulty in two ways:

First it strays from the question. This is not whether any creature or ordinance of God may be perverted or perversely used, but whether the use of lottery as such is a perversion. In the conclusion it is taken for granted that it is. Neither is the question whether men may use a lottery in playing for money, something which is incidental to other games as well. *(Cartwright, 1617)* Whether it is lawful or not, I do not need to discuss now. Much less is it whether they may be used in games for the purpose of getting another man's money out of him. This is not about the general use of them, nor would it have any place at all if there is no wagering, or where the lottery is only used at the beginning of the game to decide who shall join, who lead or the like. It is about whether lottery may be used in sport or gambling in any form.

Secondly there is more inferred in the conclusion than there was in the premise and nothing followed from it. The use of a lottery in play is always to settle some question or controversy. It may be a light one, but it is still about a question or controversy otherwise it would not be a lot.

To make amends for the faults in these argument it might be better to conceive of them in this manner: that which God has sanctified to some proper use is not to be applied to any other, especially a worse use. But God has sanctified lotteries to some proper uses, to wit, the deciding of controversies in matters of substance. A lottery therefore may not be applied to any other use, much less to a worse one. *(Perkins, 1590)* The proposition is proved by an instance *(Matth 21:12)* when the Jews were reproved because they had installed markets and merchandise in that part of the Temple which was set aside for prayer. The assumption is confirmed principally by that saying of Solomon, "The lottery stinted strife and makes partition among the mighty". For the other reference is an example when a lottery was once used by God's own appointment. It is similarly amplified by like uses of oaths. Concerning this there is a further speech of the Apostle which was brought out to prove that Solomon's purpose in those words (as previously alleged by *Balmford, 1593*) was to demonstrate the only lawful use of a lottery, namely to end controversies which cannot be conveniently ended otherwise and when each contender is too mighty to yield without the lottery to decide. This is shown thus: when the Apostle said: "An oath for confirmation among men is an end of all strife", his purpose is not so much to teach us that men use an oath to end controversies. Every man knows that God has dedicated and made an oath holy and sure solely for the necessary deciding of doubts of importance among men. In the same way similar words used of a lottery must be understood in the same sense, not so much to teach us that a lottery ends such controversies among men, which all know, but that God has ordained it only for that use.

§12. Worthwhile distinctions about sanctification

For a fuller answer to this argument and the proof of it, various worthwhile distinctions should be observed.

First there is the word 'sanctify', which is taken in different ways. In its larger sense, to sanctify signifies the assignment of a creature to any special or singular use, either sacred or civil. Thus the Medians were said by God to be sanctified for the subduing and sacking of Babel. *(Esai 13:3)* Meats are said to be sanctified by God's word for man's food. And the unbelieving mate is sanctified by the married believer. (*1 Cor 7:14)* Sometimes again it is taken in a stricter sense. To sanctify signified the setting apart of a thing from its ordinary use to some sacred and spiritual employment. An example is where God is said to have sanctified the seventh day of the world and where men are commanded to sanctify the same. By precept He enjoined that employment of it which they thereby practice by employing it according to his precept.

Now in both these kinds of sanctification the Lord may well be said sometimes to sanctify but not to appropriate. When by His ordinance He either enjoined or granted the use of a thing, so in some ways He did not restrain or inhibit the use of it in any other way. Thus the fruits of the earth may be sanctified for man's food, but they are not barred from use in medicine. The water that miraculously gushed out of the rock was thus sanctified for spiritual employment, but it was not denied for civil and profane uses, even for the watering of brute beasts. Sometimes to sanctify means that God sequesters and severs the thing so sanctified for one special or proper use excluding it from all other uses else whatsoever. And thus he sanctified and appropriated all of a species of things *(Exod 30:31),* as was the case with that curious composition of precious and holy ointments which were expressly forbidden for any other use. As with the spices, odours and ingredients of that holy ointment, so also was the tabernacle, the temple and the appurtenances of both sanctified. The elements of water, bread and wine are sanctified in the sacraments to be signs and pledges of spiritual grace.

To apply these distinctions to the present argument: if the word sanctify is taken in the stricter sense the proposition is true, but the assumption is unsound. Lotteries are not set apart or said to be so in any of the references produced solely for the holy or spiritual uses, but can also be for civil use. Taken in the larger and more general sense then, they either speak of things which are only sanctified but not appropriated, or of things both sanctified and appropriated, either in whole in part. For the things which are sanctified but not appropriated, the proposition is not true. Bread and wine are sanctified to be seals of God's covenant, but that does not hinder the lawful use of them otherwise. Oil was sometimes sanctified to anoint kings and priests and yet that did not restrain the civil use of it for food or medicine, either from necessity or for lawful delight. Or to use a more familiar instance and nearer the present purpose: The fruits of trees are sanctified to be man's food. Yet children, as of old, may lawfully play and make themselves pastimes with the nuts or almonds, as with cherry-stones, or with check-stones and the like. *(Martial)*

If it is of those things which are sanctified and appropriated, such as holy ointment and it is inhibited to all other uses, or if it is about the sacraments which are sequestered and set apart only for certain spiritual purposes then the assumption is unsound. If the sanctification and appropriation is not about the whole species but only some part of it, the premises might be granted, but that does not yet conclude anything against the use of lotteries in general.

If it is of the whole kind, then the proposition is true, though the proof may not be so pertinent, but the assumption is not sound. For the proof of it refer to Solomon, where it was shown how a lottery may be well and wisely used. But that neither enjoined the use of it nor restrained it. It only approved its use when it is good and commendable. But it is one thing for a lottery to be used well and wisely, it is another to have that as the only proper purpose of it.

§13. An oath is sacred

The apostle's speech about oaths showed what Solomon meant when he talked in the same way about lotteries, no more, no less. It is not true that the apostle's scope was to show that the only purpose of an oath was "to stint strife and controversy", nor is it. His purpose was not to show it, only to show how sacred, firm and inviolable an oath is among men and from man to man (which he proves by accepting that it is what all men know and acknowledge). How much more then from God to man, when He swore to us by whom we swear, as is the argument used by the apostle elsewhere? A man's covenant or testament once ratified cannot be annulled by any man, much less can anyone annul or abrogate God's.

That is not the only lawful purpose of an oath, for there are other purposes, such as: to give assurance of the performance of covenants and promises. Whatever controversy there was between Jonathan and David, it was ended by an oath, when they swore either to the other. Or what controversy was there between God and Abraham, or David and God, when God swore to Abraham and David to God? Or what controversy is ended by those oaths that men usually take when taking office both in the church and common-wealth?

The same may be said of that reference to Solomon. Its scope is not to stint or restrain the use of a lottery in ending strife, much less the ending of great quarrels, or among the mighty only, though Solomon expressly named them. But he spoke of contentions in general. Why should not mean inheritances be divided by lottery among mean men, as well as by a rich ones among mighty men? And do contentions never arise among mighty men about mean matters? The scope of it is intended to persuade all sorts of men to settle their controversies, be they great or small, preferably by the easy and equal course of lotteries, rather than plunging themselves into the eager pursuit of law-suits, leading to further inconveniences. This induces men of mean condition to do so simply because men of might are often keen to submit themselves thereunto.

Lotteries have often been used for other purposes and this is just one use among many that is mentioned. This has already been in part shown and will be further shown later. This is a point that some of them *(Cartwright, 1617)* that oppose me will concede.

§14. Not forbidden if not mentioned in the Bible

That was how they reasoned in the affirmative for the proper use and purpose for lotteries. But they also argue negatively thus concerning the same: if there is neither precept for nor practice of it in God's word, either general or special, express or implied, then there is no warrant for it in the word. An example of this is the use of lotteries in gaming. We do not read in scripture that lotteries were used other than for serious matters, either by Jews or Gentiles. Nowhere either is there any warrant in the word for the use of them in gambling. There is no precept, or practice, general or special, express or implied for this. *(Balmford, 1593)* There is therefore no warrant for gambling in God's word and so consequently they are unwarrantable.

This is like Ambrose's argument against merry jests, which *Perkins (1592)* (one of ours) therefore justly criticises. "We read nothing of them in Scripture", therefore they are not to be allowed. This is no good kind of reasoning. The consequence of his argument and the proposition of their syllogism is likewise unsound.

Firstly, there is some argument from the negative in matters of faith but not in matters of fact. This is to say that if something is not expressed or revealed in the word, it is therefore not a matter of faith, nor is any man necessarily bound to believe it. But that is not to say that if something is not mentioned or related in Scripture, therefore it was not done, or it never was. For example, Cain had one son only mentioned by Moses, therefore he had no more sons or children but him. Much less may a man reason from a matter of fact to a matter of right, by saying that since we never read about such or such a thing in the Word therefore it may not be done. How many things are there where there is no example in God's word and yet we use them and it is generally allowed as lawful and good? There are many things where there is only precedent for the use of them in one kind and yet they may be used also by others. No use of butter is recorded in the Word, only food in general. May it not therefore be used for medicine? Indeed there are many things of ordinary use, with no mention at all in God's word, yet which are generally allowed. Sugar for sweetening, printing of books, shooting of guns and the like, which by this argument would all be utterly condemned, or if they are to be justified, then the grounds fail.

Secondly an action may be permitted if it has sufficient warrant, precept or practice. If God has not limited the use of any creature or ordinance then He has left us the free use of it. Where He has not determined the circumstances of any action, what is not prohibited is permitted and that is sufficient warrant for it. Therefore where the circumstances have been determined, it makes unwarrantable anything that is not expressly or by good consequence enjoined, by arguing from the negative. But where they are not determined, the argument is strong enough from the negative side to prove anything warrantable that is not either expressly or by just consequence prohibited.

In the case of God's worship, the argument holds from the negative for the substance of it because God has determined it. But in civil affairs it will not be right to forbid or disallow anything just because God has not determined whether it is right or not. Otherwise what warrant is there for bowls, tennis, football, chess etcetera, which no man is as yet disbarred from?

Let one example serve to show the weakness of this kind of arguing. There is neither precept nor practice (at least allowed or allowable) for the eating of blood in scripture; therefore a man may not eat a black pudding. This is a conclusion which I assure myself that authors will disagree with, authors such as the Familists* and the new Sectaries. And yet they say more against the one than they can say against the other. One finds it to be expressly forbidden in both the old and new testament, before, under and after the law, (whatever sundry ancients may have held) but the other nowhere in either. And notwithstanding that the Christian liberty bought with the blood of Christ gives God's children a free use of the one, how much more then of the other. If it frees them there where they were bound before, then for sure it does not bind them where they were free before.

§15. Wicked men gamble, so it is sinful

There one more thing to add to this argument that should be included before we leave this point. Scripture noted that wicked men have gambled, using the lottery as sport. Sporting lotteries are therefore not allowable. *(Estey, ~1603)* Both the antecedent is untrue and the consequence is unsound. The antecedent is untrue because it was a serious divisory lottery rather than the lusory, gambling lottery that either Saul's servants used to share David's apparel, or that the soldiers cast on Christ's garments. It was not used by them, as some have supposed, superstitiously, out of a conceit of some virtue that they hoped to find in Christ's clothes, in His seamless shirt especially, which they might hope to cure diseases with, (as had sometimes been done, or yet, as others say, despite Him, was done to his garments alone). It was simply their usual custom to divide out the clothing of those they had executed among themselves and which was, it seemed, as among us also, part of their fees. This was done too in the case of our Saviour and in a manner, partly to save what might otherwise have been spoiled, and partly to prevent all contention and strife. Nor was their act evil or unlawful for any reason that I can see. Nor can be said, had it been a booty that had come to them lawfully and could not have been conveniently divided among them except by lot, since each of them had an equal interest in it. In such cases even those *(Perkins, 1592)* that condemn ludicrous gambling lotteries, will still allow them for the sharing out of prey and spoils taken in battle. There are some good writers *(Walther, 1550)* who would rather commend than condemn these heathen soldiers for their modest and equal sharing in that case.

The consequence is also unsound. It is like the argument some of the ancients *(Jerome, Origen)* use to condemn birth-day feasts because we only find them used in Scripture by two persons, both bad. Pharaoh the heathen was one and Herod who was no better, if not worse than any heathen, was the other. But this argument will not hold, any more than to reason in this manner: wicked men plant and build, marry and make marriages; therefore planting and building and marrying and making marriages is evil. Or, wicked men have sometimes kissed their friends at parting; therefore it is not lawful for good Christians to do so. Or, to

* Familists were a mystic religious sect known as the *Familia Caritatis*. Its followers were accused of asserting that all things were ruled by nature and not directly by God.

come nearer to home. We do not read in the Word of marts or fairs except when they are used by the heathens; therefore they are not now lawful or allowable among Christians. Or we only read about profane princes that kept butlers or bakers; therefore Christian princes ought not have such servants. Or, music at civil feasts is only found used in Scripture by the wicked and ungodly ones; therefore the use of it at such times is not allowable. None of what is alleged here is true, nor would it prove anything for our present purpose if it were true.

§16. Conclusion: Gambling as sport or recreation

We have now gone through the main and most forcible arguments that are produced against lotteries and gambling. The arguments that fight against the general use of lottery in sport are drawn only from the nature of lotteries or from their proper purpose and use. The rest concerns the use of them in types of games and therefore, though allowed, do nothing to contradict the main point, to wit, that gambling (the use of a lottery in sports or pastimes) is not simply evil in itself. Yet it is not amiss to hear what the rest say.

The next argument and the last (and least) of the main arguments is taken from the other matter which is questioned at this point, namely recreation or games and the right use and purpose of them. The argument goes this way: in the matter of sport and pastime the purpose and scope of it is known and is lawful. But in gambling the purpose and scope of this pastime cannot be so. Therefore using a lottery is not lawful in matters of sport and pastime.

This assumption is further strengthened: "The purpose and scope of play is either to exercise the ability of the body or the industry of the mind. But in gambling neither of these is exercised: not the mind because there is no use of art or skill, because all is put to hazard; not the body; for men sit at them without stirring anything except their fingers and hands only. In gambling therefore the aims and scope of games are not to be had". *(Daneau, 1586)* In this argument there are two things to be chiefly observed; there are also two axioms that the answer will be principally applied to:

First, it relates only to games that consist of and depend on mere chance only, not those that mix chance and art where much skill and industry of mind may be used. The author of this argument only condemns the one while approving of the other and therefore the assumption of the latter syllogism is not true of all games where a lottery is used nor should these authors extend it to them all.

Secondly, that the purpose and scope of recreation is not correctly assigned. As its name implies its principal purpose is to recreate and refresh the mind, body or both, by delight. Recreation and exercise are therefore two distinct things and however a man may recreate himself by some exercise, he may also do so by some kind of study. Exercise is no more recreation than recreation is study. The same exercise may be recreation to one that is not so to another. A man may be advised by his physicians to draw a bow in his chamber which he takes no pleasure in, not doing it for or with delight but as an exercise only. So this is not a pastime as it would be to he who shoots outside for pleasure. So when two ride together hunting, the one only to exercise his body by riding or to accompany or attend on the other and not looking at the game; the other may be doing it mainly for the game and the sport. But it is only an exercise or an office or service to the one, a recreation to the other.

The purpose and scope of an action is one thing; the means whereby this purpose and scope is effected and attained, is another. The purpose and scope of recreation is the refreshing of the body or mind and the delight of either. The means whereby this is effected are various. Sometime it is done by industrious exercise of body or mind which comes nearer to a serious business than to recreation and refreshing. In this regard it is well said of those who betake them to chess to refresh themselves after long hours in study, that they do not leave off studying but only change their studies, like one who ceases tying up bundles of sticks to go and thresh corn*. Sometimes it is effected without much industrious exercise, as in taking a nap, for that is a kind of recreation too, lying long on the grass, viewing some pleasant sight, hearing some noise of music or charm of birds and the like. Therefore the proposition of the pro-syllogism is not sound. This can just as easily happen in games which consist merely of, or with admixtures of, lotteries, as well as by others, for those that take delight in them. Neither is it simply evil or disallowable to take delight in the chance and uncertain or unexpected outcome of a thing. The thing that makes jests and witty speeches many times the more pleasant is that the answer is not what was expected. They may be light and frivolous since it is not required of recreations that they be serious.

Some kinds of games are rejected because of their frivolity. They are not well regarded by some wise and judicious persons, it must be said, not wholly without just cause. (Gataker's footnote refers to the dictum of King *James I* (1603) "Chess is over fond because it is an over-wise and philosophic folly; filling men's heads with as many fatuous play-thoughts as their affairs did before.") Things may even be too serious for matters of sport or refreshment because the proper and principal purpose and aim of them is too toyish and frivolous for wise men to be so serious in, as the curious views of some seem to require. So on the other side, these games of chance are approved or commended by some either in whole or in part as most agreeable to the prime and main purpose of recreation, namely rest, refreshment and delight

.

* Gataker's original words were: "to cease binding faggots and to go thresh hemp" which might be seen in a somewhat different light in today's English!

Chapter 8

Minor arguments against gambling

Having dispatched all the main arguments directly intended to prove that gambling using a lottery is simply unlawful and so evil in itself, we now proceed to the minor arguments. They are intended to prove that gambling is inconvenient and inexpedient and because of that it has been generally disallowed and condemned. These arguments may be ranked in two rows: the first of them is drawn from the evils and inconveniencies that necessarily or ordinarily attend gambling and the games that they consist of .

These evils they are charged with come under four heads:

- 1. Cursing, ranting and blaspheming.
- 2. Waste of time and decay of health.
- 3. Unlawful gain, or desire of gain.
- 4. And lastly, the wasting of wealth.

After the arguments based on the evils and inconveniences that are imagined as necessarily or usually accompanying these games, I will deal with the last main argument taken from the public and private testimonies of those who in their judgement have condemned them, or when those in authority have banned these kind of games. I will endeavour [in §5 onwards] to bring their legalistic arguments into some form so that we may judge them better.

§1. Cursing, ranting and blaspheming

From the first of these (cursing) it is reasoned that anything which causes horrible cursing, ranting and blaspheming is not to be endured. Dice-play does this; therefore it is not to be endured. (*Daneau, 1586)* I answer: games of chance, especially mixed (which this author does not condemn) no more cause these things than do bowls, chess or other games which can also give rise to similar outrages.

Secondly, it is not so much the game itself that makes men overshoot themselves by wasting their wealth and losing money. If this is separated out from the games themselves, then it will neither cause it among the well-disposed nor would it ordinarily make it happen at other times.

These evils and the rest that follow arise, not from the nature of the game but from the immoderate and inordinate use of it, or rather the abuse of it and from the evil and impious disposition of the gamesters. This makes it unlawful only to those that abuse it or who are affected by it. Simply in itself it does not harm those that use it with due caution.

"But these lot-plays", said *Fenner (1587)*, "necessarily draw out or at least tempt the very best into horrible blaspheming and profaning of God's name and are therefore especially condemned. In games they are wont to say, 'what luck is this, how crooked!' which is a horrible blaspheming of God's name. Lot-games necessarily draw or tempt the best so to say. Therefore they necessarily draw or tempt the best to horrible blasphemy".

This is how they attempt to prove their proposition: to say, "What a God, what perverse and crooked Providence of God!", is indeed horrible blasphemy. But to say "What luck, how crooked", is in plain words to say what is so. Therefore to say, "what luck, how crooked!" is also horrible blasphemy. *(Fenner, 1587)* The assumption is proved. It may be that in other games, infirmity or want of skill may be to blame, in gambling and lot-games there is nothing else that can be accused except God's immediate direction, unless we will brutishly give God's glory to Fortune.

To answer to this argument directly and briefly: lot-games do not necessarily tempt the best to say so nor is it blasphemy so to say. There is great difference between those two speeches when rightly conceived and as they are and may be used by good Christians. They are nothing alike at all.

As in all other chance events including lotteries there is something else beside God and His providence that such speeches may be applied to. I confess that I am often forced to repeat what was laid down before, (while I tread the maze of sundry men's fancies), namely that in chance events there are two distinct things; the work of the Creator and the act of the person using them. Persons may be accused of using such speech and so have no tang or taint at all of impiety or blasphemy. My adversaries try to build all upon the wrong ground by claiming that there is a mere and immediate providence of God in all lotteries which is not true, as has already been proved.

You may think about it through some examples of chance events in other cases where we use similar terms without any impeachment or disparagement of divine providence which even so extends itself into those actions. (We pass by such contingent actions that are carried out by man's will and forecast, which often happen during our lawful and warrantable courses, as in David's despiteful wrong done to him in the abuse of his concubines by his own son Absalom. *(2 Sam 16:21)*)

For example: Suppose a man is riding on his way through a forest when a deer rushes suddenly out of the cover and makes his horse start and throws him. If the man in this case was to say, "What luck was this!" or, "What a cross accident was this!" it would be no blasphemy or any accusing of God's providence, just a complaint about the creature's act and the outcome of it. For any man to censure such a speech as blasphemous or to construe it as if had said, "What a God is this!" or, "What a cross and crooked providence of God!" would be to make himself like one of those masters whom the Apostle James *(Jam 3:1)* reproved, when he charged them with blasphemy, yet he was unable to show the least point of impiety.

As for the name of 'fortune', if indeed by fortune we understand such a blind deity as the fabulous poets fained and idolatrous infidels adored, it is idle and impious for any man to ascribe such a thing to her. But if by it we understand the random and uncertain motion of a thing which produces something beyond its scope, then it is like that which we have heard when the Holy Ghost uses the term and that our Saviour himself ascribes it to the priests alighting upon the passer-by that lay wounded on the way thereunto. *(Luk 10:31)* "By chance, or, by fortune (for the words are all one) a priest came down that way, as also did a Levite".

There are very many differences and dissimilarities between games. But just as there are many things that a man uses to explain his loss during games besides God's providence (which even so holds sway in them), there is something else here, namely the chance events and various dispositions of thing in themselves which is distinct from God's providence, as we formerly showed. (Chapter 2, §4)

§2. Waste of time and decay of health

The second evil attending on or accompanying gambling is the waste of time and the decay of health caused by sitting at it for a long time. The argument which *Daneau (1586)* proposes is in two parts, but can be reduced to one, as:

Anything which causes waste of time, which might be much better spent would be unlawful. Gambling does so and is therefore unlawful. This proposition is confirmed by the Apostle's authority *(Ephes 5:6)* when he wills Christian men to redeem their time, that is, to spend their spare time in honest and profitable employment, such as reading God's word, visiting the sick or their friends and such like. This assumption is 'proved' by *Daneau (1586)* from the nature of this kind of sport as follows: Any recreation is a time-waster when it neither wearies the body nor ends the hope of eventual gain by its continuance. But these kinds of sport do not weary the body for there is no exercise at all in them. Nor does it end the hope of eventual gain by continuing on with them, because they depend wholly on hazard. Even the weakest and simplest may hope, despite long continued losses, that they might at length conquer and recover and that the dice might change their courses, which they may well do. Those that have won still hope to have the same luck as before. *(Pseudo-Cyprian)* These kinds of games therefore cause much waste of time, there being no restraint or end to them. Of necessity such games must lead to the body being over-wearied or the weaker side losing hope of winning for want of skill.

This case might be good enough for a caution but it hardly makes for an argument. Firstly, the proposition of the former syllogism, if I understand it properly, says that time must always be spent on the best duties only. This will ban every kind of sport whatsoever. It fights equally against all, whether it be games of hazard alone or ones which mix them with an exercise of bodily strength or wit. But that is unsound and is not the Apostle's meaning or purpose in that citation.

God's word did not propose to cut off all kinds of recreation, only to cut off idle and vain trifling forms and the needless mis-spending of time. This might be by recreation, but there are other occasions when men may dally and neglect the things that should principally concern them. This is what our Saviour would have them try to avoid in the first place, "avoiding using important matters as trivial and trivial matters as important", as *Plutarch* once said wittily, "or living for any purpose apart from what they should live for".

So it is not only in gaming and play, but also buying and selling, building and planting, eating and drinking, wiving and wedding, husbandry and tillage that we may become sinners against that injunction of redeeming our time, if we were to waste the time which was due to other necessary duties. And yet they are all warrantable and good if taken in their own time. The best works do not have to be done at all times otherwise every day would be a Sabbath day, (as *Bernard (~1120)* once said in another sense) and not just any weekday or workday. If the week is for work (I mean worldly work) then the whole week is one work-day and not a minute or moment would be left for any kind of recreation.

Nor is sin always to be found everywhere or anywhere, just as good works do not have to be done at all times. Negative commandments bind everywhere and at all times, affirmative precepts bind everywhere and at all times, but they do not bind to every place or at all times. The work that is fittest for the time is then the best work, best because of all the circumstances that concur at that instant.

Doing things in the right season is important, since there is a time and season for all lawful employments, be they serious or gambling, civil or sacred. A good action is more significant when it is done out of season, just as a meaner matter is, without sin, omitted in its season. It is a sin for a man not to recreate himself. It would also be a sin for him to do a less good thing when he might and should do a greater one. But it could also be a sin for him to be doing one thing, even though it was a better thing if he is called upon to attend to a meaner matter. As, for example, it would be a sin for a servant to be reading on good book even the Bible itself when he should be serving in his master's supper.

The Apostle's speech *(Eccles 3:4)* therefore does not cut off all recreations when they are lawful and good and warranted by God's word. If they refresh both body and mind and make a man more fit and better able to go through with and hold out in more serious employments which would otherwise oppress him, that is good. Therefore it is not wise or religious for any man to utterly neglect this. Wasting and mis-spending time may unquestionably be a great and a grievous sin and an all-too common sin. But it is not a sin or evil in itself because some men, or even many men misspend their time this way.

Secondly the assumption condemns games involving gambling such as games at tables with cards as well as bare dice. But it includes chess, which some have observed *(Zwingli, ~1523)* that men may have sat closely and continually at, neglecting all serious affairs. Chess is unlike any ordinary game in that it takes up much of the time of those that dote on it especially where two equally skilful players meet. *(Foxe, 1563)*

For the proof of the assumption it makes no sense to argue that a man will misspend his time if he spends much of it without tediousness or with no prospect of losing. He may misspend much of his time but he does not need to, unless he wants to. Nor does he sin he if he does not, because he might if he would. There are many other things that a man may waste his time on and more than he might. Many do, taking pleasant and delightful discourse with friends whose company gives special delight and could endure their discourse all day. Or it may be in journeying abroad, flitting from place to place and from house to house and the like. These things are not therefore simply evil in themselves (I mean mutual society and journeys for pleasure) if they are not evilly used, though they would be evil to them by whom they might be abused.

To this may be added by way of amplification: in one of the former arguments, that by sitting a long time at this game men may spend whole days at it, they impair their bodily health and strength and get the gout. This is an inconvenience arising from the immoderate use of gaming (and springs likewise from the immoderate use of other things which may not be evil in themselves). So no godly man would condemn and abhor something which is itself abused, especially where it may be well used otherwise.

§3. Greed: Unlawful gain, or desire of gain

The third evil that is said to accompany or that is occasioned by gambling is that it feeds covetous desires. For where is there a greedier desire of gain? Where more cheating and defrauding than in these games? They are worse than usury, yea than usury upon usury. For here is an increase of wealth without loan or a delay of time, in an instant and that is all equal without the main principal. It is worse than highway robbery, stripping those that they eat and drink with, not only of their money but of their very apparel too, even to the very shirt, something even thieves will scarcely do. *(Daneau, 1586.)*

I answer in a word: all this may be easily avoided either by playing for nothing; or if it is preferred, as it is said "without gaining, cold gaming", by playing for such trifles as may be won without much loss to the looser. Or we may make a choice to play only with what we are well able to spare and sharing whatever is so won in common between the winners and losers. In no way should these evils prejudice the lawful and honest use of any exercise when the evil may easily be severed from it.

If these grounds were to be admitted it would overthrow all playing, even playing for victory alone as well as for gain. We might as well condemn gambling, as some do, because it feeds and fosters ambitious humours, as well as other activities that nurse and nourish covetous desires. Such desires are indeed very evil, but free and innocent playing does not necessarily make them so. If as a result all gambling was to be forbidden that would seem over-harsh and to savour more of stoical austerity than of Christian severity.

§4. The wasting of wealth

The fourth evil that these games are charged with is the wasting of wealth and of men's worldly estates. These should be used to sustain and support them-and-theirs and be the wherewithal for them to be helpful and beneficial to others. For there is no game that men spend and waste more upon than these, at which so many lose land and living, goods and chattels, jewels and plate and even the apparel from their backs. There are even some who, when they have played all away have finally staked themselves, which if they lost, were to be made slaves. So much so that these games have often been the very bane of great personages and the ruin of great houses. *(Tacitus)*

I give the same answer here as was given before. The problem arises, not from the nature of the thing itself. It comes not from the spring, but from the filthy channel that the stream passes through. It may start at the source without any of filth and it is undefiled for those who partake of it there. Besides, the same grounds might be used to condemn bowls, shooting, tennis and many other similar exercises, indeed any games, because many people will also misspend both their time and their estates playing at them. For some games the waste of time is more usual and obvious, the difference being one of degree. It may make one worse than another but must, of necessity, dismiss both if it condemns either.

Here I might well pass over what is alleged by Nicolas de *Lyra*, *(~1300)* but then I might be suspected of concealing something important. In his 'Preceptory' (a little treatise of his on the ten commandments) he argued on several good grounds drawn from sundry writers, nine of whom especially condemn this kind of gambling for coveting other men's goods greatly; being a mighty means of deceit, allowing usury; causing lying, swearing, brawling and many idle words, being an offence to the godly, breaking the law, mis-spending time and so forth. He thereupon concluded that such games are not to be tolerated or endured among Christians. It is true that *Lyra* in his 'Hostiensis' named nine circumstances, all of which, said he, are the deadly sins that accompany gambling and often are. But instead of those nine he might as well have reckoned up 16, because that is how many that he had cited in certain verses of Hostiensis. To which we may also add, ignoring those that allege fewer *(Gritsch, 1477),* that Antoninus and some others have raised up a whole alphabet of evils that usually accompanies gambling, even as many as there be aces or points on the dice. There are also some other friars who find them in dice-play, as the late Rev. R *Parker (n/k)* found a breach of the whole of the ten commandments.

As I said, I might as well pass all this by, partly because in effect they bring no new matter; and partly because these evils are equally common to all games and so do not much concern the nature of this kind of play, but contain general abuses of all kinds, though they may apply more especially to these. They are the faults of the gamesters not of the games. As *Baronius* well said of gambling, writing of this argument about lotteries and of the lottery used in games, (and I agree): "The lawful use of them must be distinguished from their unlawful abuse. For it is a game in so far as it is a game, another thing to speak of how it is abused". The scope of these authors *(Petrarch)* seems only to condemn such games in so far as they are so used or rather so abused, as too commonly they are. In this regard I may well say that they are not always sincerely cited, but forced to say what indeed they do not. They do not to quarrel with light gambling, nor do they pass a peremptory sentence against the use of all such games in general, although others from the same texts try to.

Let me add a word or two concerning the clause added to this argument, so I can leave it and pass to the next. The Lord forbids all appearance of evil and all occasions of evil. It is true that the commandments forbid any sin and forbid those things also that may be occasions of that sin. But they do not generally prohibit the use of everything that anyone does or may take occasion of evil by. They forbid them to those to whom they are in that way dangerous, not to those that may and do use them without danger of that kind. And it is no less true that Christian men ought to abstain from all appearance of evil. That is, that they are to avoid what they may justly suspect to be sinful, though they do not evidently see it or certainly know it to be such. They also must avoid what may make them suspected to be sinners, or which rightly they ought to do by the rules and laws of Christianity. As I take it, this precept does not extend any further than these two branches. How the use of any lottery at all in games, or the use of a lottery alone in this kind of game should be brought within the remit of either of these two branches, I cannot see. This is especially so when they are used by those of a godly and religious disposition and when they take such cautions as will be given later.

§5. Legal prohibitions on gambling

First they seem to reason in this manner: whatever is forbidden both by the civil magistrates and the spiritual governors cannot be used without offence. But lot-games are forbidden by both so therefore they cannot be used without offence. This assumption is confirmed by many instances, which may be referred to under two heads, civil constitutions and ecclesiastical canons.

The civil constitutions may derive from Roman law and are said to include a general forbidding of the use of those games to all, either in public or private, either as partakers in them or spectators at them, subject to a discretionary fine of four times the money lost in them and also denying relief or redress to anyone who was wronged in the game by fining those who entice or compel others to play. *(Daneau, 1586; Babington, 1583)*

Some other laws are specific, forbidding some groups the use of them. This could be for ecclesiastical persons only, or condemning a particular abuse such as where men gamble away more than they can afford. There are positive laws in some nations such as our own which generally forbid all dicing. Convicted dicers are to be punished with six days imprisonment and with sitting in the stocks. Keepers of dicing houses get three years, players two years imprisonment. In the state of Geneva even the making of dice is condemned and forbidden. *(Babington, 1583)*

The ecclesiastical canon laws produced on this point can be either general and universal such as the Canons of the Apostles (as it is commonly termed). Inserted into the body of the decrees is that every clergyman given to dice or drunkenness shall be deprived of his living unless he reforms. According to one report *(Peter Martyr, ~1560)*, a certain clerk in the decree section was deposed for being a dicer and a usurer. Two general Councils produced cannon laws: the one which was held at Rome under Innocent III in 1179 AD, forbade clergymen either to play or to be present during play with dice and hucklebones. The other council was at Constantinople under the Emperor Justinian in 553 AD, banned forever after, to all in general, lay-men as well as clerics, to play at dice under pain of excommunication.

Particular canons of national or provincial synods produced laws. A Spanish council held at Eliberis [Elvira, Granada in 306 AD] decreed that every Christian man who plays at dice or gaming tables was to be suspended from the Lord's table for 12 months and only a promise of amendment would allow him to be received again. Two French Synods were held, the one at la Rochelle, the other at Nîmes, both condemned and forbade the use of these games in general. *(Babington, 1583)*

§6. If unlawful then evil?

From the proposition of this argument and the conclusion following from it, as it is conceived it comes nowhere near to the main point in question. If it is conceived correctly that whatsoever is forbidden by the civil or canon law is therefore simply evil in itself, then it is not true. This is also admitted by some (as was before alleged). We now deal directly with this point. Human laws restrain the use of some things without discrimination. These things do not cease to be indifferent in themselves and in their own nature. So by making them unlawful, it is only insofar that the laws bind and no further. But the main question here is not whether the use of lottery in games is prohibited by man's law, but whether it is inhibited by God's law or not. Many things may be lawful by God's law, but are unlawful in man-made law. For example, to transport certain commodities may need a special licence, as does trading and trafficking into some foreign parts, eating flesh at certain times, bringing some sorts of fish into the market for sale and the like. All of these things are not evil simply or in themselves.

Yet take their proposition as propounded: that whatsoever is forbidden in man's law cannot be done without offence. But that is not all true neither. For how many cases have there been where the Summists and Casuists* both civil and ecclesiastical agree with the Schoolmen, that things may be done without offence even though declared unlawful by the letter of some positive law? It is more common to find rules like this in their writings: "We should mark the cause that moved the law-giver to make the law than the words of the law itself". *(Aquinas, 1270)* Or that "a law will have ceased when the reason for it ceases, though the letter of it does not". And that, "a law which is enacted in regard of some inconveniences does not bind when such inconveniences are no more". *(Cajetan, 1525)* And that "a reasonable cause will always excuse a man who breaks some human law". And that "if a cause is just and sufficient then even a law-giver would excuse himself from it. Common equity ought to hold sway both in the exposition of laws and in the exaction of things enjoined by law". And that, "man-made constitutions admit the favourable constructions that he is no transgressor when, though he break the letter of the law, that act had not crossed the mind of the law-maker"(mostly *(Aquinas, 1270)*). Lastly we note that custom interprets laws and gives strength to them, just as disuse of laws is a kind of abrogation of them.

Let me add that that a transgressor can, in common equity be sometimes excused when it is said that "he did not keep to the law when it was difficult to keep it and when he would be counted a fool if he should". *(Gersonides, ~1320)* In some cases, therefore, a thing may be done without causing a scandal even though the doing of it is prohibited by human laws. Nor, I suppose, is there any man who is so extremely censorious, that, because by law we are forbidden meat on Fridays we would therefore hold a man guilty of sin by eating a small bit of meat while in the company with others, or having it ready to hand when he is hungry, especially if he is not doing it out of any contempt and is otherwise regardful of the law.

§7. What is forbidden and how

From the assumptions of their argument let us consider both what is forbidden and how it is forbidden. As to what is forbidden, not all lottery use in games is generally condemned. There might be the use of it in those games that the civil laws expressly allow. This could be for joining and leading games, taking turns and the like. These are often used in the kind of games allowed by our laws, as when in shooting arrows men are shuffled and cut again to be sorted into sides or to decide who shall lead. (We omit what some good lawyers suppose; that a lot-game is one of them although what for is not certain)

Nor are games that consist solely of a lottery or depend on it prohibited; much less are they rejected or condemned on those grounds. In all games at gaming tables (including even chess too, whatever some say to the contrary), apart from bare dice, have expressly been approved by those authors whom I now deal with.

* Summists were 12th Century dialecticians; Casuists used case-based reasoning, as opposed to principle-based arguments.

Indeed all games whatsoever which require sleight and skill to manage are approved by law, with just five named exceptions [Gataker does not name them]. These games are not condemned simply as evil in themselves, which they admit as having once been used to good purpose. It is to restrain their use from forms of abuse and to forbid all playing for gain at them. Yet there are some other games where they allow playing for gain when played privately and with some kind of caution and on somewhat stricter terms.

So it is not the games themselves that are simply condemned but the evil and hurtful usage of them. This could be by the immoderate, customary, excessive or expensive use of them. It plainly appears by the letter of the law and the best interpreters are in accord and the authors also cite that, as *Peter Martyr (~1560)* well puts it: "A man is not to be condemned, if being weakly or evil at ease he recreates himself by playing at hazard, but does not hazard his money". The scope of those laws must be specially observed for what is forbidden in such kind of games: that men should not waste their estates. For this purpose it was enacted that no man should hazard above a shilling [5pence, 10cents]. So the scope and drift of this law was to ensure that monies might not be misspent, which if they are not, then the law is not broken.

§ 8. English laws against gambling

The laws of our land are now alleged *(Babington, 1583)* to be unfit for the purpose of proving that dice are evil and should be utterly condemned and generally prohibited, although cards and gaming tables may be allowed and approved. This is the conclusion to be drawn from a detailed survey of the laws for that purpose and of others that have been enacted in later times.

The first Law *(12 Rich 2 c. 6)*[*] where dice are said to be generally forbidden, enacted only that: all servants of husbandry, labourers, servants of any artificer or grocer shall have bow and arrows and use the same on Sundays and Holidays; and shall leave off all playing at tennis, football, quoits, dice, casting of the stone, kailes and other such troublesome games.

The next Act *(11 Henr 4 c. 4)* imposed a penalty of six days imprisonment upon all offenders against the former.

In the third of them *(17 Edw 4 c. 3)* we discover the main scope of these Acts, namely, to bring in a more frequent use of the bow, because the defence of the land was then mainly by archers. For this purpose it gives various other grounds for the previous prohibitions, reviving and renewing them. Sundry unlawful games were named such as closhe, kailes[^], bowls, queckboard &c. all newly invented. Gaming houses had been erected and so commonly employed that gamesters were thereby impoverished, murders and robberies were occasioned &c. So it was enacted that furthermore there would be a penalty of £20 and three years

---

[*] that is, the 6th Act of Richard II in his 12th year.

[^] closhe, kailes and logeting are all forms of skittles

imprisonment against everyone that shall keep and of £10 and two years imprisonment against every one that shall haunt any such house.

The fourth *(11 Henr 7 c. 2)* commanded that no servant or labourer play at gaming tables except for meat and drink, nor at any other unlawful game except at Christmas and then only in his master's dwelling house only. Every one so offending was to be set in the stocks and he that allowed it in his house was to forfeit at least a noble (£0.33).

To this, though not alleged, may be annexed another Act *(19 Henr 7 c. 12)* of little later date, forbidding the same persons to play at gaming tables, tennis, closhe, dice &c. save as above, with the same penalties imposed on persons therein delinquent. And these are all, indeed more than all the laws that are particularly cited. But because we were referred to another work *(Pulton, 1618)* for more matters of this kind, let us also see what later laws were enacted concerning such games, if we shall not tire out our reader with such trifling proofs.

The later laws *(33 Henr 8 c. 9)* forbid keeping any common house, alley or place of bowling, quoiting, closhe, kailes, tennis, dicing, gaming tables or carding for gain, lucre and living and the haunting of places so kept without a special licence expressing what games are played and what persons may use the same. It also covered private playing at tennis, gaming tables, dice, cards, bowls, closhe, quoiting or logeting by any artificer, husbandman, labourer, apprentice, journeyman, serving man &c. except at Christmas and then also nowhere other than in his master's house and presence. It was further enacted that playing at bowls by any man at any time in open places out in his garden or orchard would merit the several pecuniary penalties imposed upon the former offences. But any servant is allowed to play at cards, dice or gaming tables with his master, or any gentleman repairing to his house, so long as it was done openly in his house and in his presence. Any nobleman or gentleman of £100 lands per annum is permitted to allow his servants, at his discretion to play at cards, dice, gaming tables, bowls or tennis within his house, garden or orchard, either among themselves, or with others repairing to them. Inn-keepers were warned not to allow such games in their houses. And lastly all wandering persons using unlawful games were to be punished as rogues and vagabonds.

To any dim eye it might on first view plainly appear that this particular recital of the several laws that either have been or might further have been alleged in this argument shows that the laws of our land justified and approve the games in question rather than condemned them. They forbid some use of them, but they also forbid bowling, quoiting, tennis, logetting and throwing the stone. Some of these are exercises of art and skill, some of industry and activity, or of dexterity and agility, which applies more strictly to bowling than either carding or dicing, yet no man that I know condemns them or concludes that they are unlawful.

Again though they forbid them to be used by some persons in some places at some times, yet they allow them to other persons and those of best note. They also allow them to the same persons in other places at other times. It is evident

(Dalton, 1618) that they only restrain the use of the games and do not condemn them as simply evil in themselves. Rather they approve them, in that they reserve the common and ordinary use of them to great personages. Do we say that laws licence the great ones to sin more than others? Should not their greatness restrain them from anything that is simply evil, especially regarding the hurt that their evil example might give? Are we therefore to allow and tolerate any evil which poisons and corrupts the public well-springs and common conduit-heads and so breed and bring in an epidemical infection upon the main body of the state?.

The purpose and scope of the law is partly to reform some of the abuses about these games, such as the mis-spending of time and coin in common gaming houses or elsewhere; and partly to bring into use other kinds of exercise instead of them. There are a variety of games which are much neglected; to wit, shooting with the longbow which was matter of much use and of great weight when we were at war.

For my own part I am far from disliking these laws, which, when considering the great and general abuse of the games they prohibit, limits both the waste of precious time and the throwing away of wealth and thrift at these exercises. I wish rather that the laws were even more severe than they are and that the laws that be were put in execution better than they are, for the most part .

As for the French state and synods with their canons and constitutions, having not seen them, I can say nothing but this about them. If they have utterly abandoned the use of those games among them (which I doubt) this does not prove that all gambling is simply unlawful nor does it make games in that regard evil for us.

§9. Canon-law condemnation

As the Glossers* and Summists have expounded before, canon law condemns dicing and tabling just as civil law does, both more especially for the clergy. *(Cajetan, 1525)* This is because there are many things that might be lawful for others yet are not so fit for or so well beseeming men of their rank. It is the same canons and councils together with others that forbids them the use of these games, as it also forbids to them all secular employment and traffic, the baser sort of it especially: Not to go into any tavern or to eat and drink there except for necessity in journey; Not to play openly at tennis; Not to use hunting and hawking and the like. (As do the statutes of our universities and civil laws likewise restrain students from many such activities.) Yet these things to this day are neither simply condemned as unlawful to all Christians, nor are they generally forbidden to ministers if they are seasonably and soberly used by them, although there may be abuse in this kind and is doubtless over-great.

It seems that the canons of old were not very precisely kept in this matter (neither kind of exercise being wholly forgone by bishops or ecclesiastical persons

* Glosser: one who explains, especially with sophistical explanations

who were otherwise of good note), but neither are they commonly understood to prevent all use of those games that are condemned by them. A clergyman who was reported *(Cajetan, 1525)* to have been deposed from his post. He was said in the decree to have been a common dicer and an open usurer. According to that constitution all such voluptuous games are condemned in clergymen and just because they affect a courtly kind of carriage they can still fall into dishonest and dissolute courses. But of that more anon.

§10. False testimonies from the 'ancient fathers': ***Cyprian***

I pass on to the next argument which is much of the same nature as before: whatever has been condemned as evil both by Christians and heathens cannot be lawful to Christian men. But dicing has been generally condemned by both. Therefore it cannot be lawful to Christians.

The answer to this argument must consist in a survey of the particular allegations which are produced for proof of the assumption. (I admit that it does not home in on the main question concerning the general use of lottery as sport, even though all which is said here be granted still stands.) To begin with, some Christian writers condemn all use of dice as simply unlawful. But they are not as many as it would partly appear. Those who allege these testimonies will themselves allow some use of them and such uses as these authors allege by them are as often condemned as allowed.

The Ancient Fathers whose testimonies are alleged are not past two or three in number, besides those that were discussed in the former argument and of those they either carry no weight at all or have nothing pertinent to say for that purpose. *(Daneau, 1586)*. I will omit their condemnation of some other exercises, such as hunting and hawking that have been as commonly and sometimes more generally and peremptorily condemned by them but which are confessed not to be simply evil or unlawful therefore in themselves: "Cyprian", said *Daneau* "was as holy a man as any other in his time, had said that it was the Devil himself who was the first author of this harmful invention. Hence that godly man testified that it ought to be accursed and abhorred by us with our whole heart since we can have no safe or saving traffic with the Devil or any of his devices". Cyprian was also reported (by *Daneau*) to have said that "it was the Devil, according to one source, or the heathen god Mercury according to another, having invented both cards and dice, caused his own image and the images of other idols to be painted on the cards (instead of the other pictures we have upon them now) so that he would be adored forever by the gamesters, with a cup of wine and a kiss at the entrance into game".

A man might with better grounds, equally argue in the same way against the work of medicine or the goldsmiths, thus: *Tertullian*, an ancient Father and one that Cyprian commonly called his master, said that "the use of herbs for medicine and the curious working in costly metals were both invented by evil angels to please women. Enoch himself said so in a work of his yet extant, taking his authority from the epistle of Jude. *(Jude 14:15)* He concludes that Christians may have no dealing with the Devil or with any of his devices so therefore may not meddle in way with herbs or metals. Nor should Christian women wear any gold about them". And as Tertullian supposing the Apostles also spoke for him concluded: "Nor should Christian men or women use the benefit of medicine", as some other of the Ancients *(Macarius)* have held. But this argument is too weak and yet the other is far weaker; being built upon the testimony and authority of a mere counterfeit author.

There is a trace indeed of that argument in the late editions of *Cyprian,* but not in earlier ones. The author of this whoever he was, was surely not Cyprian; the rudeness of the style shows it to be none of his, who for purity of Latin phrase and fineness of speech is specially commended by all. He tells an idle tale concerning a certain learned man, who after long study invented the game of dicing by the instinct of the Devil. He then caused his picture to be drawn including his invention – the dicing table which was to be adored by the Gamesters at the beginning of their game. (As for playing-cards or any of the images painted on them there is not a word in this book). Next he termed the dicing table to be the Devil's hunting ground and ordained that whoever played at dice must first make sacrifice to the Devil as the author of that game and so polluted his hands with diabolical sacrilege. If there was any such custom in his times it would have been impious. But the story itself seems idle and frivolous and the author is an uncertain authority of no weight.

And the foolish friars, (who may well have forged this counterfeit Cyprian, because they *(Landulfus, ~1498)* were the first to cite it) have even more idle matter in them for this purpose. One *(Paris, n/k)* tells us that 'hazard' is the same as Astaroth (or Astarte as the Greeks say), which is the proper name of one of the principal devils and that the dice are therefore the Devil's altars, the points on them his eyes. So it is that men are calling on God and the Devil together when they say: "God and good Hazard". Those that play either at gaming tables or with cards are with the idolatrous Jews, spreading a table to Fortune, putting themselves in play with her. Another writer *(Pepin, 1530)* claimed that just as God had invented an alphabet of 21 letters with which to make up the Bible, so the Devil had invented an alphabet of 21 abuses, the same number as points on the dice, which make up his black book or his Bible. A third author tells a long tale of a parliament held by Lucifer in hell, where this game was agreed upon and a church was constituted of those that followed it; Lucifer himself should be pope or chief head, with the other Devils as his cardinals, the common dicing houses would be the cathedrals, the taverns to be parish churches and each family house would be a private chapel for the 12 days of Christmas. The dice would be the missal or mass-book with its 21 black letters. And so he goes on in his apish manner to apply it to all the priest's mass-attire and all the mysteries of their mass to this devilish device. This may well suit the one with the other; it is all of the same stamp as those friars' fancies, mere poetical fictions that are counterfeits of Cyprian. In both the phrase and the frame of the work they betray what the real author was.

§11. False testimonies from the 'ancient fathers': ***Augustine & Chrysostom***

It was *Augustine* who said that the Devil invented dice. *(Elliot, 1531; Babington, 1583)* This can be found in that authentic work, his fourth book of the 'City of God'. It is true that those words are found in Augustine's index but refer to a place not in Augustine's fourth book of the City of God, where there is no such matter, except for a comment that "Stage plays are esteemed by Varro to be a part of divine worship and that the devils are greatly delighted in them". However, there is a reference in *Vives*'s *(1522)* Commentary on Augustine where Augustine says that "there is a society of ungodly men who live not after God but after man, following human traditions and doctrines of devils in worshiping false gods and having contempt for the true God". *Vives* adds that "It is learned that devils have delivered magic, astronomy and all kind of divination except prophesy unto men". *Plato* writes in Phaedrus (a dialogue of his so titled) that a spirit or devil called Theuth invented writing, arithmetic, geometry, astronomy and dice and presented them to Thamus who was then King of Egypt. "And there is no doubt", said he, "but that this wrangling and cavilling logic proceeded from some devilish disposition. It loves always to strive so against the truth, refusing to yield to any that shall speak to better purpose and by falsehood rejoicing to overcome truth". *Augustine*'s Index therefore deceived the author of this argument and made him put words in Augustine's mouth which he nowhere said by taking from another words that were not his own either, only as reported of an other. It is a fable of *Plato*, whose works are full of such poetical fictions, although always aiming at some moral matter. Among other kinds of tales that he tells is the one about Theuth whom he sometimes styled Daemon. In his own language that is what they call a good spirit (for so they esteemed them and it was because of their singular skill and knowledge that they gave that title to them), or sometimes they were titled 'deum ant divum', either a god or a divine man at least. They used this term for such persons who were authors and inventors of anything that might be useful for a man's life. Now of this Teuth, whatever he was, he was reported as having invented many arts of special use, including numbering and counting, geometry and astronomy, also dice and gaming tables and the use of letters. He came and presented his devices to Thamus who was then King of Egypt. Among his inventions he had highly commended the use of letters and writing as a singular means for the increase of wisdom and to help the memory; Thamus answered him, "that on the contrary, this was a means to make men more careless, if they put their trust in it and so they would become more forgetful than before. It would make them self-conceited rather then soundly wise, by stuffing their brains more with a variety of opinions rather than a sufficiency of matter and sound judgements".

Whether this is true or false is not greatly material. There is a great variety of opinions among authors about the origin and invention of these games. Some credit them to the Lydians as the inventors of most games and sports, (and the Grammarians are therefore supposed, though with small probability, to have their usual appellation in Latin from them). Others credit the Grecians and they most credit Palamedes, who was the one that helped to furnish Greece with letters, although one of them ascribed it to Helen. Isadora's conceit that it was one Alea, a soldier at Troy, was much like his other toys and akin to the learning of his times. Some others have it that it was Attalus, King of Asia, but this has little, if not less ground, because the invention is far older than that. I would say that if we accept the main current of the authors and writers from Plato's era in this point we might as well use the same grounds to condemn grammar, astronomy, arithmetic, geometry and the use of letters and ciphers, as well as the use of gaming tables and dice because they are all diabolical inventions. In his fable Plato credited them all to the same origin and author. It was common for these heathens to ascribe the invention of every art and matter of moment to some idol or other or to deify or idolise the inventors themselves.

I will conceal nothing that may seem fitting to this quest. It was *Chrysostom* who spoke in general terms saying that "Play or game is not of God but of the Devil" and "We read that Christ often wept but never that He laughed, or so much as once smiled" or "None of the saints in Scripture are reported ever to have laughed, except for Sara, who was soon reprimanded for it". Yet, said that reverend Father, "I do not ask you to abandon laughter, but to banish looseness".

So said *Chrysostom*, but is it all sound and true? For did not Abraham laugh too, as well as Sara? He was not taxed or rebuked for doing so, nor indeed was Sara simply rebuked for laughing, but for doubting and, if I may say so, for mocking Abraham's laughter. As the ancients have well observed, it proceeded from joy, while Sara's savoured of distrust. Not that it matters in our present purposes. I cannot see how some have thought that *Chrysostom* was alluding to the fable of Plato or that others have applied that speech of his to the games that are in question here. In truth it is apparent that he had an eye to the Israelites sport, which he also mentions, which was used by them during the worship of the golden calf. He speaks only (as the sequel of his discourse plainly shows) of the stage plays and such like that the heathens put on to celebrate and in honour of their idols (as some of the authors observe). This may well be termed a devilish invention both as they then used them and as they are used at this day. Further on that grave father *Chrysostom* also said that the Devil was the first builder and founder of theatres and as *Tertullian* put it, "the Roman theatre was the Devil's temple". There was surely some good ground for *Chrysostom* to take the origin of stage plays from him, for whose honour and at whose command they first came in, who was directly and evidently honoured in them and who ever and anon enjoined them and called for them in honour of his idols. But for dice and gaming tables both *Plato* and the counterfeit *Cyprian* speak without ground, the one professing but to tell a tale, the other pretending to relate a true story, but an idle one, the one as improbable as the other. However I do not deny that, as the apostles term some heresies as doctrines of devils or devilish doctrines, so *Vives*'s wrangling sophistry (for so I suppose his meaning) is a devilish device. It is the abuse of these games because of any impiety that accompanies them that leads to them being termed, as some do, "a devilish invention and a service of Satan" *(Chaucer, 1476)* and our common dicers may well be marshalled among the flock of his followers.

§12. False testimonies from the 'ancient fathers': *Bernard*

Thus far we have examined two of the Fathers produced in this point and have found one to be a forger and the other to be forged; the one a counterfeit pretending to be who he is not, the other having something attributed to him that is not to be found in him. There remains only one other of the ancients though not very ancient and that is *Bernard (~1120)*. He is reported to have written that "the godly Christians at Jerusalem detested the use of these games". But let *Bernard* speak out and he will speak very little on this point. "Chess and dice", said he, "they detest; hunting they abhor; hawking, as the manner is, they take no delight in". And again, "They live altogether without wines or children, in evangelical, or angelical perfection", as he termed it at other times. So he joined chess and dice together, as some others *(Pepin, 1530)* also do when passing the same sentence upon either. The author *(Daneau, 1586)* who cited him, approved the one, but does not utterly condemn the other. He claimed that hunting and hawking as well as gaming are all abhorred by them, but he actually is speaking about the Knights of the Temple, a company of persons retired from the world and worldly things, addicted to a monkish course of life, restraining themselves from the lawful use of the good ordinances of God and affecting a superstitious and more austere manner of carriage than God or his word has tied any man unto. Their example therefore is no precedent to others so it does not prejudice the use of games by any that have not sworn away from the same.

§13. Ancient heathen views

From the ancient Fathers we pass on to the 'heathen' [non-Christian] writers. *Cicero* was said by *Babington (1583)* to object to dicing by Catiline and his accomplices. He would even spit fire into Antonio's face as he laid his charge that he was a dicer and his house a common receptacle of such. It is true that *Cicero* placed dicers and adulterers and filthy folk of all fashion in the sixth rank of Catiline's companions and as he also elsewhere noted that many of them have been dicers and drunkards. He accused Antonio likewise of being a common dicer and a drunkard and that he favoured and restored things that had been condemned. Among other things, he is described as running riot and revelling and by dicing and drinking and other riotous courses he had suddenly wasted away and that on the great Pompey's fall he then made away with all those ample spoils that had come into his hands. His excess and prodigality was so great that it soon consumed the riches of whole realms. Those who read what *Cicero* wrote can easily see what he condemned in both them and their crew.

But does *Cicero* therefore utterly condemn all use of gaming tables or dice? Nothing less. Elsewhere he allows the use of them to men wearied with other ordinary labours or restrained by weather from other outdoor exercises abroad. They should not show excessive fondness for them as some tennis players* do and with other exercises too. But in a more special manner he deemed them to be very fit recreations, as *Sidonius* said, "for sick and weakly persons and also for old men grown unwieldy and past games of activity". This was the *Sidonius*, an ancient French bishop who advised that the young men should be set to tennis and the old men to gaming tables. In these writings we also find that learned men and divines too, ordinarily used such kinds of sport in his time. The bishop himself made use of both, in private, playing both at tennis and at gaming tables with his familiar friends in his own house. The Emperor Theodoric also sometimes kept company at that game. His civil, moderate and courteous demeanour was thus very wittily described in an epistles: "In the afternoon he often betakes himself to the gaming tables, where he catches the dice nimbly, views them warily, shakes cunningly, casts speedily. He calls for his chance merrily and expects it patiently. In good casts he is silent, at evil ones he smiles. He is angry with neither, he carries himself wisely in either. A good chance he scorns either to fear or to make, with its opportunity refused when it is offered to him. He lets it pass when it goes against him. He is neither moved if defeated nor uses cheating to win. He behaves himself at the game as if he were at his weapon. His care is all how to win. While he is at play he sets aside his royal state. He invites those he plays with to frolikness and freedom and fellow-like behaviour. To speak as I think, he is afraid to be feared. In a word, he loves to see those who he has beaten in play moved, scarce believing that they played badly if they are not thoroughly angry". *(Sidonius)* And having been told how often many win their games with him by watching and taking their time, he is said to have remarked that "he is also glad to win, when he is lucky enough to beat them". But he was also content to lose.

§14. Dicing Emperors of Rome

But to return to our task. "Augustus", says *Babington (1583)*, "was reproached for his dicing with an undying phrase, which counted him a dissolute man. It was said to be his notorious vice although he was otherwise a very great and very good Emperor, but this infamous blot blemished all his other great virtues". *Suetonius* reported that when Augustus was taxed by many for his common dicing, he thereupon made up a rhyme to this effect:

At sea twice beaten and his ships lost twice;
To win yet once, all day he plays at dice.

---

* This would be 'real', that is indoor tennis.

Yet *Suetonius* and others seem to excuse him in part, alleging that he played simply and openly for delight alone, even into old-age. But there were other more foul matters that blemished his fame, some shrewdly suspected of him, some confessed even by his friends. His fault was twofold: in part that he was somewhat too profuse and spent more at play then was fitting, (though nothing compared to what some of those who succeeded him did); and partly that he used gaming somewhat unreasonably, (as also some of his successors did) in bestowing time on his sports that other serious affairs might more justly have laid claim to. This he was taxed with, not gaming in itself.

Again, it was said by *Daneau (1584)* of Claudius that "he was especially noted to be of a dull and foolish disposition because he took so much delight in gaming tables and dice". Claudius was indeed noted to have been a very serious dice-player. He even wrote a discourse on the game and used to play along as he rode in his coach, having tables fastened to the seats so that the dice might not mingle and the game be marred. In derision *Seneca* related that after his decease he would sent to hell with this penance; "to take his dice up with a box that had a hole in the bottom" and so make him always lose in his labour. But I do not find anywhere that his behaviour in that way is seen as a mark of his stupidity, neither do I see how that should be so, (since the game he used required art and dexterity to manage it) or if it was, that it would be at all material to the point that is at question here, namely the lawfulness or unlawfulness of the game itself.

§15. Dicing kings and princes

There was a Spartan called Gobilo,(or Cobilo, Chilo, Stilpo, or some other name; they cannot agree) who came to Corinth to set up a league between his countrymen and them. He observed that the Corinthian governors and people were generally into gaming. He went away again without conclusion or any treaty, deeming it to be too dishonest and dangerous to be in league and amity with such idle persons and gamesters such as they. *(Daneau, 1586)* In another tale, the King of Persia, (some say of Parthia) sent Demetrius, King of Asia, golden dice as a present, thereby noting his sloth, say some, his childish lightness, say others, that such toys were used in that royal household.

All this needs no long answer. The Corinthian looseness both in dicing and otherwise (which no well-minded man will either excuse or defend) might well discourage a Spartan of generous and warlike disposition from proceeding with important business. This story, however, cannot be found in any authentic source and the allegers of it vary in their reports. But even if true, neither does it prove that no lottery in or about a game may lawfully be used. The Spartans as well as other Greeks joined together in the Games they held for their youth, to stage fights with each other. It is known that lottery games were sometimes in use in Sparta, from the common byword with one of their commanders, that "their children had been cheated with balls and dice (or hucklebones, which were then used as dice) and that men cheated with words and oaths". *(Plutarch)*

The story of the dice, which one king is said to have sent to the other is mistaken or at least misreported. *(Justinius)* The dice were indeed sent by Phraartes, king of Parthia to Demetrius, who had been king of Syria. He was a valiant man, as the Parthians well knew, having often been beaten by him. But, surprised by an enemy column, he was prisoner in Parthia. Though honourably treated, he was still desirous of liberty, having twice attempted to break away and twice being brought back again. So he had these dice sent him, not to accuse him of sloth for tending to such toys, but to note, says my author, his childish inconstancy, or rather (I think) to show him that he must tend to these and not attempt greater matters unless he grew weary of his life. But we must admit that one king had sent such a present to another in derision.

This is similar to what we read in a present-day story *(Holinshed, 1577)*, that the Dauphin of France once sent a ton of Paris-balls [tennis balls] to Henry V, though without just cause and with no great good success. Another tale has Magus *(Plutarch)* sending dice or hucklebones and a tennis ball to Philomen the poet who had defamed him on the stage. Yet that would not prove that the use of the one to be evil or unlawful, any more then this proves the other. It is indeed unseemly and disparaging for a king to addict himself to those sports even though they are good and honest in themselves. Neglect of state business and serious affairs has been a foul blemish for many princes and great personages, especially so when they come from parents who took a clean contrary course. It would be better if they were exercises more beseeming to a king's place or person. In this regard our royal sovereign *(James I, 1603)* right wisely advised his son, that a hopeful prince (that then was, but, to our woe, is no longer hopeful*), "should leave the ordinary use of dice to debased soldiers to play with on the drum-head and leave tumbling tricks to players to win their bread with". What he should choose is "riding, tilting, hunting and the like, exercises that are more seemly for a prince and may make him fit for military affairs". Even so, the evil practice of the former no more prejudices the morals of any prince than the preferred exercises of tennis or gaming tables in a sober and seasonable way But the riotous courses of luxury-loving princes should be a restraint on the royal entertainment of others when performed at such occasions and ought to be agreeable to their state.

§16. Poets and dicing

Lastly come the poets who are produced to condemn dicing. Poets and satirists especially are the common scourges of the vices and abuses of their times. Now it is not my purpose to pander to any sin or to be an advocate pleading for it, nor will I excuse or extenuate much less justify or acquit any abuse used in game. Let my tongue first stick to the roof of my mouth, let it rot to the very root, if I should ever once attempt anything like that. But we consider these games only, separated

---

* Prince Henry, elder surviving son of James I, who died aged 18 in 1612.

from their abuses and that so men may use them, if they will and no doubt many do.

"The poets put Dice, Wine and Women among the common cancers that consume men and make beggars of them". *(Babington, 1583)* When I first read this, I remembered a Greek epigram in which Baths, Wine and Women are joined together as the cancers corrupting and consuming men's bodies and making a speedy dispatch of their lives. Some writers, turning to Latin to mend the matter, add that these might equally well prove to be restoratives or preservatives as much as they are cancers and corrosives when they are used and taken as they ought.

I have found an obscure author *(no ref)* who comes close to that allegation about dice, wine and women. Authentic though it may be, it no more enforces an absolute and general condemnation of dice than it does of wine and women, which have all be joined together. No wise man in his right wits will therefore utterly condemn them. What more can be said than (I say not of poets alone) that the Spirit of God itself has said, (not to draw too much from the Apocrypha *(Pepin, 1530)*) of the other two, as well of women and of wine? How is it that the vines in foreign parts have not all been uprooted (as some *(Scopeliano, ~1250)* have attempted) and all use of wine (a good creation of God) to be wholly forbidden us? We might live well without it because wine is much abused by many. Nor should women be abandoned or deemed evil though necessary, just because of the abuse of them or other's abuse of them, confirming what the Spirit of God says. Marriage being God's own ordinance, is in itself helpful, beneficial and comfortable, it is holy, honest and honourable and in that respect should be well-regarded. But the use of either should be limited, the abuses stripped from them, as required by both the rules of reason and religion.

Yea another grave author *(Daneau, 1586),* reckoned this game among those vices that most grievously and easily are wont to corrupt a whole family:

If wasteful Dice the old man please,
His son's sick of the same disease;
Where father sits at cinque and sise,
The child in side-coats loves the dice.

And one of our own poets, *Chaucer (1476* in Pardoner) has said:

Hazard is very mother of leasings,
And of deceit and cursed for swearings;
Blasphemy of God, manslaughter and waste also,
Of cattle, of time and other woe,
It is a reproof and contrary to honour,
For to behold a common hazarder.
And ever the higher he is in estate,

The more he is holden desolate.
If that a Prince shall use hazardie,
In all governance and policy;
He is by a common opinion,
Holden less in reputation.
Lords might find other manner of play,
Honest enough to drive the day away.

In a word, it is no wonder that we can take any author, Christian or heathen and find, almost to a man they have something against dicing. There is nothing in this I willingly yield to and indeed nothing at all to the point or the purpose. For first, do not all those authors and authorities impugn and condemn gaming tables and dice as well as bare bones? How is it then that those who cite these games divide between them, allowing one sort and alleging testimonies against the other sort, yet which equally concern either?

Which of these heathen or Christian writers was ever so scrupulous or censorious that he conscientiously utterly avoided all such games himself, while condemning them in all others besides himself? They showed what they disliked and condemned in them, namely the immoderate use of them, or the wastefulness of expense at them, which no man would defend. (This can be found in writers such as *Paschasius (1618)* who defines that distinctly; others describe it in more general terms, for example in *Osorius (~1590)*). But all of this says nothing about the game itself. It is not warrantable for a man to spend more time then is fitting at any recreation or to waste himself and his worldly estate at it.

Lastly I would add that in whatever book a man might lightly lay his hands on, he shall find something in it against drinking as well as against dicing. Usually there is more against drinking. It may be true that as *Paschasius (1618)* said, that before himself, no-one, whether a poet, orator or philosopher had ever directly and professedly railed against dice. But that does not prove that all sorts of men condemn drink any more than that all sorts of men detest dice.

To draw near land at length. "A dicer", said the heathen man, "the better the worse". This was a speech that *Diogenes* used of another kind of sport, but not one of hazard but of skill. And if a man, as one of our countrymen said (*Elliot, 1531)* hears that someone unknown is a dicer, then he is judged to be a light and a vain person and of no credit or account. No marvel this, for to be a dicer suggests a habit, profession, a practice or trade; and to make a trade or practice or a man's living out of any recreation such as this is not commendable even though the recreation itself be such. It is one thing to play at dice or cards, quite another to be a dicer or carder. Just as it is one thing to drink wine and another to be a wine-drinker, or as we used to say 'a wine-bibber'. In a word, they are not all courtiers that live at court (if we take courtiers in no very good sense, with prince's palaces much abused). Not all fishermen fish, for a man may angle or cast a net sometimes for recreation even though he does not live by this trade. So those that use dice and cards are not all dicers or carders, only those who make gain or common trade of them. To do so is most base and is a course greatly condemned by Christians as well as heathens too.

To conclude this argument, I join the condemnation willingly as much as any of the authors do. But not one of them condemns all which they allege in them and therefore they say nothing at all that concern us. But to reply to the argument: it is not whether it is lawful for men to use dice, but whether it is unlawful for children to play at even and odd, cherry-pit, or at heads and points, push-pin, or at cross and pile, or at span-counter. None of these authors, either heathen or Christian, would judge this last question to be other than a jest and unworthy to be answered in earnest. And yet no-one asks whether such children's sports are lawful, but the question is ignored by those who condemn all gambling and lusory lotteries which is our main concern here. We had better see to it that the grounds are good and sure on which to condemn that which hardly any heathen or Christian had ever made an issue of before.

§17. Abandon things of bad report?

But there is something further to be pressed and enforced on the last point: first, as some say *(Philip 4:8)*, "All things of evil report are to be banished and abolished. But cards and dice, it appears, are things of evil report and therefore ought to be utterly abandoned among Christians". *(Ammianius Marcellinus)*

I answer: it is the immoderate use or abuse of them is of evil report, while the moderate and sober use of them is not. To be a tobacconist [smoker] or a common tobacco-taker is also a matter of no great good report. *(James I, 1604; Sylvester, 1617)* But the seasonable and profitable use of tobacco should not be utterly abandoned and abolished for that reason. There are reverend divines, as well as others who find benefit by it and should not be restrained in their Christian liberty in that way.

Secondly, we encourage others that abuse them by our use of them. *(Fenner, 1587)* We ought indeed to be wary that we give as little bad example as may be. But by the discreet and moderate usage of them, we could teach them how they may use them well, even if they could never be wholly weaned from it. It is obvious that the faults that are found are not because of the thing itself but the men who use it; it is man's corruption that abuses it.

Thirdly, It scandalises those who condemn these games both within the Church and without it; so things which are indifferent ought not to be done. (*Fenner, 1587)* For those without, there is little fear of offence being given by the sober and seasonable use of them. We heard before what they condemned. For those within the Church, it is true indeed that it is not good to do anything whereby a weak brother may be offended. To do anything with offence is evil. Men should not use these games among those that are diversely minded and who might therefore be scandalized and grieved thereby. But for those that are otherwise minded, they ought not to be so peremptory in censuring and condemning those that use them, or that differ in judgement from them. Neither ought they to take offence at them for doing that which they know to be lawful and approved by many others, both learned and religious, just because something is condemned or questioned by a few, especially when it is not a main point or matter of faith.

§18. Differences among the learned make men doubtful

Lastly, it is said that differences among the learned are bound to make men doubtful and to use them doubtingly is a sin. *(Estey, ~1603)* I answer: first, if this simple and general consequence is granted it will infer grievous inconveniences and drive men into strange straights. If a man may not do anything when there is any difference about it among the learned, how many matters will then be utterly cast and cut off, despite it not being condemned? Men shall continually encounter and entangle with a troop of dilemmas concerning where shall they stand. Being unable to take part they cannot take sides, which some saying is a sin, others say not. This is similar to the controversies between the Separatists and our ministers and even between our own ministers among themselves.

Secondly, differences among the learned are not generally a just cause of doubt. Two special cases are: when a man discovers the evident weakness of the grounds against it and when a man finds sure ground for one side which he should therefore stick close by. How many main points are there in Divinity, which many, nay most among us, now do not doubt, notwithstanding the differences among the learned about them? What troops of the ancients have condemned second marriages, which yet no divine that I know makes any doubt of today? How many of them have held that a man who had been twice married was, by the Apostle's own constitution *(1 Tim 3:2)* incapable of the ministry? May no man therefore so disqualified undertake that office or execute it, without scruple and doubt and without sin? Are there not a great many differences about the real presence of Christ in the Eucharist between Papists and Protestants? Were there not also great differences between Luther and Zwingli, with eager opposition about the same point by many of the learned and religious taking part on either side and continuing the controversy even to these times? Cannot a man therefore without wavering, even a plain ordinary Christian, join himself to either side? Yes! Doubtless he may and many do so without question. Differences among the learned give good cause of disquisition and discussion but are not necessarily just cause of doubt[*].

Thirdly, faith may withstand some doubt and special Faith may stand with some kind of wavering. Every sudden injection, or idle scruple, or snarling objection which a man is assailed by does not make that man's actions unwarrantable or bring him Apostolic censure. "He that doubts is condemned because of what he

[*] As good an advocacy of religious toleration as might be found anywhere in those times: An excellent description of the confessional turmoil and its uneasy resolution can be found in: Benjamin Kaplan (2007) *Divided by Faith: Religious conflict and the practise of toleration in early modern Europe* Cambridge, Mass: Belknap Press

does and does not do in faith: and whatsoever is not of Faith, is sin". *(Rom 14:23)* A man may be certain of the lawfulness of a thing, having sure or sufficient ground for the same and yet have some scruple in his mind about it which he cannot avoid. A man may hold firmly to some points of doctrine, as the articles of his faith, though he cannot answer every subtle sophism that some may throw at him. Casuists may say that in civil actions words which are not precisely and expressly determined are enough to keep a Christian man from incurring God's displeasure; having done his best to inform himself aright and being ready to yield unto any better information.

I hold it to be a moral certainty that this should apply on points concerning gambling, despite the differences among the learned and religious. For example consider what a reverend Minister of our Church now with the Lord *(Bradshaw, ~1590)* said in conference with certain Separatists: "It was sufficient to prove the truth of our ministry when wrangling and cavilling with companions such as they, that they could not object to anything which might be well and easily answered." It may be thought a sufficient warrant for the use of these lotteries that the opponents of them who are learned men, well-read in God's word, say nothing against them (for that is what they do say, when they try their best) but that has been sufficiently answered by others.

Lastly if any man wants good ground for the use of them and has just cause for doubt, he should best leave off until he has better assurance for the use of them. But he should not be censuring others that use them when they have warrant to do so.

Chapter 9

Cautions to be observed in the use of gambling

§1. Games as a special refreshment, not ordinary employment.

I have answered the arguments against gambling produced by learned men and proved that it is not unwarrantable in itself. It would be appropriate, as we did before, to annex some caveats and cautions to be observed in its use, applying some of same advice as before, as well as adding some more. This may deal with those abuses to which such kinds of lottery are prone, so that things which are lawful when used correctly may not become unlawful by our abuse of them. Gambling therefore, as with all other recreations, is to be used soberly, seasonably, honestly, inoffensively, prudently and religiously.

First, I say, soberly and moderately: remember that for this purpose that the Holy Ghost has recommended Christian sobriety and temperance as a principal virtue: "As a nurse and a staff of godliness and righteousness". *(1 Pet 4 7)* This consists at least in the sparing and moderate use, not only of meat and drink, but of all bodily benefits especially those that are merely or mainly for recreation and delight. *(Fenner, 1587)* Heathen men have, by the light of nature, discerned that there is a measure and a golden mean to be observed in all things. *(Pindar)* There are certain bounds and limits prescribed in nature and if men transgress them they swerve from the right use of them. Even the best things used immoderately become inconvenient, just as waters breaking their banks or surpassing their bounds grow incommodious and dangerous. So meat and drink taken unreasonably or excessively will hurt rather then help. As with all other things, a middle course should be held especially in these pastimes, partly because of time and expense and partly because of our manner of using them.

Regarding the amount of time we spend, they should not take up too much of our time nor should we spend too much time at them. They who spend, as we say, 'the live long day' at gambling cause offence. For some of them it is both day and night at game. The evil practice of Saturnalia which is all too common in many of our places has been condemned by a reverend prelate *(Edmund Grisdal in Fulke (1560))* and others besides (*Travers, 1574)*. They publicly complained that it defiles the usual solemnity of our Christmas. Around this time, which for heathens is Saturnalia (14th Jan)*, *(Macrobius)* they were wont to give themselves wholly

* This is the date given by Gataker, but currently it is taken to be 17th December.

to gambling and revelling. So too do many (too, too many) among us who profess ourselves to be Christians, setting aside all sage, serious and sober demeanour, giving ourselves up completely to games and play of all kinds, mis-spending our precious time which should be better spent. We carry on in a loose and dissolute manner so that if a stranger should come among them by chance, not knowing what religion we were, he would by our behaviour guess us to be worshippers either of Bacchus the revelling and drunken god, or of Saturn the riffling and gaming god rather than the servants of Christ Jesus who preached and practised sobriety and temperance. As the Apostle says: "My brethren, these things ought not so to be". *(Jam 3:10)* Although the heathens behaved thus, but were ignorant of God, yet we, that have learned of Christ must not do so. "We have heard Him and have been taught of Him" *(Ephes 4:20),* and we profess ourselves to be so. Christian religion gives no liberty for such behaviour at any time, much less at a time when we should (if we celebrate aright the memory of God's mercy toward us in Christ) carry ourselves most religiously and conformably to the life of Christ. We ought therefore to remember both then and at all times that recreation is to other affairs as sauce or salt is to our meat. As the use of sauce or salt is to prepare our stomach for food or to help our appetite in eating; so the use and purpose of recreation is to refresh us after labour and to make us fit for labour. It should not be an employment in which our principal and precious time is spent on. This was the fault of those both in Esau's days *(Act 17:21)* and in Noah's time *(Matt 24:38)* (whom the Holy Ghost therefore taxed) who gave themselves wholly over to delights and pleasures, regarding nothing else and minding nothing else. This was like the idle Athenians that applied themselves to nothing else but to hear or tell news. *(Plutarch)* It is surely a preposterous diet to use more sauce than meat which will then cloy the stomach rather than whet the appetite. It is no less preposterous to have the greater part of men's lives taken up with sport so that it becomes a method to keep them from that which they ought to do.

Rule 1: The rule therefore is that: games are to be used as a special refreshment not as an ordinary employment. (*Aristotle)* So just as medicine is for restoring the health in times of sickness, so recreation is for the refreshing of the spirits in times of weariness. As the saying which was applied when it seemed better to play than it was to study: "We must play but a little". Delights of this kind are compared well with the use of honey which should be taken up with the finger rather than with the whole hand. *(1 Sam 14:27)* We must not spend our life in sport. (*Fenton, 1611)*

§2. Only hazard what may be easily spared

As for the expense of gambling, great regard should be had so that we spend no more then is fit or that our estate can well afford upon our sports. In our lawful recreations we should not go beyond our ability. Therefore we should play without any stakes or wagers or at least not staking and wagering more than a man's estate allows one of his rank to spend on his lawful delights and without disabling himself from doing what God requires of him to do otherwise.

In this context such play is justly condemned by a reverend divine (*King, 1597)* if "the matter engaged in jeopardises a man's stock or his estate". Civil law also prohibits these games (among others), because so many men did not so much play at them as throw their wealth away, playing night and day for gold, silver, jewels and plate. Soldiers are to be found pawning their weapons and armour by this play. This is why the same law, although allowing some games, expressly forbade any man to hazard more than a shilling-a-game at them even though he might be of good ability. It should be a much lesser sum staked if he is poorer and the loser should not sustain notable losses. Our laws *(33 Hen 8)* also prohibit all but the richer and better sorts of persons to use these games or others like them. Games where much may be quickly lost are allowed but only at certain times. This aims to prevent the wretched practice of constant playing which would be continually crumbling away the wealth of those ordinarily using them. To do so is no better than plain stealth for any man. It takes from the poor whom he ought to be relieving, for by this method he disables himself from doing so and their necessity gives them a right to his wealth. It robs his family, which he ought to maintain and if he does not provide for them, shows himself a counterfeit Christian worse than a professed infidel. It robs himself, and as Solomon said *(Proverbs 28:24)*, "He that robbed father or mother and says it is no sin is first cousin to a murderer or a destroyer", so he who robs himself by wasting his own wealth on such gambling is little better then a murderer or a destroyer. And surely if a self-murderer cannot be discharged of sin, any more than he that murdered a mere stranger, so neither can he be acquitted if he robs himself. In one case a man deprives himself of life, in the other of the means whereby he can live and without which his life may be no better and may become many times more bitter than death.

Yet is it lamentable to consider how common is this kind of abuse both at these games and at others and among men of all sorts. Sometimes a great man may attend a race, a sitting, a match at bowls or an afternoon's cock-fight. He may gamble away what could have maintained many an honest man in good estate for a twelve-month or more. By this means the poor may remain unrelieved and the servants unrewarded. Their rents may be racked up to maintain the estates and the tenants are thereby impoverished. As with the Pharaoh's lean cattle *(Genesis 41:21)* when they had eaten up the fat ones, they were never a whit the richer or better able to do king or country service, for all that they had scraped and gathered together in that manner.

Even for the poorer sort on the other side, though they may complain of penury yet they will not be discouraged from play. Some will pretend poverty yet will make great efforts to get the wherewithal for a game. When they have spent all that they had in that way and hoping for some means to recover soon or suddenly again, but being inured to idleness in such thriftless haunts, many are forced to use methods which may bring loss of life as well as of living to them in the end.

But the question that is mooted amongst the learned is whether a man is permitted to play or wager anything at all. This question requires a larger discourse to discuss it thoroughly than this present work will well permit, which is already growing too great. Some utterly condemn it. I have lately seen a long discourse by *M.W.*[*] *(in Judg 14:12)* containing sundry arguments tending thereunto, of which I am not yet able to apprehend the force and validity, any more than those that *Balmford (1593)* has put into print. (Here I speak my mind freely and honestly and without exception to this author of whom I think reverently of otherwise, though I dissent in judgement from him on this point.) I can discern nothing which should make it unlawful for a couple of familiar friends to engage in a bit of gambling, where either may pay a trifle over to the other, just as either of them might lawfully spend the same on his own pleasure or that they might otherwise freely bestow on each other.

Others allow, as does the civil law, that in some cases something may be spent in common between them when men play together to decide who pays the charge for their supper. Yet men may go too far that way, feasting their friends to excess (a fault all too usual in these times). It was said of Nabal the Oaf that he made a feast like a king. *(1 Sam 25:36)* By feasting, a rich man may soon bring himself to poverty and a poor man to beggary: either may do the same, some have observed, by hazarding overmuch on play.

For my own part, I approve the judgement of the reverend *Babington (1583)* who decided this doubt as follows: "When little is played for so that it does not prevent a man from fulfilling the duty of his calling, or if the money being not much, is bestowed in some meeting for the maintenance of love, or if whatever is won is a reward agreed for the exercise, (bestowed by those that are in charge), then I think, with others, that it is not unlawful".

Rule 2: So the rule is: only hazard what may easily be spared or what a man may lawfully spend at present on his lawful delights. As we may not spend our life in sport so much less may we spend our life on sport. Nor should we spend our livelihood or the estates that our lives depend on as many do, on sport.

§3. Sports to be used sportingly

So far we have cautioned about keeping the measure or quantity of both time and expense within bounds. Now we give some consideration to the manner in which games should be used. Here there are many who offend when they are too eager upon play or are overmuch transported and carried away with delight in it. When, as *Fenner (1587)* well said, that "they either sleep on it or are drunk at it; that it has so occupied men's minds that it makes them unwatchful against the motions of sin, or the delight of it so overcomes them, or with other passions procured by

[*] I cannot discover who M W was.

it, that it makes them break forth into an outrage of swearing, blaspheming, fretting, cursing, quarrelling and such courses that would never happen if they were sober". A man can be drunk both with wine as without it. So too the dry smoke of tobacco may affect a man as well as the drink. As is well said of prosperity, "that it so transports some that they are drunk with it". Some sorts of mirth and music are also said to effect men similarly. So we might as well say that men are drunk with gambling when they are so addicted to it that it stirs up distempered passions in them, such that men who are soberly minded would condemn and abhor and which they themselves would equally dislike in themselves if they were besides themselves in that way at that moment.

So therefore, as it is well advised by *Bernard (~1120)* that "men never give themselves wholly to sleep", so we have even more good cause to be wary that we do not set our minds wholly upon play all the time as if sleep-walking at it, (a dangerous form of sleep), or allow our desires to be carried away with it, lest we become as dangerously drunk with it as are some with wine or strong drink. For our worldly cares it is good sometimes to turn to bodily pleasures, to games amongst others. Though not evil in themselves they may become spiritually prejudicial and dangerous unto us if our hearts are wholly possessed by them or we become over-eagerly and earnestly addicted to them.

This excess is particularly reprehensible because the business itself (if it may be so termed) is light, relating to recreation and ordinary delight only. But it is no less a condemnation for a man to be over-serious in trifling matters, than to be over-trifling in serious and weighty affairs. As *Plutarch* well observed, "those who are wont to be over-serious in the one are seldom as serious as they should in the other". They usually prove over-slight and light in matters of weight. and in toys and trifles they are over-serious.

Rule 3: The rule here is that sports are to be used sportingly. We should be equally content to win or to lose at them and be indifferent whether conquering or being conquered by them, whether going well or being crossed in them, as it shall fall out. Our desires should be no more fixed or fastened on them than the weight or worth of them may warrant.

§4. Only spend time in play that is free after serious and religious duties

Just as recreations should be used soberly so too should they be used seasonably. For there is a time and season for all things and for recreation too. "There is a time", said Solomon *(Eccles 3:4)*, "for laughing and mirth and a time for dancing and delight". There are times for recreation and sport and times for sad and serious affairs. Recreation is good when it is seasonable, when it comes at its due time; otherwise it is like the fish and fowl when they are served out of season, a thing that is evil which would be good at another time.

In this men offend not only when they take up too much time with it, but when they take it up at times not fitted for it. Just as a man may spend too much time at it, sinning by using it immoderately, again he may also spend a little time but not a fit time because he sins by using it unseasonably. Men may game and take recreation unseasonably when they ought to be otherwise employed, either in the works of their own special callings, or about the holy things of God.

Firstly, when they should care about the necessary duties that concern their estate and place or their means of their maintenance and the good of themselves and theirs. In condemning this it was said by *Virgil* of one that "he neglected his own business to attend others at play". It cannot be justified for a man to sit at cards and gaming tables indoors or be in the bowling alley outside when other affairs of great consequence require his presence elsewhere. The use and purpose of recreation is not to withdraw or withhold us from our more serious employments, but to make us fitter for them and better able to go through with them. As peace is the end of war and peace is aimed at in war, so business is the end of recreation, it being ordained for business and not business for it. Indeed as the right purpose of war is peace so the main purpose of peace is not so much the taking of our pleasure (though we enjoy the benefits of it) as the freedom it allows to follow our own serious affairs. The time therefore that ought to be employed in the one must not be unseasonably misspent in the other. Only our vacant time is allowed for sport. Then it is most seasonable, as is food when hunger craves it, or as is sleep when heaviness after watching called for it, so when weariness after other employments requires it.

Secondly when they should tend to the holy things of God either in public or private: It is a sin to follow games on the Sabbath as the Jews used to do and even to this day do so, both on their Sabbath and on solemn feasts. The Popish sort are also noted for solemnizing their festivals in this way. *(White, 1614)* This is not the way to sanctify or consecrate the Sabbath as holy to the Lord. The Sabbath indeed is a day of rest but of holy rest, not of worldly recreations but heavenly meditations, giving rest to pursue religious and spiritual employments. It is sacrilege to follow games on the Sabbath when we should be plying the service and worship of God. It is time stolen from God if we spend it on our sports. It might be less of a sin to spend some time on more serious affairs; according to *Augustine,* who says that "on the Sabbath it would be better for a man (in such manner) to plough rather than to play and to dig and delve than to dance all day". For the lighter the occasion of sinning is, all other things being equal, the greater the sin is.

It is also the case that those that waste time in this way on other days when they should be about their own private and personal devotions or in instructing their families in the performance of holy duties, are no more justified than the former. The one turns it to sin as well as the other in neglecting duty in order to follow their own pleasure, when God Himself has enjoined them *(Deut 6:7)* and will one day require it of them.

Rule 4: The rule here is that the only time that may be spent in play is time which we have free from other serious and religious affairs.

§5. Play for game not gain

Recreation must be used honestly, freely and liberally, but not with any greedy desire of lucre and gain. Recreation should never be a trade or course of life that a man uses to try to make a living out of or to live by. But it is not so much in the playing but in the spending that men waste themselves. Nor it is by the playing but by the preying on those we are seen to play with that causes their pillage and spoil. It alters the very nature of sports and pastimes if we make a trade or a traffic of them. This turns it from a playful to serious lot, or even a serious, sad and heavy lottery, as sometimes happens. An example given by *Travers (1574)* was of the man who hanged himself in Trinity College Hall when he had lost his money gambling the night before. It should be merely for recreation and delight. Whoever you are, you make yourself a sinner by taking from your brother that which he should not part with or that you should receive. You become a partner in sin when you allow him to misspend or hazard mis-spending that which he ought to employ otherwise. But can it ever be lawful then, some may say, for a man to receive any gain or live in any way by gambling? I answer: that in some cases it may and that may be either ordinarily or extraordinarily.

Ordinarily, people may be said to live lawfully by gambling when their trades or professions are employed wholly or in part in the making, providing, selling and issuing the instruments and other furniture that are commonly used in gaming. These could be bowyers, fletchers, turners, dice-carvers, card-makers and haberdashers of small wares. If the games themselves are lawful then these callings are not unlawful and men may be set to work to provide necessaries for the same *(Pepin, 1530)*, which could not otherwise be had so commonly or conveniently.

Extraordinarily, a man may sometimes receive gains through gambling. Suppose a man of good wealth is ill-at-ease and desires to recreate himself. He calls in a poor man from the trade or work he is employed at to accompany him in his game, because he cannot play on his own. It would not be unlawful for the poor man to so accompany the rich man, nor to receive some gain from him as a reward for his employment and in lieu of the loss he sustained by interrupting his own work. But when it is among equals who play together for mutual recreation and delight, for one of them to enrich or to desire to enrich himself by the others' damage and loss would be a sign of a base and an illiberal disposition and against the nature of sports, which ought to be free. *(Aristotle)*

Rule 5: The rule then is that play should be used as play, for pleasure but not for profit; for game but not for gain. *(Ambrose)* Just as no man should waste his precious time or threaten his estate by buying his recreation at so dear a rate that it leads to great expense or loss, nor should any man seek or desire to increase or advance his estate by making prey and spoil of those he plays with.

§6. Do not gamble if forbidden

Recreation should be used inoffensively and without causing offence. *(Fenner, 1587)* This applies in recreation as it does in all things. Eating and drinking is more or less a matter of necessity, but lighter things of less weight are a matter of mere delight only, so things may be otherwise. The offence that may be given by gambling is either general or special. It relates to public or private matters, or it is in regard of our superiors or our equals.

Public offence may be given if the laws of the state we live under have made the common use of such games unlawful. It may be true indeed *(Field, 1580)* that laws as such do not also bind one's conscience or alter the nature of things which are lawful or indifferent in themselves. Nevertheless, by breaching the law men may also become guilty of sin in God's sight. Where the laws restrain the use of things which are neither good or bad but do so for good and wholesome purposes, it is a contempt of the authority enacting them to break them. If the public utility aimed by them is hindered then any man may stand guilty of sin against God by breaching these laws severally or much more so if jointly.

The same can be said of those that live by such religions where the use of particular forms of games are held to be unlawful and banned. For peace and quietness sake everyone should conform in things indifferent to the church that he lives by. *(Augustine)* This applies to those that live under the ministry of pastors who are of contrary judgement on this point. It was the Apostle who said *(Hebr 13:14)* that Christian men "were required to yield unto them that have the oversight of them and of them that watch over them for their souls' safety". That is to say, that they must not only be ruled by them for all necessary dutics and others that they shall be able to convince them of by the evidence of God's word, but that they should also be over-ruled by them in matters of indifference, when they shall deem something to be unlawful that might well be forborne, even though the grounds of such judgement of theirs might be insufficient or their people may not be thoroughly convinced of the same.

Nor should children or servants take liberties in the use of such games. Their parents or masters under whose government they are should be prepared to restrain and to prohibit games in their houses when the laws of both God and man give them a power of command and when breaches may cause the guilt of sin in God's sight.

Rule 6: So the rule here is that men should be content to be restrained in matters of the ordinary use of games by the Church and State they live in, by the pastor they live under, or by the master they serve with.

§7. Do not cause offence when gambling

Just as offence may be given publicly or generally to those that we live under or among, so too may offence be given to those that we converse with in private. Because of this, these games should be forborne in some cases out of regard for our brethren. They may have scruples and doubts about gaming, being persuaded that in their judgement they are unlawful. Hence they may be either offended with us or at us. It is not a matter of indifference that something should be done without offence since we ought not give offence to anyone unnecessarily. We should seek to please others as well as ourselves, even if that means that now and then it might displease us. We do this for them just as Christ once did it for us. And therefore "It is not good", as the Apostle said *(Rom 14:11)*, "to eat flesh, drink wine or do anything to cause your brother to stumble, be offended, or be weakened". Doubtless if it is evil for a man to eat offensively then it is no less evil to play games which cause offence. Now we may offend two ways in this:

Firstly, by causing others to sin and so to offend with us, not because what we are partaking in is sinful, but because they believe it is a sin for them. As it is said: "He who holds that a thing is unclean, to him it is unclean" *(Rom 14:14),* so it is to one who delights in doing it or in dealing with it. So if you encourage someone to do like you then you lay a stumbling-block for him, who either by dimness of sight does not see it or by weakness of limb does not avoid it, so it is your fault that causes him to stumble and fall.

Secondly we may cause others, in good conscience, to be offended at us and to think evil of us by our courses. Because we are using that which they suppose to be sinful they must also suppose that we cannot but sin. Most men think that everyone else should see things as they do. So to give offence in a case of this kind is a wrong to ourselves. It causes others to think evil of us, although unjustly and undeservedly. It makes our commodity and Christian liberty to be spoken of as evil. It is a thing not to be lightly regarded what our brethren shall think of us or speak by us. "A good name", as the Holy Ghost said *(Ecle 3:1)*, "is better than a good ointment and a good report is desirable above riches and much treasure". Consider the old saying that "The efficacy of the agent consisted much in the disposition of the patient". As the worthy divine of ours *Hall (1606)* has well observed, "It is hard for a man ever to do good on others, unless he be reputed good himself". We need to take great care to keep our credit good with men as well as our conscience clear with God, to ensure that our name and fame remains unstained in regard of men, as our hearts and hands are untainted in regard of God. Otherwise, relying wholly upon the one we grow careless of the other, we might not only deal cruelly and uncharitably concerning our brethren, but also unwisely and inconsiderately concerning ourselves. It is a wrong therefore to allow yourself to be thought of as evil without cause. It is also wrong if we give our brother an occasion to offend by his misjudging you. It is a sin against charity, for it is a breach of charity to needlessly do what may vex a weak brother's mind. It is against peace and concord to give occasion of vain and needless disagreement. It is even against piety too, for "in offending your weak brother you sin against Christ". *(1 Cor 8:12)* By occasioning him to stumble and fall, in so far as you do, you destroy him that Christ died for. Therefore when you find that your liberty does or may in all likelihood offend, for your own sake and for that of your brother's and for the sake of his weaknesses too, for Christ thy Saviours sake, forbear! "Hold on to thy faith within thyself" *(1 Cor 8:7),* and keep your knowledge to yourself; and say with the Apostle *(1 Cor 8:13)*, "If cards or gaming tables offend my brother, I will never play at them while the world lasts, so that I may not offend him".

Rule 7: The rule here is, in a word, that it is not right to needlessly play in front of or with those that hold such games unlawful, or who are likely in that regard take offence from it.

§8. Only play if you can stay calm

So our recreations are to be used prudently and providently both for ourselves and to be inoffensive to others. It is a point of spiritual wisdom therefore that we forbear to use such games that either in whole or in part have been found to be occasions of sin to us. As they are inconvenient, so they are inexpedient when they may endanger us by sin. In part they are to be forborne, not because of the game itself, but of the way it is played (which can be changed by us) occasions the evil. Also to be condemned is that eagerness in the game that we spoke of before. Also, gambling for great sums is, not only in itself and the loss that it brings with it, but that it may cause further grievous abuses and enormities that men may break forth into. Men may well say that whether they win or lose, it is all the one for them. But as Bishop *King (1597)* (a prelate yet living, whose words I often willingly use in this argument) has well said, "That in such profusion of substance as the loss cannot but pinch, so men's passions cannot but be moved and a troop of wretched sins commonly ensued: swearing, forswearing, cursing, ranting, defying, heart-burning, quarrelling, fighting, spilling of blood, unsupportable sorrows of heart, cursed despair, self-executions. Weeds are able to blemish and disgrace the most lawful recreation that is, wherever it may be found, just as in *Virgil* the Harpies defiled the cleanest meats"

Because of this, sometimes such games must be wholly avoided. When a man finds that by his own disposition he cannot ordinarily use them at all without much distemper and that he cannot contain himself when the cards or dice go against him, so that he is ready to break out into profane and bad language. Or when he cannot endure to be beaten at play without wrath, vexation and disquiet of mind. Or even though he can sometimes and with some effort suppress his unruly passions and perturbations in this kind, yet that ordinarily and usually he is overtaken on these occasions and therefore in danger of being ensnared and entangled. In all these cases it is best for a man to take the safer side and as Job made a covenant with his eyes *(Job 30:1),* so he should make a covenant with his hands not to handle cards or dice, which the rule of inexpediency here strikes out of his hands. Indeed, taking the previous Rule into account, a man should only join in play with those whom he knows to be no less evil than he and that they will use it as he does.

Rule 8: The rule then here is that we do not use these games unless we can rest quiet and content with the outcomes in them. If so, then we can use them, knowing that we will not be tempted into disquiet and discontent by them. The golden rules of our gracious Sovereign King *James I (1603)*, which he laid down for his son are: "First, before you play, consider that you do it only for your recreation and resolve to hazard no more than you can lose in all that you play. Next, play no more then you would care to cast among the pageboys. Otherwise, if you cannot keep to these rules, my counsel is that you utterly abstain from all these plays, because neither a mad passion for loss, nor a falsehood used for the desire of gain can in all truth be called play".

§9. Play reverently, but without calling on the Almighty

These recreations are to be used reverently and religiously with regard for God's majesty and His presence and providence in so far as the nature of the business exacts or admits. Christian men should do all things whatsoever for the glory of God and in the name of Christ Jesus as a thanksgiving unto God. All their actions are to be sanctified by word and prayer.

This caveat excludes two extremes: Profanity and Presumptuousness. As for profanities, we should not behave in play either profanely and in an ungodly way. As we play we should not we shut the door on God, nor should we make the Devil our play-fellow. *(Marbury, 1602)* Remember that we play just as we pray in God's presence and that the providence of God watches over us there while we play, just as while we are asleep. By His goodness we also have the freedom and liberty for our sports, pleasures and lawful delights, as well as for our wiser and more serious affairs. It is as well therefore to acknowledge God's mercy and goodness and His gracious providence when we enjoy freedom and liberty for gaming and that we do not dishonour Him from whom we have the free use of them.

Presumptuousness should also be excluded from games. Insofar as we take notice of God's providence in general, we must be careful when we attempt to draw down or call on His immediate providence or special presence during play to regulate the contest between us and those we play with. "We should not be so gross" (to use again the words of that worthy prelate Bishop *King, 1597*) "on the one side as to try to make Fortune our goddess, assigning good or evil luck unto her. On the other side we should not be so saucy as to call down God's majesty from heaven to guide our games, to further our play or to determine our doubts. Do not look on high in such frivolous and gamesome quarrels, but as we carelessly undertake them, so we follow them lightly and end them merrily". And therefore to say, as some do, in play "God send me such a card, or such a chance of the dice", or, "I pray God I may win this or that game", is saucy and malapert behaviour for any.

But may not a man, as some will say, lawfully desire to do so during a game? or may not a man lawfully pray for whatsoever he may wish or desire? or are not "all our actions to be sanctified by prayer" *(1 Tim 4:4)* as was formerly said?

I answer: it is true that every action of a Christian man could be sanctified by prayer either general or special, but this does not cover every action for every sort and manner of petition or prayer. A man may pray that in his recreations that he will carry himself soberly and without offence and that by playing he may even be better fitted for better things. Such a prayer would be sufficient to sanctify the games either in general or in particular, as he finds and feels his heart to be affected and as the occasion and circumstances admit or require it. In gambling this ought to be a man's general desire and he may lawfully pray to impart this to God if he pleases.

But there may be a more particular desire that a man may have in a game, such as: to win rather then to lose; to overcome rather then to be conquered. Such desires are not evil if they are moderate, but would be idle and frivolous, dangerous even when they grow excessive and immoderate, not fitting for the nature of the thing they concern. Yet it may not be unseemly to acquaint God about them. To better understand this consider this: that every desire does not by-and-by become a prayer, ("to desire is not to pray, but shows what we approve") although every prayer should ordinarily include some desire. Nor is every lawful desire a fit matter for prayer, for prayer is a wish or desire of the heart directed unto God. But there are many things that we desire and may lawfully desire which are not matters of moment that would be fit to acquaint God in particular with or to direct our petitions in special manner to Him for them. Much less would we expect or require God's hand to show any special work or help of His to effect them. These are the kind of desires which might be said in a game, such as "I pray God I may win", or, "I would to God I might have such a card or such a cast", is much too much presumptuousness and does not stand well with that reverent respect that each one of us owes to God's majesty.

Rule 9: The rule then is that just as we do not exclude God's presence in play, nor do we call on His providence to further our play. It is one thing to play before the prince and in his presence, another thing to call him in "to stickle [adjudicate] between us" *(Estey, ~1603)* over some question about measuring a cast. So it is one thing to play as if before God and in his presence, it is another thing to make God our play-fellow or to call him in to help and further our game. That is something no Christian man may do.

§10. Gambling with these cautions, or a complete ban?

These are the cautions that I have thought good to propose to limit and rectify the use of these games; cautions, which I confess are mostly about games in general, (in which equally well with more serious and sad matters, both civil and sacred, account must also be rendered unto God). So they are not directed properly or peculiarly towards gambling in particular. Yet I do not think it is amiss of me to point out these cautions nor to press the case for them. I do so partly so that I might not be taxed and censured as a pleader for sin or other such abuses that are common both in these games as in other pursuits. It is by these means that those who condemn all lotteries used in games are wont to take the opportunity to make them seem more odious in general. It is also so that any profane person who abuses these or any other games might be prevented from taking any hint of an advantage from anything I have said about the lawfulness of the games of themselves and in themselves, simply considered, to justify his own abuse of them in mis-spending his time, wasting his estate at them or otherwise inconsiderately and irreligiously abusing them. That may be what some would have done had I been silent on this part and proposed only such cautions as the nature of the lottery itself might seem to require.

Yes but, some will say, would it not have been much better to have passed over all this with silence, knowing your judgement in this point to be different from many other very reverends and religious? Or is it not in this case, as *Tertullian* said of Images, "it is an easier matter wholly to take away the use of them, than to keep them free from abuse"?

Here is my answer: first, these abuses are common to all kinds of games. They accompany all other games as well as those that the evil-minded and profane engage in. Therefore whatever may be said of all other games may also be said of any particular game, at least in its ordinary use.

Secondly, it is true that where the uses and abuses of a thing are so enwrapped and entangled together that they cannot easily be separated one from the other, then the use of the thing itself, if otherwise unnecessary, should be completely abandoned. But in these games the use and the abuse may for the most part be separated (some special dispositions only excepted) by those that desire to walk in the fear of God. Those with no conscience will not be dissuaded from them anyway, whatever is evidently discovered about their manner of abusing them. It is the abuse of them that makes it evil and unlawful to themselves, which otherwise it would not be of itself. For those that fear God, they may easily rectify and sanctify their gambling to themselves as they may with any other games they use and they can just as easily sever the abuses that are commonly committed in them from its use, just as they can in other sports and pastimes, such as draughts, bowls and the like that are both commonly used and generally allowed.

Thirdly, though many of the godly dissent from my views, yet I am sure that many, and I suppose more than many, of the reverends and religious agree with me. And if the truth was known, especially concerning matters in common practice, it is right that men may have the wherewithal to inform themselves aright.

And lastly, though the minds and judgements of others may be unknown, I am not concealing any truths. Because a few of the godly have denied or opposed it and none publicly by writing have contradicted them in it, then I consider it to be especially needful that the opposite point of view be known.

§11. Why I entered the fray on this question

For my own part, I entered into this discourse on the use of lottery by the general pursuit of that part Scripture that dealt with them *(Jon 1)*, although it was then far from any purpose of mine to publish anything about this argument. I was first induced to deliver my judgement on this point largely upon the following considerations:

First I considered that it is faulty to try to either straighten or widen God's way and that there is a subtlety of Satan as well in both. For straightening is like when a conjurer puts a pair of false spectacles on a man's nose which makes a bridge or viaduct seem broader than it indeed is, so that if the man was to cross over it, he might step to one side and not fear falling in. (This is how they who are at fault deal with the dissolute.) In the case of widening, this is like a magician showing a man the bridge that he is to pass over and using a false glasses of another kind which makes it appear to be as narrow as the edge of a rapier or the point of a needle. It would terrify him from attempting to go over it. (This is how they deal with those who are over-timorous and full of scruples.) It is not good to fill men's minds with unnecessary scruples, discouraging them when they might come to love and like the good ways of God. Nor is it right for those who have already come to God to throw them onto snares of men's making *(Cicero),* tying them into stricter and straighter bonds then God Himself had done and making more things unlawful than God's word makes. In truth this is no better than a spice and a branch of superstition, to make men suspect that these things displease God which indeed they do not, just as it would be if men were to imagine that a creature could do something which indeed it cannot do.

Secondly, I am verily persuaded that there are many who truly fear God and are sincerely religious but yet have used and are commonly using these games. I also consider that there are many who are and have been constrained by scruples about gambling to strain themselves to the point of inconvenience by refusing to play when invited occasionally to do so by those on whom they depend or have familiarity with. It seemed right and proper to let it be known what grounds or warrant one has or might have for the use of theses games. Due and diligent discussion over a long period of time has undoubtedly persuaded me that I am sound and firm in my views. Were this not so, then far should it have been from me to have ever opened my mouth in this argument.

Thirdly, I consider that the arguments and grounds which are used to condemn these games have made many wary about using a lottery to resolve serious and necessary civil matters, a thing which they are often forced to use when bargains are bought in common between them and others. They may have doubted whether it was lawful to consent to the use of lotteries. That was indeed the first occasion which required me to narrowly search and sift out the nature of lotteries in general. It is certainly the case that if we admit the principal arguments against this kind of use of lotteries then we utterly overthrow the use of any kinds of lottery whatsoever.

Fourthly, I considered the great offence and scandal that is taken by many of contrary judgement to mine against those that use these games. These views, though, were never put as soberly and seasonably as they suppose, or on good grounds. They often caused much heart-burning and of breach of Christian affection, even the peremptory, uncharitable and unchristian censuring of one on the other. Our own corruption and our natural disposition to a diversity of judgments, commonly breeds alienation of affections, especially when manifested in practice, although indeed it should not do so. As *Yates (1622)* puts it: "Why should any be angry with me that I am not altogether of his opinion, feeling I am not angry with him, because he is not of mine?" Considering therefore that these games can hardly be wholly eradicated because they are so common, general and usual with most people everywhere, I supposed it would not be unfit to investigate further. If I discovered the truth of the case for or against them, then scandal and offence might be prevented and Christian concord and amity could in part be procured and maintained between those who were previously of diverse minds in this matter. This might apply to any of those who at least might hear and apprehend the force and weight of the arguments and be brought to see the invalidity and insufficiency of their own grounds against these lotteries. It has been my endeavour to do this. Let the judicious and impartial be my judges.

To draw to a conclusion, I could wish in this case, as the Apostle *(Act 26:29)* did in another, that everyone who was affected in this point thought in the same way as myself; that their judgement be rightly informed of the truth concerning the lawfulness of these games in themselves. Nevertheless (and without prejudice to those who use these games as they ought to) I would hope that in godly discretion they would abandon gambling and give it up because of the all too common and ordinary abuses and that many people could then remain unresolved and unsatisfied concerning the lawfulness of gambling.

But this is more a matter of wish than of hope, so my second argument shall be like that which the Apostle makes in a similar case: *(Rom 14:10)* "Let not him that played condemn him that played not; nor let him that played not condemn him that played. For, I may as well say to the one: why do you condemn your brother? as I say it to the other". Why do you condemn your brother for being too strict and strait-laced because of scruple and doubt, so will not engage in something which is unnecessary anyway? And why on the other side do you condemn your brother as too dissolute and loose, for doing something which he has sufficient ground and warrant for from God's word? And to both sides I would say: (and would to God that I might prevail with both sides, not just on this one alone but in all other controversies which are afoot among us at this present) "Let us follow those things that may further peace", *(Rom 14:19)* and "Seek after the truth between us in love". *(Augustine)* "Be ready to yield with Apollo to anyone" *(Jerome),* however humble, that is otherwise minded, so we shall be more able to thoroughly instruct ourselves in anything that we were not so fully informed of before.

Chapter 10

Extraordinary divinatory lotteries

§1. Divinatory or consultative lotteries

So far we have considered the sort of lottery which we termed 'ordinary'. These were of two types, either serious for division of goods and offices, or lotteries which were used for gambling. Their use only requires the ordinary power that is used to put them into effect for the purposes for which they are employed. We have shown them to be lawful when lawfully used. We now consider another sort of lottery which we term 'extraordinary' and is commonly called a divinatory lottery by most divines. *(Peucer, 1572; Krackewitz, ~1610)*. Extraordinary lotteries are such that they require an extraordinary power and providence in their disposal or direction, or in regard of the things to which they are applied.

It is not within the power of those that use them or in the nature of these lotteries themselves on their own to produce the effect for which they are employed. This is the main difference between this kind of lottery and the former ones. It is a difference which is not sufficiently considered and has bred much confusion and occasioned a diversity of opinions amongst authors in this argument. In the previous lotteries all that was necessary lay within the natural power of those using them. By using them they could effect a result, it being natural for it to fall this or that way. Together and by mutual consent they could determine matters that were in the power of the users. But in these latter lotteries, which we are about to consider, it is not at all in the natural power either of the persons using them or of the things used in them to produce the effect that they are necessarily used for. There is some other secret work, either divine or diabolical, that of necessity is required for this. These lotteries are most commonly termed 'divinatory'. Under this heading we may well include some of those that are called 'consultative' lotteries, *(Aquinas, 1270)* which are used for divination and consultation by way of divination. Ordinary lotteries are merely for dividing or deciding and are merely civil; divining lotteries are either sacrilegious or sacred.

These extraordinary divinatory lotteries are used for two purposes: either for the discovery of some hidden matter in the past or present; or for the presaging or foretelling of some future event. For either sort we have examples both great and good in holy writ and from profane writers, as well as the daily practice by many among us here as elsewhere.

In holy writ we find that lotteries have sometimes been used to discover some hidden truth about things present or past, and have also been used in matters of distribution of offices and of retribution in justice. They have been used to discover and make known whom God deemed to be fittest, or who He had secretly assigned for some place or estate. And this is the difference between lotteries used ordinarily for the selection of officers and disposition of offices and the use of lottery in the cases that now we treat: in the former it is in the power of the parties doing the choosing to choose who they list and like best, so they may agree to make their selection at random by lot; there is nothing else required of the lottery but to light upon any one of those that are proposed by them. In the latter form of lottery it is not wholly within their power. Either they require the further consent of others whose good-will they are uncertain of, and they seek to know what it is by means of a lot: or the choice is to be made by God's special appointment, whose secret will and purpose they desire to discover by this means. *(Aquinas, 1270)* Examples in Scripture of lotteries used in this manner include matters of marriage, of the magistracy and of the distribution of offices, both civil and sacred.

§2. Choosing a marriage partner (Bible)

For Eliezer, the man-servant of the elderly Abraham, arranging a marriage was something in the nature of a lottery. *(Genesis 24:12)* He had been sent to fetch a wife for his young master Isaac. Standing by a well-side, he desired to know from God which of the maidens that came there to draw water he should request to drink from her pitcher and would also offer to water his camels. In this way he would know that she was the party that God had appointed to be his Master's son's wife. This then happened, with one of them accordingly, and he used it as an argument to persuade her parents that God had so appointed it. They too were persuaded thereby to likewise rest thereupon and agree thereunto. A different story is told by *Josephus:* his idle conceit is that Eliezer in fact prayed that Rebecca, who his master and he had already chosen, would be approved by God as their choice. So when those wenches came to draw water, he might know which one of them she was, since many were coming at the same time. She gave him a drink when all the rest would have denied it to him. Accordingly when all but she refused to let him drink, excusing themselves that they drew it for other necessary uses and that it was not easy to draw, Rebecca thereupon rebuked the rest of them for their un-courteous demeanour and herself offer kindly to fulfil his request. But these are but mere surmises and fancies having no ground in or agreement with the story, as others *(Lyra, ~1300; Peter Martyr, ~1560)* have also well observed.

There are also some of the ancients *(Augustine; Lyra, ~1300)* who distinguish this from the usual manner of divination. But they spend much pains to small purpose, for it is apparent that this was used as a divinatory sign for the manifestation of God's mind concerning His hidden purpose and pleasure. This is like making a lottery about the result or success of a journey and the business for which it was undertaken. It is no more warrantable than those courses that they compare with it. Nor is it what some others *(Zwingli, ~1523)* have concocted from this example: his meaning and purpose may have been to pray to God that one of the maidens among them that came to draw water should, by her behaviour in that particular, show herself to be of a free, courteous and honest disposition and so might well be the wife that God had appointed for his young master, Isaac. And so it would not have been a lottery nor a sign of God's design, but rather shows that the maid's inward disposition was right for such a match. Now there are great odds indeed between these two. On the one hand to pray that the party by such an answer shall show herself to be thus disposed and could be a wife to such a one; on the other to pray that that party that God in his providence had appointed to be one's wife may be certainly known and distinguished from all others by such a random sign. I have heard of someone who, having cast his wandering desire on that kind on a woman, would try to pass it off as a sign to himself: that if at church, he asked to see her book so that she could point him to the preacher's text, then she would be the woman that God had assigned to be his wife. In the former there is no lottery or divination at all, to speak properly. This is but a human and moral conjecture by the outward behaviour of an inward disposition, with the desire of matching with such a one and to try to see if God would also make it good. In the other there is a sign which comes from the nature of lotteries. They try to discover what lies hidden in God's secret counsel. Such a course has of itself no kind of natural congruity with the thing to be discovered. Eliezer's act is of this latter kind rather than the former and would not be justifiable unless it was done by some special instinct known only to the conceiver of such prayer for the use of such a sign in that way.

§3. Magistrates and government (Bible)

Again, as the lottery has been used in matters of marriage, so has it been used in matters of magistracy and government for the distribution of offices both civil and sacred.

Firstly civil: Saul was chosen by lottery to be king. This was not just a divisory lot used only to determine who should govern God's people but more a divinatory one used to discover whom God had secretly appointed and set apart for that place as then fittest for the same. The business was thus carried, with Samuel *(1 Sam 10:17)* having the chief hand in ordering it, first by causing the people to be sorted into their several tribes to appear before the Lord (that is before the Ark of God and the High-priest, say some) at Mizpeh, each by the chief heads of their houses. Then, upon prayer conceived and lottery drawn or cast, the tribe of Benjamin was taken. And of that tribe, appearing in the heads of her houses by a second lottery was the house of Matri chosen; and the several persons of that family being put all into a third lottery, it was Saul the son of Kish who was taken and thereby manifested to be the man whom God had made choice of to be the ruler of his people. All this He had signified secretly beforehand to Samuel and Samuel had likewise afterward imparted it to Saul and so he had solemnly, though privily and privately, by a visible sign with sacred oil sanctified and set him apart to that office. Afterwards he did the same for David too, on a similar occasion and case.

Secondly, sacred offices of employment have also been disposed of by lot. This was how Matthias was set apart to succeed Judas as Apostle in his place. They (that is the whole assembly) presented two men, said the text *(Act 1:23)* and with a solemn prayer first conceived, so that God, who knows all men's hearts, would vouchsafe to show which of the two He had appointed to that place. So they gave out their lotteries. And the lottery lighted on Matthias, who was by common consent thereupon reckoned one of the Twelve.

This is a course of action reported by some, (if their words be not mistaken) and assented to by others, to have been used for some time afterwards by the Apostles in similar cases for the re-supply of the ministry. But this is unlikely because the holy story of those times reports that things were rather otherwise. There is another conceit that some of the ancients *(Aquinas, 1270)* have, that the Apostles should have used the lottery for the choice of Matthias, but for the want of God's spirit which they lacked, not having yet been baptised until afterwards at the Pentecost. (The former report of it crossed a recording of a later use of it, so one falsehood often commonly breaks the neck of another). Others *(Theophilus)* have said that they did not use any lottery at all, instead asking for some visible sign from God, a streak of light or some such to make known His own choice. All are without ground of Scripture and the other against the express terms in the text.

Nor are they *(Walther, 1550)* of sound judgement that propose that this is a precedent to be ordinarily imitated, any more than is it their judgement to exclude all lotteries from ecclesiastical elections. This example was extraordinary, done no doubt by special instinct and direction of God's spirit, and the lottery itself was not merely divisory, but manifestly divinatory, discovering God's secret counsel and choice in that business, as by the prayer conceived before it plainly appeared. And thus divinatory lotteries have been used in the distribution of offices.

§4. Justice and retribution (Bible)

Lotteries have likewise found further use in the matter of retribution and justice, in deciding questions of the offence committed. That happened when it was altogether uncertain whether an offence had been committed or not. Or it might have been when it is certain in general that some offence had been committed but it is not known in particular either who is the offender or what exactly the offence is. Or lastly where it is known in particular what the offence is, but the offender is not known. The lottery has sometimes been used in these cases to discover whether there was any offence done or not; sometimes to decide who were the offenders, sometimes what the offence was and sometimes who were the offenders in an offence which was known to have been committed before.

Sometimes a lottery has been used where it was wholly uncertain whether any offence had been committed or not, where the offence, offenders and party offended have been altogether uncertain. Once when there was a plague upon the Philistines *(1 Sam 6:7)*, but they did not know from whence or for what it came, they were advised by their wizards to send away the Ark of the God of Israel, which had been captured in fighting by them. They took it in a cart drawn by two new-milch cattle that had calves. If the cattle were to draw it towards Beth-shemesh, they would thereby know that it was the God of Israel that had plagued them; if any other way that it was nothing but some chance that befell them. This course was accordingly put to trial and the cattle drew the cart directly to Beth-shemesh. They thereby discovered both their offence and the party offended with them, the author of the evil that had lately befallen them.

I dare not say (as some might) that this practice of theirs was undertaken by them from divine instinct rather than any such instinct that they themselves were aware of, for both these must concur to make such an act as that warrantable. It seems rather to have arisen from the magical superstitions which were their wont, yet no doubt it was accompanied with a special providence of God, as the same authors and others have well observed, thereby convincing themselves that it was by their own evidences and so gaining glory to Himself by their wicked courses.

§5. Spot the delinquent (Bible)

Again lotteries have been used where the offence in general has been certain but particulars about it are uncertain. So once found, the offender on being apprehended might by his confession also bring the offence to light.

Jonathan was discovered in a wood by his father Saul. *(1 Sam 14:24)* He had tasted the honey that they found in the wood. Then his father Saul had cursed all that had eaten anything at all, because he would not have his people held back for any reason from the pursuit of the adversary that they had been chasing. Then Saul began to ask advice from God whether he should follow the adversaries by night or not; God gave him no answer. He concluded that God had been offended, but he knew not how or by whom. To find it out, he cast a lottery between himself and his own family on one side and the people on the other side. He entreated God to give a right or a perfect lot, (though some *(1 Reg 21:10)* expound his words otherwise) and the result was that he and his were the first taken, with the people being passed over. On the second casting between himself and his son, the lottery lighted on his son Jonathan who thereupon confessed to his offence in tasting the honey with the tip of his staff, against his father's order on that score, something which at the time was unknown to him. This is a lottery which, although it was used without warrant (as the prayer was made without faith) yet was guided by God in a special manner to deservedly punish Saul for his ill-advised act and to show what snares men may enwrap themselves in, as did Jephta by inconsiderate vows, so in Saul by idle, rash and unnecessary oaths.

Jonah *(Jon 1:7)* was also discovered in this way. The ship was suddenly in strange danger and distress, so they presumed that it was God's hand upon them for something which was amiss with them. But for what or whose sin they were not able to guess, until a lottery was cast by them, with the lot lighting upon Jonah. He was the offender and the offence he had committed was in flying from God when he should have gone another way on his errand. He thereupon confessed and both were by that means discovered.

A learned linguist *(Arias Montanus, 1593)* has gathered a number of changes in the words of that story: "They gave out their lotteries; and the lot lighted on Jonah", is taken to mean that they should cast a lottery often, over and over to be more fully assured of the certainty of the thing and that upon every casting the lot would still light on the same party. This is not unlike the instance where rabbi *Solomon (~1090)* gathered from a later change in gender in the same story, that Jonah should be in the bowels or belly of two different whales, a male and a female, one after the other. But this is idle and senseless and a groundless conceit. Genders in that language are often indifferent and indefinite. So there might as well have been three whales as well as two picked out of the text, their gender being also once again afterwards changed. So the change of numbers, passing from the plural to the singular, or sometimes from the singular to the plural is nothing unusual for the penmen of holy writ, as with other profane writers and those of the best note. This help is not needed here anyway, because there is an article of some emphasis in the original: "They cast their lots", which may have been many, as was usual. And 'the lot', or 'that lot' was assigned to show who was the delinquent. "That lot lighted upon Jonah", who being thereby discovered, showed them what had been done by him.

This recourse to a lottery was undertaken by them, not because of any general light of natural grounds, as some great ones without good ground have declared, (for then men could imitate them now in similar cases, as some *(Torreblanca, 1618)* have also concluded), nor was it done by any special divine inspiration, as some others with as little likelihood have taught. Rather it was done in the common manner of their own heathenish superstitions, observed (as is likely) by them then also in the use of it. It was therefore not lawful or warrantable, as some have said, but a wicked and unwarrantable course by them. There are some *(Lavater, 1586)* who warrant that they were all bad men and all their other acts were evil. *(Hagg 2:13)* So the lottery took effect and fell out as it did, not, as some have imagined, by force of the lottery used or through the faith of those who used it, nor by any ordinary course that God had tied Himself unto, nor in regard of any prayer conceived by Jonah as a prophet, (unlikely, considering his state at that instant, in God's displeasure and guilty to himself that he was the man aimed at) but because it pleased God extraordinarily. By making good use of their wickedness He secretly guided them and disposed the outcome of that action, not by regarding them or any act of theirs, but only to effect and work His own purposes, so that his fugitive servant might be reclaimed by that means and brought back to His obedience and His power and providence be proclaimed among those that were altogether ignorant of either before.

And thus have divinatory lotteries been used where both the offence and the offender have been equally unknown. It has also been used where the offence has been known, but not the offender; or where the offence has been known for certain in general and discovered in particular exactly what it is, but the delinquent party remained as yet undiscovered.

Thus there was a lottery used for the discovery of Achan. *(Josh 7:11)* God had told Joshua that an offence had been committed, the offence being the retaining some part of the accursed spoils of Jericho which ought wholly to have been destroyed. Because of this, the wrath of God was kindled against the whole army. But the offender remained unrevealed and undiscovered. By God's special appointment, a lottery was used, (as *Gersonides (~1320)* agrees; however some idle rabbis dream of other means of discovery) and Achan was thereby made known as the delinquent party. For this result the lottery had been cast for the tribes first, with the Tribe of Judah being taken. Casting again for the families of that Tribe, Zerah's family was taken and cast lastly again for the houses and persons of that family or kindred, Zabdi's house and in it Achan was at length caught and discovered. He thereupon confessed his fault.

§6. Divinatory lotteries in later Christendom

These were all examples of extraordinary, divinatory lotteries. There are those that define a divinatory lottery to be only that by which men enquire into future events, as the great Schoolman *Aquinas (1270)* did, with most following in his tracks. *(Lyra, ~1300, Perkins, 1608)* But they come far short of the true extent of this form of lot, because it includes sundry other kinds as well. It includes any lottery which attempts to discover any hidden truth by a chance or random event, which no power of human wit or skill on its own can directly reach, being simply able to discover it by such means.

This is the procedure which seems to be alluded to in the tale of Joseph and his steward (as some of the soundest *(Abraham, ~1140)* take it). It was said of a cup that was pretended to have been stolen either by Benjamin or one of his brothers, that "Is not this the cup that my Lord drinks in; and whereby he divined, or conjectured what you are?" *(Gen 44:5)* And another afterwards said to them, that "Know ye not that such a one as I am can certainly divine?" or, "take some course as certainly to discover your thievery, as if either I dealt with diviners or were such a one myself? This has been a usual practice with sundry nations, seeking by such means to try to discover persons suspected or guilty of some crime".

We pass by the Russians' manner of deciding controversies by lottery in lawsuits. *(Hackluyt, 1560)*(of which we spoke before). The ancient Frieslanders [in the north of the Netherlands] were accustomed to try those suspected of or charged with manslaughter in the same manner, having first offered to purge themselves by oath. *(Delrio, 1618)* The French in olden times were wont to use a similar trial with persons apprehended on suspicion of theft, where there were some grounds of presumption but pregnant proofs had failed. *(Chlothar)*

It is said that Marcian, a Nestorian [heretical ~430 AD] abbot asked for a lottery to be cast, *(Baronius)* following the example of the Apostles. This was to decide between his heretical monks and the orthodox bishops to establish which of them were telling the truth. Once cast, said the story, it went with the bishops, whereupon he and most of his monks recanted. And so lastly in our English writers Roger of *Howden (1178)* we read that one Peter of Toulouse was on trial being accused of heresy and had denied it on oath. A bystander peradventure suddenly opened the Book that he had sworn upon, wherein the first words he lighted on were those of the Devil to our Saviour, "What have we to do with thee, thou Son of God, Jesus?"*(Mark 1:14)* That, said the man who reported it, sorted well with such a heretic who indeed had nothing to do with Christ. We shall enquire further into this type of book-lottery again in §10 in this chapter.

As for the divinatory lottery itself, it is all too common among us even to this day to use a lottery to make enquiry after thieves, *(Delrio, 1618)* and for things stolen or lost. Some use a hollow key and a book, some an axe and a helve, some a sieve* and a pair of shears or other toys and some repeating part of a Psalm, others abusing the name of some saints. The reverend prelate Bishop *King (1597)* has well said of this practice, "that it is the Devil whom such persons use to gratify themselves by their sorcery and who also produced scripture and saints' names to as they do to no good purpose; that they have sifted them to the bran and scarce left a grain of good Christianity in them". Both Canon and Civil laws condemn it.

§7. Turning ordinary into extraordinary lotteries: Whether to do it.

Extraordinary lotteries have also been used for the discovery of some hidden matter from the past or present and for presaging or foretelling future events, and thereby directing men as to what course they should take in their affairs or what success they might expect in them. Just as the previous extraordinary lotteries were partly divisory and partly divinatory, so these ones are partly consultative and partly divinatory, being used partly for consultation and partly for divination, or for consultation by way of divination. *(Aquinas, 1270)* Using a lottery simply to divide out something makes it ordinary and such a lottery is merely divisory. But to divide or share out anything by lot and expecting to have the division by lottery made exactly and precisely according to the rights of those amongst whom the thing is divided, or according to the truth of something that has been thereby enquired into by that lot would make that an extraordinary lottery and turns it into divination. Again, if offices are simply distributed by a lottery which simply decides who shall have this or that place, or who should be admitted and who excluded, that is an ordinary divisory lottery only. But to expect that God should

* The sieve, an everyday kitchen implement, has been long known as a witch's device, with a mention in *Macbeth.* It used to convict at the Salem trials of 1692. Using the sieve for magical purposes is known as 'coscinomancy'.

thereby reveal whom He deemed fit or unfit, or whom He had fore-assigned to any office makes it an extraordinary and divinatory lot. So the situation here is that if we determine by lottery which of two equally and indifferently proposed courses a man should take, it is an ordinary lot and such a lottery is merely divisory. If it is a consultative lot, then it is improperly termed as such. To try to enquire or determine what would be the best course to take, or which was likeliest to prove the luckiest or the most successful makes it extraordinary and makes such a lottery properly termed divinatory and consultative. The attempt to turn an ordinary into an extraordinary lottery can be found when a thing itself is questioned, or where the business of it is to be resolved but the circumstances of time, place and person are still undetermined.

An example of this attempt, where the thing itself was not fully resolved comes from the tale of Jonathan and his armour-bearer. They had agreed to show themselves to a garrison of the Philistines. (*1 Sam 14:6)* If they were discovered and the Philistines asked them to stay with them, they would then not proceed with their attack. But if they were challenged they would attack straight away, taking it as a sign that God would give them victory. They then put this plan into action. The Philistines invited them to come up unto them, they clambered up the rock on their hands and their feet to them and God so discomfited the Philistines that they fled and they slew twenty of them within an acre of ground. But it was not a conjecturing of the minds or the courage of their adversaries that gave them their answer, as some of the rabbis *(Gersonides, ~1320)* have supposed, but a sign that Jonathan had set for himself, much like that of Eliezer, Abraham's manservant before mentioned, whereby he minded to discover whether God would be pleased to further his plans and give success to them in that enterprise or not. This is like the manner that many superstitious Jews (as reported by their own writers *Solomon, ~1090*), have usually resolved whether they should go or stay on some journey. They take a staff in their hand and measure it inch after inch, or span by span, saying on the one while "I will go" and then "I will not go" and so resolving the matter down to the last inch of their staff. (*Godwin, 1616)* This is the kind of divination that was intended when Hosea said "My people ask counsel of their stock and their staff teaches them" *(Hosh 4:13)* though others explain it otherwise.

§8. Turning ordinary into extraordinary lotteries: How to do it

Lotteries have also been used once the business itself has been resolved but the circumstances of time, place, or persons are as yet undetermined. Sometimes they are used where deciding which of two or more persons be dealt with first. Which of them is then the question to be decided by lot.

It is said of Nebuchadnezzar, King of Babel, that he stood at the head of a crossway where two turnings were, one leading toward Judah and Jerusalem, the other toward Ammon and Rabba (the head city). At that place he consulted with his divines, that is, his soothsayers or sorcerers. Among the methods used, as well as inspection of the liver and entrails of beasts sacrificed (a practice much used among heathens) to conjecture what success he might have, he would also draw a lottery to try which way would be best for him to take and whether to bend his forces in the first place against Ammon or against Judah, against Jerusalem or against Rabba. And the lottery in his right hand came forth for Jerusalem, God in His secret providence so disposing it, as was foretold by the prophet, for the deserved destruction of his own rebellious people. *(Ezek 21:19)*

Now this divination of theirs was performed and practised, some think, by mingling of arrows with several inscriptions. *(Jerome)* First they were secretly shuffled and afterwards openly drawn out. Others think that it was by casting up of a rod or shooting of an arrow as directly as could be plum upward into the air and observing on which side it lighted when it came down. *(Josephus)* (The clause that both build on is somewhat ambiguous and by many others turned otherwise.) Others again think that it was by stones with inscriptions or marks on them, one saying for Jerusalem, the other for Rabba, which is not altogether unlikely. However it was done, it is apparent in this reference that some kind of lottery or other was used for that consultation of his and in this all the authors agree. Senacherib, King of Assur is also though to have used a similar course. *(Esai 36:10)* However it had not the same effect as the other, because it did not please God to grant success to him, although He had thought it good to vouchsafe the other.

Sometime lotteries are used when all the circumstances are resolved on, with only the time of it still undetermined. Thus it was when Haman, having resolved to do what he could to destroy and root out the whole Jewish nation, caused a lottery to be cast to decide the day and the time for it. He had made enquiry by lottery as to what would be the fittest and most fortunate time for the enterprise. Lots were cast in the first month Nisan (about our March), day by day and month by month. And so it fell out on Adar, their twelfth month (much like our February), with nearly 12 months in between. The time for it fell out contrary to Haman's expectation and so the success that his sorcerers had promised eluded him. *(Est 9:3)*

A similar delay from the same sort of process was the means which saved a noble Roman who was in enemy hands. It also gave Caesar a famous victory against the Germans *(Caesar)* when they looked to have had won against him*. The ancient Fries-landers are also reported to have a similar custom. This happened when a Christian Bishop and his disciples were being threatened, but by

* "When Caesar inquired of his prisoners, wherefore Ariovistus did not come to an engagement, he discovered this to be the reason – that among the Germans it was the custom for their matrons to pronounce from lots and divination, whether it were expedient that the battle should be engaged in or not; that they had said, 'that it was not the will of heaven that the Germans should conquer, if they engaged in battle before the new moon'." (Ch 50 Gallic War) Ariovistus was defeated by Caesar in the Battle of Vosges in 58 BC.

casting lottery it never lighted upon him, or on any of his company, apart from one alone, who by that means was made a Martyr. *(Baronius)*

§9. Divination among the heathens

This kind of divination was very common and usual among heathens *(Pindar)* whose idols were often used to give their answers by some form of lottery. This is how their oracles became to be called sorts or lotteries, among other names. Their wizards or soothsayers were called 'sortilegi' or 'sortiarij', which is the name for sorcerers and sorcery that we now give generally to witches and witchcraft of all kinds*. The means and manner of their performance were many-fold, as were the matters and affairs for which they made use of it. The Slavs, as the Jewish rabbis wrote, *(Moses, n/k)* used to peel a stick or a green piece of wood on one side, leaving the bark on the other side; then casting it up into the air, would conjecture about the good or bad success of their intended business, as it alighted with the bark or the bare side upwards. Something similar was reported *(Linschoten, 1598)* about the Chinese: that they use two sticks tied together with a length of string for the same purpose, one side flat and round on the other. If the two sticks alight and both lie alike on the flat side they account it a good sign; if unalike, an evil sign. There are also many barbarous people in Germany where is was recorded *(Tacitus)* that some of them conjecture using little pieces of wood, white on the one side and black on the other. Their women do it by drawing lines at random with ashes to see if they fell out even or odd. Others use little sticks or sprigs marked with several inscriptions which are first shuffled together and then solemnly drawn. Some of the ancient Scythians used bundles of willow-wands, others of them did it with the rind or bark of the lime tree. The Gauls made lotteries using the leaves of a vervain [verbena] to foretell if their businesses would succeed in any of the things they were likely to do. (*Herodotus)*

Among many other superstitions practices of this kind, one of the most famous and which is reported by *Ammianus* (and mis-reported by *Cassiodorus*) and by many others, is the example of Valens, Emperor of Byzantium [AD 364 – 378]. During his time as emperor, there were some who made inquiry as to who should succeed him. This was done, say some, by an enchanted ring hung by a silken thread in the middle of a basin with an alphabet of letters engraved round about on the sides of it. As the ring was stirred to and fro it struck various letters. Others say the letters were drawn in the dust with a corn of wheat or barley grain laid on each of them; a cock was brought in and turned to pick up any of them he pleased. Both reports agree that the four Greek letters θ E O δ were found in that order, either being struck by the ring, or picked up by the cock. They thereupon concluded that it was Theodore, a noble man of special note who was the person

* 'sorcery' derives from the Latin 'sortes' – lottery, hence the Italian, Spanish 'sortilegio' – witchcraft; and the French 'sortilège' – magic spell; English 'sortition'. These words have also become associated with an alternative form of democracy where representatives are chosen, not by election, but selection by a lottery, as in ancient Athens.

that their oracle had aimed at. When this came by some means or other to the Emperor's ear, it was the occasion not only for the death of Theodore, but also of many others whose names began with those letters. But Valens had missed out Theodosius who afterward did indeed succeed him as emperor.

Of special note was the use of lottery at ancient Latin city of Praeneste [Palestrina, near Rome]. *(Cicero)* This was so famous among the Romans that Carneades the sceptic used to say of them that he never knew Fortune anywhere so fortunate as there. Cicero reported and derided their fabulous origin: certain oak-wood pins or suchlike, which had several inscriptions on them, were kept in a box or a chest wrapped up in woollen bands. The emperor Tiberius is said to have removed it, taking the box or chest Rome. But once there, the lottery was found wanting and so it continued to be, until the box was brought back again to its wonted place of abode. Back at Praeneste the drawing took place ordinarily on new year's eve to foretell what should betide them the following year. When it was drawn by Domitian, during the last year of his reign, the lottery was said to have given him "a heavy and a bloody chance". That accordingly was what happened afterwards, whereas previously they had always given him "light-some and lucky" ones before.

Instead of wooden pins or wands, some places used dice or hucklebones which had the same function as dice. *(Pausanias)* Among those that used them was the Oracle of Hercules in Achaia, where they used to cast dice with certain marks upon them. According to how they fell, it directed them to a place on a table on which they found their fortunes. Another example could be found at Padua where Tiberius ordered that a lottery be drawn at the Oracle of Geryon. Golden dice were to be cast into a spring which was at hand. From the fall of the dice he was afforded the highest chance of being able to foresee the empire's fate. *(Suetonius)*

§10 Divination by book-opening: Foolishness by the wise

But the most usual form of divination to be found both there and elsewhere is by taking a book or verses of some famous poet like Homer or Virgil, or of some of the prophecies of the Sibyls. From these they either wrote out some verses on to several scrolls and afterwards drew from them, or, opening a book suddenly, took whatever they first lighted on for an answer to their present doubts or demands. This is how Hadrian is reported to have had his advancement to emperor by Trajan foretold, using certain verses of Virgil. So too did Claudius Albinus find out about the lack of further tumult after the death of Pertinax and that he would be victorious against the Gauls. So too did the future emperor Alexander Severus while still a child and had his universal sovereignty confirmed to him in certain Greek writings after consulting the verses of Virgil *(Lampridius)*. Again also, Heliogabalus [Roman emperor] sought to use the same means to be informed about what should betide him. And so too, lastly, by this means is Claudius said to have been informed of the length of his own reign, the short continuance of his brother Quintillus's authority, that his nephews would succeed him in the place of supreme government and that they would continue there for many generations. It is still an ordinary practice among the common vagrant fortune-tellers (such as our counterfeit Gypsies) that folk have their fortunes read out of such lot-scrolls or fortune books. (*Plutarch)*

All this seems to confirm what the Psalmist said *(Psal 106:35)* of the Jews, that "being mingled among the heathens, they learned their superstitions". Superstitious practices first used by the Gentiles grew afterwards to be far too common a custom, not just among the Jews and their rabbis alone, but among Christians also, many of whom were otherwise of no very great evil note. We pass over the popish practice of casting lotteries among the saints to choose which of them should be their special Patrons and Protectors to depend principally upon; *(Bonfinius, 1568)* or which saint to commend themselves or their dear friends unto in times of some danger or distress; *(Lopez, 1552)* or which saint to offer up their daily service to. Although these practices differ in their manner and circumstances, yet they are superstitions all the same.

We pass on from something which may seem far off and to come nearer home. Instead of the works of poets which have been used (or abused) by the heathens in this way, Christians have made use of the Bible, God's own book, using several parts of it, both old and new testaments, Epistles, Gospels, Psalms and Prophets. This has given rise to the terms 'the Apostle's Lotteries' and 'the lottery of the Saints', *(Delrio, 1618)* which we find condemned in so many canons and constitutions. (Not condemned, as some *(Baronius)* have supposed, from the Apostle's use of lottery in ecclesiastical elections.) Thus the Emperor Andronicus the elder was at odds with his nephew and in some doubt what to do about it, he had recourse to his book of Psalms and by chance lighting the verse "When the Almighty scattered kings in it, it was white as snow in Zalmon" *(KJV Psal 68:14)* he was thereby persuaded to give way to a reconcilement.

The Byzantine Emperor Heraclius [610 – 640], when his war against the Persians was at a standstill was in doubt whether to go back or stay with it. After a three days public fast, he took himself off to the Gospels and on opening up on a text, he took it to mean that it advised him to winter in Albania. *(Theophanes)*

Gregory of Tours has reported that Merovech son of Chilperic [King of the Franks 539 – 584] was thirsting after his father's royal estate. He had received an answer from a witch that gave him good hope of it, but to make yet another trial of the truth of it, caused a psalm-book, the book of Kings and the Gospels to be laid on the shrine of Saint Marius. After fasting and solemn prayer he came up and opened them and he lighted, little to his comfort, on these words in the first of them: "Because ye have left the Lord your God and walked after other Gods and done evil in his sight, therefore hath God delivered you into the hands of your enemies". *(2 Paral 12:5)* In the second book he opened it said (in vulgar Latin) "But for their deceitfulness hast thou laid evils upon them. Thou hast cast them down, when they were advanced. How became they desolate? they perish for their iniquities". *(Psal 73:18)* In the third book he came upon: "Ye know that after two days the Paschal feast shall be; and the Son of man shall be delivered up to be crucified". *(Matt 26:2)* These sayings were like something of the sort which afterwards happened.

But it must be said that Gregory himself was not free from some taint of superstition of this kind (although *Delrio (1618)* seeks to excuse him). When a report was brought to him that some of his clerks had been apprehended by one Leudastes, he resorted to his psalm-book. In there he alighted on the verse: "He led them out in hope and they feared not and their enemies the sea over-whelmed". *(Psal 78:53)* He noted that this had taken effect in part for Leudastes, who was shortly in great danger of being utterly drowned.

A similar tale is also reported by Gregory of Tours which seems to indicate that divining from books was no strange or unusual matter even with the best of them in those times. Tetricus, Bishop of Langres and his clerks desired that God would show them what was to become of Chramnus who was then in arms for the crown. They took the books of the Prophets, the Apostles and the Evangelists and laid them on the Altar and on opening the books they lighted on the Song of the Vineyard to be Laid Waste *(Esai 5:4)*, the prophecy of Christ's second coming to the sudden destruction of secure persons *(Thess 5:2)* and the Parable of our Saviour of the house built on the sand, in the Gospel. *(Matth 7:26)*

Lanfranc, Archbishop of Canterbury [1070 – 89] is reported by *Higden (~1340)* to have read the destinies of three youths that attended him using certain passages of the New Testament. They had been seeking their fortunes and were told that one of them should be bishop, another an abbot and a third an apostate, which accordingly, says my author, afterwards happened. Another author's report tells that enquiry was made in the same way for the self-same Lanfranc (whether by himself or others is not said) and it afterwards proved that he would be a great alms-giver. *(Malmesbury, 1120)*

Peter of Blois when Archdeacon of Bath reported dreaming once or twice of a friend of his whom he saw being invested as a bishop, but with omission of some ceremonies. Out of a natural curiosity he betook himself to his psalm-book by way of a lottery. The first words that offered themselves to his view were: "Moses and Aaron among his Priests". (*Psal 99:6)*

Thus Saint Theodora/Thodorus, as she is styled (if we may believe the reports of *Voragine (~1260)* of her) had yielded to an adulterous act by ungodly persuasions. She went to a prioress and desired that she produce an evangelical lottery to know what should become of her. As a consequence, she put herself into men's clothing, ran away from her husband and became a monk and so lived undiscovered to her dying day*.

The last of this troop is the foolish Saint Francis (as I may well so term him, if everything that the papists like *Leo (1318)* report about him). When a man of

* This bizarre story is acknowledged in the Catholic Encyclopedia. There have been several Saints Theodore, but only one trans-sexual Theodore/a.

wealth called Bernard [of Quintavalle] wished to be a follower of his, Francis advised him to first consult with God about so weighty a work. This he did, said the story, by going with Saint Francis to a priest who, after Mass had ended, made a cross on his mass-book and then opening it at random in three places one after the other, lighted still on some text or other that tended to that purpose. Whereupon Bernard, on the advice of Saint Francis, left all his wealth behind and became one of his followers*. This is the same Saint Francis who is said to have reported himself being tempted to have a book which seemed contrary to his vows, which should have denied everything except a coat, cord and hose and (in case of necessity only) shoes. He resorted for advice and, after prayers, took the Gospel and there he alighted on the sentence: "To you it is given to know the mysteries of the kingdom of God; but to others by parables". *(Matth 13:11)* He thereupon concluded that he could get by well enough without books and required all of his followers never to have so much as either a Bible, a breviary or a psalm-book.

It is hardly surprising if the ordinary and ignorant people have been carried away with such superstitious fooleries when we see bishops and other learned men addicted to them, despite their being greatly esteemed for their knowledge and holiness in their times. And this notwithstanding the fact that all such kinds and courses of divination and lottery were generally disallowed and prohibited both by the civil and canon law; also banned for everyone by various synods from time to time, especially for clergymen. It not only condemned those that practiced it themselves, but also those who dealt with it or gave heed or credit to them. Some of the synods which were held and which made constitutions against it, are reported *(Malmesbury, 1120)* to have been at fault themselves in this matter.

* This story is also true, and even the 'American Catholic' website is a bit coy about it. I am saddened that my beloved St. Francis is branded 'foolish', not least because of my experience at a Franciscan school.

Chapter 11

The unlawfulness of divinatory lotteries

§1. Divination: Once lawful, but not now.

Considering the extraordinary divinatory lotteries mentioned in the last chapter (for that is what they all were), some were lawful and some were unlawful in their times, but none of them would be lawful nowadays. Those that were lawful in the past were used either by an express word and warrant from God, like that used by Samuel for the election of Saul *(1 Sam 10:18),* and that used by Joshua for the discovery of Achan. *(Josh 7:14)* There were those which used the special instinct of the Spirit of God. That is certainly what was used by the Apostles to replace Judas. It is probable, though questionable, of the divinatory lottery used by Eliezer, Abraham's servant; the outcome did not prove the point, any more than in some others, nor that used by Jonathan and his Armour-bearer *(Gen 12:14),* which parallels it. Though approved by God, they are not to be imitated by us because they are extraordinary examples of the use of lotteries and as such are outside the rules and therefore set no precedents or patterns for us. We must work by ordinary precepts, not by extraordinary practices.

Unlawful uses of the divinatory lottery were: either, when the result was expected from the true God, as in the lottery used by Saul that lighted upon Jonathan *(1 Sam 14:41);* or from false gods, devils and idols that were used by the Philistine sorcerers and soothsayers *(1 Sam 6:7);* or that used by the mariners for the discovery of Jonah *(Jonas 1:7);* or that used by Nebuchadnezzar by way of consultation for the siege of Jerusalem *(Ezech 21:19);* and that used by Haman for the destruction of the Jewish nation. (*Ester 3:7)* Some of these extraordinary lotteries did indeed take effect in unexpected ways. In Nebuchadnezzar's lottery for his journey and expedition against the Jews, God bent it to His desires, effecting His own will in punishing those people. Likewise, in the lottery cast on Jonah and Jonathan; sometimes they had no effect, as in Haman's lottery for a fit time to destroy the Jews, where God turned the outcome clean around and contrived his downfall that day.

However there are some grave authors *(Palat., n/k)* who do not accept that some of these were done by divine instinct. It is true indeed that God takes a secret hand, power and providence in directing and ordering all projects and purposes, both of good and bad. But we cannot safely say that there was such a special and immediate instinct in some of them that made their actions warrantable, or that in others which makes their courses unwarrantable. The difference between them is that, on the one hand there is a lottery which speaks and works at random *(Bernard, ~1120)*, as happened to Caiphas which did not intend or require any such divine motion or direction; however God secretly directed the business that they and their actions dealt in to produce an outcome that He saw as good. On the other hand, a special instinct of God makes an act warrantable, when the party employed in it knows it and understands it to be such, and concurs with God equally in will, work and intention of His purpose in the execution of His will. The former alone will not serve to justify an action, any more than will God's secret counsel, purpose, predestination or preordination acquit the cursed Jews from sin in the crucifying of Christ.

None of these divinatory lotteries are lawful to us today, nor do any of those kinds of previous uses afford us warrant for them. Some can be admired as being marvellous, others abhorred as superstitious *(Calvin, 1584),* but none of them are to be imitated by us nowadays, because we have neither the warrant, as they did, nor may we do anything without warrant or against warrant as the others did.

§2. Types of unlawful divinators

The point we propound concerning these extraordinary divinatory lotteries is this: it is not lawful without express warrant or special revelation from God to use lotteries, either for the discovery of any hidden truth or to foretell or presage any future event. Discovering hidden truths includes: attempting to tell where treasure lies hidden; to discover a theft; to recover things lost; and such-like. Foretelling things to come would include; what fortune in general a man may have (using fortune-books to do so); what success he is likely to have in some particular affairs, such as in matters of marriage, in going to war or to sea, journeying by land or the like. These all come under the heading of consultative lotteries and like the rest are condemned as well. It was God himself by His own words *(Levit 19:26)* who has expressly forbidden all such kinds of divination including sorcery by lottery (for that is what this word signifies) by name.

We pass by that reference in Leviticus *(19:26)*, where God prohibited his people from using sorcery and other superstitions like it; pass lightly, although it is of great and sufficient weight in this point. The book of Deuteronomy gives the same message against many other detestable and abominable courses which were practiced by the heathen. He threw them out and prohibited His people to have any dealing with them: "When thou come", said He, "into the land that the Lord thy God gives thee, do not learn to do after the abominations of those Nations that God casts out before thee. Let none be found among you that makes his son or daughter pass through the fire." *(Deut 18:9)* This was a foolish ceremony, as many take it *(Maimonides, ~1200)* which was used by heathens; they supposed it would purify their children and preserve them from perils of spells and witchcraft. The children were made to pass between two fires, or were drawn hastily through the flame of a fire. Others *(Calvin, 1584)* explain as burning their children in sacrifice to idols and devils, which some idolatrous Jews did in imitation of the heathen. *(Psal 106:37)*

Divination was also prohibited. *(2 King 17:17)* This could be for the discovery of hidden truths or foretelling of future events, but without engaging man's natural skills. There are those who deal in divination in general but they are of the same nature and stamp as those who engage in particular forms of divination. We will deal with them in detail later on. But first let us view the particulars of those who practise certain forms of divination:

The first of the divinators uses **time**. Some use observations of times and account some days to be lucky and some unlucky or dismal days, but have no grounds in nature for this. Our common almanac-makers do this and as do other superstitious people who have an idle conceit about Childermas-day [Holy Innocent's Day, Dec 28th] as they term it, as an unlucky day to undertake anything at all that year and the like. There are those *(Heydon, 1603)* who say it is mere juggling or deceiving of the sight by casting a mist before men's eyes.

The second is a **sorcerer** or **conjecturer**, who casts lotteries. Haman did this *(Ester 3:7)* as some also think the King of Babel did by drawing arrows out of a quiver. *(Ezech 21:19)* Gentiles were wont to do the same using a sieve, which is a by-word in their books *(Erasmus, 1515)* and as many of the superstitious ones among us still do; or they may throw dice, stones or bones; or they may do it by opening a book; or by marks and figures made in the dust, ashes and the like and writing drawn and done out peradventure; or by using sticks or leaves, shuffled and severed, or left to blow in the wind; or by any other chance or random course which attempts to conjecture or guess at hidden or secret things.

The third is a **witch**, one that does mischief by hurtful confections; or seems to alter the nature of things and so works miracles using sleight and collusion. Such were those Egyptian magicians Jannes and Jambres *(Exod 7:11),* and sundry false Prophets *(Apoc 13:13)* that in later times under the kingdom of the Antichrist have attempted to do so. Under this heading we should include conjurers. *(Perkins, 1608)*

The fourth is a **charmer** or **enchanter** (the two are the same). They use spells and charms, or characters and ligatures to: enchant serpents, prevent harms, staunch blood, assuage swellings and the like. "These are merely superstitious" said the heathen man *(Sophocles)*, "which no wise artist will use, his cure requiring another course".

The fifth is a **consulter with spirits** or with **familiars**, ones that deal directly and immediately with the Devil (whom the others also deal with, but indirectly), requiring and using his help either to hurt or heal, or to tell or foretell anything; or by being possessed by some form of impure spirit, helps thereby to divine either by telling things that are hidden or by foretelling things for the future. Because some of them used to speak a low and hollow voice as if they spoke out of a bottle, or their words came out of their bellies, as was supposed by some *(Galen)* to have been so termed*. Others call them this because their breasts and bowels were so possessed that their bellies used on such occasions used to swell up like a bottle.

The sixth is a **wizard**, or a wise-man as they termed him, a soothsayer or fortune-teller, who professes to foretell future events by the flight of birds (auspices), shrieking of birds or entrails of beasts. This has been quite usual among the Gentiles. An example of this is reported about Xerxes. He made his army stand to for a while so that his wizards could observe the flight of a bird. A watching Jew in the troop who understood what was going on, shot the bird stark dead. He then asked how the bird could tell what was going to happen to them, when it had no foreknowledge of what was about to happen to itself and would surely not have flown that way at that time had it known. (*Hecataeus)*

Lastly come those that ask **advice of the dead**, that go, as the Prophet says, *(Esai 8:19)* from the living to the dead, consulting with those who raise up the souls of the deceased, just as the Devil takes men in hand and makes many believe in him.

These methods of divination which are joined together here all hang on one string and they are all prohibited and condemned by God as being practices that pollute all that use them, if not in body then yet in soul; and that make them abominable, if not in men's eyes, yet in God's sight. The text says it expressly *(Deut 18:12)*: "For all that do such things are an abomination to the Lord thy God, who will not therefore suffer any of His to do so". What could be more plainly or pregnantly spoken for the condemning of these courses? But men are commonly heard to object: "What harm is there in these things? What evil is there in a spell or a charm as long as there is nothing but good words in it? or what harm can there be in casting lotteries, or in drawing cuts, or in pulling an arrow out of a quiver, in holding a sieve between two hands, making a child run between two fires, or of breaking a wish-bone between two people and the like?" "Yea but", said God, "these are courses that I utterly abhor when they are used for those purposes. All those that use them or have dealing with them, or who cause such things to be done by others for them, they are not only abominable themselves, but an abomination in My sight". *(no ref)* That should be a sufficient argument for us if we do sincerely love Him, to hate and abhor them even though we may not see any hurt or harm at all in them.

To better conceive why God forbids and abhors these courses and why this prohibition is not without special reason, let us next consider in more detail the manifold evils that are to be found in these practices. From these it is evident that men make themselves guilty of Curiosity, Superstition, Idolatry, Presumption, diabolical Impiety and of high Treason against God's majesty. We will now deal with each of these.

---

* the description seems to be that of 'ventriloquist' – speaking from the belly.

§3. Why it is not harmless: Curiosity

Firstly Curiosity: it is vain even impious curiosity to enquire into those things that God has concealed and kept in His own power. In was in that regard that our Saviour reproved his Disciples when even by lawful means they enquired into things of that nature. He also rebuked Peter by name for being over-inquisitive in that kind. *(John 21:22)* When God has denied men ordinary means of discovery, He thereby reserves and keeps things in His own power. So the rule of God's Spirit concerning these things holds that: "Things concealed belong to God, things revealed to us". *(Deut 29:29)* This applies even though they are about things that concern us or might be of some use to us if we could discover them by ordinary means or direct courses. When God has either concealed them or suffered them so to be concealed from us so that they cannot be discovered by ordinary courses, then it is not lawful for us to seek to try to find out about them by extraordinary means, any more than it was for our Saviour Christ as a man and so made for us under the law, to ask His Father to have stones turned into bread when food failed Him. *(Matt 4:3)* We must be content with the good pleasure of God and rest satisfied with as much as may be known by lawful means, otherwise we will make our selves guilty of unlawful curiosity.

An examples of this is found in the curious arts. There were books which the good Christians at Ephesus had believed in before converting to Christ. Afterwards they burned them as a token and testimony of their renunciation and condemnation of them. *(Act 19:19)* This reference, however it is understood, relates to some form of curious craft or mystery which would tend towards the furtherance of idolatry. But most, or generally all interpreters explain this as a kind of curious art applied to divination which (as heathen stories also testify) were frequently used at Ephesus and were so famous that 'The Spells of Ephesus' had become a common by-word.

It was death for any man to look into the Ark or even to so much as peep into the holy of holies. *(Cajetan, 1525)* And so it is sin for a man to search and pry into what God has concealed; to search by such means as He has not warranted, or to search into such things that it is apparent He has concealed from us and wishes to keep hidden, in that He has taken away all ordinary means of discovery and offered no extraordinary means of finding out. We should accept, indeed we ought not refuse God's offers and suggestions about them to us. To do so would be to condemn God. We ought not to desire or request from God's hands, much less frame them to our selves when God shall see no good reason to do so. That is manifestly to tempt God. God promised His people His word and spirit to direct them and that He would raise up Prophets *(Deut 18:15),* and as the occasion requires from time to time instruct them in whatever shall be necessary or needful for them to know. So they shall not need to seek any such indirect courses, nor can they probably or profitably acquaint them with His will being taken up beside and against his will.

§4. Why it is not harmless: Superstition

Users of divinatory lotteries can become guilty of superstition. It would be superstition to ascribe a power to a thing or to use a thing for some purpose that it has no natural power or efficacy for and for which its use is not enabled by any divine ordinance. Such lotteries use a thing which is held to possess strengths, not by any natural power of it own nor by any ordinary ordinance received from God. Neither can it achieve such strength through the will-power of those who make use of it. This is the difference between any previous divisory lottery and these divinatory lotteries. It also marks off the difference between a special lottery used at God's express appointment and these. Divisory lotteries can only be applied when they have the power to effect in themselves, a power given by the will and consent of the users. True divinatory lotteries have power to effect a result only by virtue of God's covenant or appointment joined with them.

For example: A lottery has the ability to alight with uncertainty, although with certainty of a kind. It is uncertain because it has the possibility to fall a number of ways; but it has some certainty because it will actually light in one way alone. It has this power naturally in itself; but besides this power, men may by mutual consent choose to confer further power on it to arbitrate over such things as they are free to dispose of. But a lottery has no power of itself, nor can any man give it any such power, from his own will or even the will of many mutually consenting to make the lottery alight so that it necessarily discovers something that is hidden or is secret from the lot-users. Therefore to do so is mere superstition.

Sometimes a lottery may have power by God's will and appointment to reveal and discover some such matter and it did so in the lawful, extraordinary lotteries which were mentioned before. But in the lotteries we deal with here there is no such appointment or agreement of God between us and Him. They cannot be sure to have any such power now from Him. To show what we mean more clearly, take an example: Water has a natural power to wash and to cleanse the body and men may therefore use it for that purpose. But it is a sign and seal of God's covenant of grace *(Matth 28:18)* and that by special appointment from God therefore it may not be used for any purposes save those alone that are in covenant with God. Bread likewise has a natural power to nourish a man's body, but only if he receives it, retains it, concocts and digests it. But if bread is to be a type of Christ's body, which it can have only from His institution, there no power or skill of man that could make it to be such. Otherwise might not any piece of flesh do as well as a bit of bread? It was once, but is not now a type of Christ's body, because there was an ordinance then for it, whereas now there is none. *(Coloss 2:17)* Again, the Samaritan is said *(Luk 10:34)* to have washed his neighbour's wounds with wine and oil mixed together. But our Saviour Christ cured the beggar that was born blind with clay tempered with spittle and another that was both dumb and deaf was cured too, with spittle alone. *(John 9:6)* The first has warrant to be used still because it had and still has power from nature to heal and therefore is not superstitious. The second cannot with any good warrant be now used, because it had its power then, not from its own nature but from the special will and pleasure of the Creator. This power ceased with His pleasure then and to use it now for that purpose would be mere superstition. In same way, to use a lottery for something for which it lacks either the natural power or human help to effect is not unlawful because of that inability. It is mere superstition for a man to attempt to do something by a lottery which it lacks power to perform, either by its nature, or by using a human ceremony, or where there is no ordinance of God enabling it.

§5. Why it is not harmless: Idolatry

Those that use a lottery also stand guilty of Idolatry. For what is it but idolatry to ascribe to a thing what is properly the Creator's? This happens when a power to foretell things in the future, such as a lottery having no connexion or congruity at all with the thing foretold, is ascribed to something without cause, grounds or natural signs. This should only properly be ascribed to the Creator. Previously we sorted events into three categories: Necessary events which keep in a constant course naturally; Contingent but not chance or random events, that fall out for the most part alike, though they may vary now and then for some reason; and Contingent and Random that are altogether uncertain, as are the causes on which they depend. In the first sort are eclipses of the Sun and Moon which may be foreknown and foretold with certainty because the causes of them are constant and certainly known to us. The second sort include disease and death, which in some cases may be preconjectured and guessed at by those that are well seen and experienced in the signs and causes of either with some good probability. It is the third sort, depending on causes that are utterly uncertain and unknown unto us, which cannot be foreseen or foreknown and therefore cannot be foretold with certainly except by God himself alone. It is in this third sort of events alone that constitutes a divinatory lottery which no wit or skill of man is able to predetermine or foresee. *(1 Sam c14)* Therefore this kind of divinatory lottery and the practice of divination by lottery is not only, as canon law justly charges it, a step to idolatry, but is also a spice for of idolatry and sacrilege in itself because it robs God of His proper due, attributing something to an object which is peculiar to the Creator.

§6. Why it is not harmless: Presumption

Such lottery-use also makes men guilty of presumption against God. There may be some who will say: "Yes, but we do not expect the result from the thing used when we cast lotteries, we expect it from God the Creator Himself." My answer is that it would be impiety and presumption for any to do so. For what is this but a tempting and a stinting of God? What is it but requiring what God should do? It is not therefore true or sound, as some say *(Aquinas, 1270)* that men may require an immediate verdict by lottery from God in some cases so long as it is done with certain cautions and that an extraordinary, even miraculous hand of God may be expected thereby, when human help fails. *(Gersonides, ~1320)* This suggests that it would only be unlawful for men to use lottery in this manner if there was no necessity urging and enforcing them to use them.

In an argument which one of those authors *Peter Martyr (~1560)* lays down to support his opinion in this point, he claims that "where there is no faith, no act done can be free from sin". *(Rom 14:23)* But there can be no faith in this case because there is no ground or warrant for it out of God's word. And faith without grounds is no faith but a fancy; it is but a mere presumption where there is no promise. God has nowhere promised to work for us or relieve us either in the one case or in the other by such extraordinary courses.

Besides, as the heathen man *(Seneca)* once said, though for another evil purpose: "It is a miserable thing for a man to live in necessity; but there is no necessity at all for any man so to live". So I would say here that it is hard for a man to be so driven by necessity that he must partake of such courses; but there is no necessity at any time that he should do so. For what is the necessity they speak of; who would warrant such a course? If it is absolute necessity then there is none such. There cannot be any case where a man is so constrained that he cannot avoid it, so that of necessity he must do it. If it is a conditional necessity, that a man must either do it or he might sustain some damage perhaps even dying if he does not do it, even here is no such necessity that might justify such an act. For it is not only a tempting of God, as *Aquinas (1270)* has described it, when a man requires some extraordinary work of God for his pleasure or to test by it what God either can or will do when there is no need to have anything done. But for a man to require some extraordinary work of God, even for his profit or his safety rather than for his pleasure, but done without special warrant from God to do so, that too is to tempt God. If God's influence is not admitted in such cases it neglects and condemns Him; and to so require it before He offers it is to tempt and to stint Him. The Jews are said to have tempted and stinted God, not only when they required to be fed with flesh, having insufficient other food already, but then they even required to have water by miracle, when they were about to perish from thirst and had nothing else to drink. And how much more then is it a tempting and stinting of God when we prescribe Him to work extraordinarily for us, simply for the recovery of some trifling loss or the discovery of a thief? *(Gersonides, ~1320)*

§7. Why it is not harmless: Witchery

This kind of lottery or sorcery (for that is the right sense of that term) is nothing more than plain witchery and we often find them both coupled together in scripture. *(Deut 18:10)* Can we really think that God will be at our command to work for us at our pleasure, when we like, just for the finding of a rag? No. It is indeed the Devil not God that we work with when we either deal so ourselves or make use of those that deal in such things. From where did these practices spring or who brought them up? So who suggested discovering a thief by a key and a book, or a pair of shears and a sieve? Or foretelling what shall befall a man using fortune-books, or by the opening of a Bible or any other book at random, or by throwing dice, or by the drawing of tickets? Are they found anywhere revealed in any word of God? Or were they ever delivered by any Prophet of God? Or are they grounded on any principles of reason and nature? Or were they learned from any form of natural or ordinary observation? It is no such thing at all. They have nearly all been brought into use either directly by Satan or by some limbs and instruments of Satan. It is from blind, superstitious and ignorant persons who are wholly addicted to vanity and to ungodly curiosity. *(Augustine)*

There are some things for which we have some ground in nature either for them or the use of them; it is unimportant to know who discovered them. They simply discovered what lay hidden in God's work and applied it to whatever use that God had ordinarily imbued it and power to effect. But to require an extraordinary power, divine or diabolical, to work together with such things when they cannot effect such things on their own! What can we say about those who were the first to broach or teach us these?

Rather than listen to the authors and masters of them, we first turn to one grave writer who said of someone who would use them: *(Gersonides, ~1320)* "You that by lot-use profess to tell fortunes, or to discover a theft or a thief: either you must do this by a miracle, or by nature, or by some evil act. If it is by a miracle (I am sure) you would not dare say so because it is not likely that God would work miracles by you. If it is by nature (I am as sure) you cannot say; for there is no such natural efficacy in the thing you use. It must therefore be that it is done by some evil art and so consequently by the Devil who is the only author and ordinary assister of such arts."

It is the general belief of all divines that there must be at least a secret if not an open league and commerce with Satan in the practice of such superstitions, (which no Christian ought to have) whatever men may pretend or even intend in the use of them. As the Apostle warned the Corinthians *(Cor 10:14)* who were in the habit of attending the heathen's idolatrous feasts just to please or pleasure their heathen friends: "Nevertheless, by doing so you put yourselves in league and amity with idols and devils by the very act of associating with them". This shows that the use of these diabolical courses, even though many intend nothing much in the use of them amounts to trading and trafficking with Satan, something therefore all good Christians ought to abhor.

So then if you make enquiry into such things which God refuses to disclose by ordinary courses you becomes guilty of curiosity. Do you use something for a purpose that is has no natural power to deliver? That is mere Superstition. Do you expect that sort of outcome from a thing used that way? Then you commit gross idolatry and you are making an idol of it. Do you expect a result from Satan? Then that is plain and evident witchery. Lastly do you use some of the superstitious courses which the Devil's limbs or instruments have produced and which can have no efficacy of themselves without him and his help? If you do expect the result from him then it is no better than Witchery; and a heinous impiety and (which in the last thing we now charge it with) it is high treason against God's Majesty which he has punished most severely at various times.

§8. God versus the Devil

In all this it should be remembered that there are two adverse powers and two contrary kingdoms in this world. The one is of light, the other of darkness; the one of God the Creator, the other of His adversary the Devil *(Act 16:18)* who for that reason is called the god of this world, of the wicked of the world because they replace God with him by following and obeying him rather than God. Now so opposite are these two powers and parties to each other that no man can be a subject of one when he belongs to the other. He would fall from and rebel against the one if he flies or seeks to have anything to do with the other. When a prince proclaims open war against some foreign foe or even if he shall have proclaimed some of his subjects to be rebels and traitors they will never qualify for a pardon, or receive grace or mercy again and it shall be prohibited and forbidden for any of his subjects to resort with them or to have any commerce with them or with any of those that follow them or fight under their colours and will each be required to have taken a corporal oath for that purpose. If any of his people now, notwithstanding this charge publicly given and oath solemnly taken to the contrary, shall resort to such people and have intercourse with them, directly or indirectly, in person or with those that deal between them, he will undoubtedly be held guilty for so doing, guilty of perjury and disloyalty and high treason against his Sovereign and accordingly suffer and that deservedly, as a perjurer, a rebel and traitor to his prince. In like manner then our Sovereign Lord and Maker, having proclaimed open war, if I may say so, against Satan, indeed an eternal hostility without hope of reconcilement and having pronounced him a rebel and an irrecoverable one at that, such a one as he will never be received again on any terms whatsoever. He rightly charges and binds all his subjects and servants by a solemn oath under pain and peril of His perpetual displeasure, never to have any dealing, either directly or indirectly, either with him or with those that associate themselves with him, either by seeking to him immediately, or by using such methods that he has been the author and adviser of, or to require his helping hand. If any of God's people shall be found faulty on any of these grounds, must not such a one also be held guilty of perjury and disloyalty and high treason against God's Majesty and look to suffer accordingly as a breaker of his oath, as a violator of his vow, as a forsaker of God and the Christian religion and a follower of Satan and his accursed faction?

Besides which, if a Prince shall have disgraced or fined one of his nobles or other subjects and deprived him of goods or dignity for some offence upon some displeasure, or (as it may be) but to try him to see how he will take it and what course he will take in it. If the party so used by his prince seeks out a rebel to help him against and by his aid recovers such losses and damages as he had sustained at his sovereign's hands, would not his sovereign take such an act as exceedingly evil? It might also move his sovereign to deal in the like manner with him, as he had done before with another whom he seeks out for succour. Not only to proclaim him a rebel and a traitor but even to deny him all hope of grace or favour again? Now all Christian men know well (or at least they should know; and cannot but know, if they have read and observed anything in God's word) that there is no evil that could befall any man in the world, be it loss of life, health, goods or good name, (by what means so ever it be effected, or by whosoever inflicted) but it comes from God, either to exercise and try his obedience and patience or as a punishment justly laid upon him for his sin. If any man who has sustained loss or damage in some way in his person or in his worldly estate (which must be acknowledged will come to pass only by the holy permission and just judgement of God) shall seek from the Devil, who is God's utter and professed enemy, or from his wicked and wretched helpers, any help or relief for the recovery of his losses, or for the discovery of the party by whose means he sustained them, as if he meant to try out what the Devil in hell can do for him, when the God of heaven had afflicted him and refuses to relieve him. How can it not exasperate the wrath of God against anyone who would set so little by him, so that for so small a trifle he is so ready to forsake Him and resort to an enemy, whom He is known to hate so extremely? How mean a man would take it, any one that had tenants, children or servants, if some one of them that depended on him or belonged to him should, by his hard usage of them, or because he refuses presently to right and relieve him, when he may in some wrongs that he had sustained at some enemy's hand, or by means of a bad neighbour, take himself instantly off to his deadly and irreconcilable enemy, one that he knows his landlord, father or master cannot endure or abide of all men in the world. I will leave to each one's particular heart to determine how offensive such a course would be to even the meanest of us. And can we think or hope then that God will take it better at our hands (God, I say, on whom we wholly depend and who has graciously promised to right all our wrongs and not to discover only but take vengeance upon all our wrongdoers, if we will await but for His time) when we deal with Him in the same sort? And that when He has so often, so expressly and so strictly forbidden us to do so and enacted grievous penalties against all offenders and inflicted fearful punishments upon the transgressors.

§9. Penalties for the use of divinatory lotteries

We have already seen some of the prohibitions; we now consider further the fearful penalties and condemnations which are imposed for them, together with some examples where God has made good with them. As God therefore has rightly forbidden such courses, so also has He set the penalty of death on their practice or use. "Thou shalt not", said He, "suffer a witch to live." *(Exod 22:18)* The warning mentions a woman witch (for that is the word in the original) partly because women are more prone to offend in that kind and partly also to show that no infirmity or weaknesses (with woman being the weaker) shall serve to privilege or excuse anyone whatsoever in that case.

Elsewhere *(Levit ch 20)* laws are enacted against capital crimes, mention being made of many that He would have punished by death such as idolatry, adultery, incest, sodomy and such like, sins so horrible and unnatural that they are almost not to be named. Next after idolatry is placed, showing the heinousness of the sin, between it and adultery, comes the sin of witchery. He said this again in the conclusion of those sanctions (because that which comes last is wont to stick best in the mind) where He includes them all within the scope of the former constitution that condemns the witch and the wizard as well as the witch or wizard him- or her-self. But let us weigh the words themselves *(Levit 20:27)* a little. "Whosoever, man or woman shall have a familiar spirit, or shall be a wizard, let them die the death; their blood be upon them", or "they deserve well to die; they are the cause of their own death". And again, "If any turn aside after such as work with spirits or wizards, to go a-whoring after them, I will set my face against that person and will cut him off from among his people". Observe how God said that it was not only witches and wizards but those who seek them out, turning aside and going from Him; they also commit spiritual whoredom or adultery, that is, idolatry, in making the Devil their God, while they seek help from him against God, or for help at least where God refuses to help them. God therefore threatens even these, as well as the former, saying that He will set his face (or his wrathful countenance) against them. (It is a fearful thing for God in anger to turn His face away from one, much more fearful than for him in anger to set his face full against one.) He will set himself against them, as they set themselves against Him. And He will both cut them off by temporal death through the magistrates' hand here and He will also keep them in eternal perdition, cut off from the society of his saints in heaven forever hereafter. Or, as He has said of some idolaters and of other similar transgressors elsewhere that even though men and magistrates may wink at and neglect their crimes He himself will take vengeance for them, both on them and theirs.

§10. Just meant to terrify?

There may be some who might either say or suppose that many things of this kind are only spoken of so as to terrify men *(Giraldus Cambriensis, 1188),* and that notwithstanding, God being a good and a gracious God will be better than His word and not so fierce in the execution as He seems to be severe in His sanctions. So that we may see that God's threats and denunciations of this kind are not idle or formal, ritual words only, consider some examples of the fiercenesses of God's wrath against various persons and people that have been faulty this way. To begin with the Canaanites and those other nations that God drove out for the Hebrews: God Himself propounded them as an example of His wrath and indignation against them, in exhorting His people against these practices. "Be thou upright", said He, "with the Lord thy God; and take not such abominable courses as these nations do, whom the Lord expelled before thee, to put you in their places." *(Deut 18:13)* This implies that if we do not walk uprightly with God and we are not sincere and entire with Him, we are like the Israelites who sometimes halted between God and Baal. So we too sometimes halt between God and Belial, or between God and Beelzebub when we use courses of this kind. "For the nations whom thou succeeds, they give ear to diviners, astrologers, witches, sorcerers, wizards, charmers, conjurers and necromancers *(*for all these abominations had He formerly recited as usual among them) and because of these abominations doth the Lord cast them out before thee". *(Deut 18:14)* This can be explained, as was said elsewhere in another case that they must look for suchlike who were similarly at fault and "that their land should spew them out, as it had spewed those out that were before them in it". And surely God destroyed those Gentiles, not for doing these things themselves, so much as for listening to those that dealt in them. He destroyed those Gentiles, I say, for doing something that these laws had never given them, but which by the general light and law of nature alone would direct them. How much more justly may He destroy those who after His will has been so particularly, so precisely, so expressly revealed to them in this point, shall notwithstanding make no conscious effort to forbear such practices, which appear plainly to be so offensive to God and may prove so prejudicial to themselves.

§11. No escape from punishment

Although God may be sharp with others, He may not deal so rigorously with his own even though they are at fault in this way. He destroyed those heathens for these practices, yet He did not spare His own people when they took the same course. The judgements inflicted upon them remain on the record, equally for the prince as the people, indeed on the whole body of them together for sins of this nature.

Consider the examples of this; firstly of two Kings, then of two kingdoms and states. Ahaziah sent to Baalzebub, the god of Ekron *(2 King 1:2),* to enquire whether he would rise and recover again as he was then lying sick and sore-bruised after a fall. If there had been a God to advise him, as in Israel, he would have had this answer returned to him from the true God (that he should have consulted). His minister Elias on meeting the king's messengers, said that therefore he should not rise again from his sick-bed that he was laid on, but he would assuredly die. The other example is of Saul of whom this is noted as the main cause of his overthrow: "Thus died Saul for his sin, whereby he sinned against God, in that he regarded not His word; and in that he sought to ask the advice of one that had a familiar and asked not of the Lord; and therefore the Lord slew him and turned the Kingdom over to David". *(1 Chro 10:13)* There are two sins which are especially pointed out as the principal causes of Saul's downfall, as is said elsewhere to be witchery and idolatry. *(1 Sam 28:8)* Saul's case was more excusable than usual for most of those who used such practices, for he had not merely lost some sorry trifle and desired to know what had become of it. He stood in jeopardy of loosing life and living, crown and kingdom. He had tried all the courses he could whereby he might be resolved of the issue of it, before he consulted the witch. For it is said, "He asked advice of God and God would give him no answer, neither by Vision, nor Prophet, nor by Urim and Thummim." *(1 Sam 18:6)*. And how can it be said of him then that he did not ask for His advice? But the Holy Ghost accounted it as no worse than not asking at all. When God refuses to reveal things by lawful means, men do not rest there but seek the knowledge from those people as by such courses God would never counsel or advise them to use. Again his request to the witch was to have a word or two with Samuel, a good prophet of God lately deceased only and not with the Devil. Nor did he suppose it was the Devil that he talked or dealt with; he took the person that he saw to be Samuel although he was mistaken. However the Spirit of God has expressly condemned him principally for this lapse and the Lord deservedly deprived him both of sceptre and life.

To these two kings we add two whole states, entire kingdoms even. There is the kingdom of Israel of the ten tribes and the kingdom of Judah, consisting of the other two Tribes. The kingdom of Israel was first destroyed under Hoshea. And the cause? There were other sins, but it was the sins named precisely as divination and sorcery. *(2 King 17:17)* Such an enormity is to be branded with this mark: that it is a selling of a man's self to sin and to incense God's wrath against himself. For the destruction of the kingdom of Judah begun under Jechonias and completed under Zedekias, God determined to destroy Judah, as he had done with the ten Tribes. And the cause of this? It was said to be mainly for the sins of Manasses. And what were their sins (amidst many other indeed) but witchery and sorcery? If there are any who surmise that the oppressions and murders were the main cause of all those miseries that befell that state, because there is special mention made of them in some references, they are wrong. The Holy Ghost came in with them in the story of the Manasses afterwards as a by-matter. The main cause, for which God would "stretch over Jerusalem the line of Samaria and the level of Ahab's house and do with that famous City as a man doth with a dish in that he wiped and whelmed upside down" *(2 King 21:6),* when he had done with it. So this explained not only his fall but the ruin of the whole state by idolatry and sorcery and sins of that sort.

§12. Conclusion

To draw all this to a head then and so to conclude. Since God has restrained us from all forms of resort to Satan, *(1 Cor 10:10; Torreblanca, 1618)* and we ourselves in our baptism have renounced all kind of dealing with the Devil, we would break our faith which we have solemnly plighted to God and make ourselves guilty of rebellion and high treason against God whenever we seek to Him and ask advice of Him about these courses, whether we believe and trust in Him or not.

Again, we see that the sin of witchcraft (of which this sorcery is one kind) is so heinous and so capital a crime that God commanded the witch to be put to death whether she helps people or hurts them, just because she is a witch and has dealt with the Devil. We ourselves, in our own consciences must condemn such kind of people because it can be said of them, more truly than usually, as we are wont to say, that they have sold themselves and their souls to Satan. It must surely be the most damnable and detestable practice to employ any, or to use the employment of any in such actions, when we know that we hazard the casting away of our souls by them, although there may be no other sins on our part but these. We might as well make use of some swaggering butcher to revenge us by murder on someone who has wronged us; or procure some knight of the realm to perjure himself for the recovery of a just debt which has been unjustly denied to us; or hire some light housewife to entice a man to lewdnesses and to play the whore with him as Delilah did with Sampson *(Judg 16:5),* and thereby discover something that we suspect him to have wronged us in. For murder and witch-craft are alike, both sins, both notorious in God's eyes. He has therefore assigned the same penalty for both. Sorcery and perjury are very nearly of the same nature, since by the one a man wilfully casts his soul into God's hands and by the other he solemnly puts his soul into the Devil's hands. Fornication in itself may be simply considered a far lesser sin than this. As is plain to be seen, God has only assigned a fine or a money payment for this but has appointed capital punishment, loss of life, for the other. (*Deut 22:28)* But more than that, when God himself has passed the death sentence on those who seek such, he also punishes the parties involved. He sealed up his hatred and detestation of such courses by removing two kings, Abaziah and Saul, the one by sickness, the other by his own sword, by himself, not just killing Saul himself, but rooting out his posterity and cutting the crown off from him and his. He further destroyed whole nations and overturned whole states for these sins, as the Canaanites and others that He cast out before his people. And His own people too were cast out when they took the like courses. We must see that we should never wilfully wink and shut our eyes against the light of God's truth concerning this point, which so clearly shines forth in His words and how heinous and horrible a sin it is in God's sight. We cannot but tremble to think of the heavy wrath of God which is justly provoked and procured by such practices. If we know ourselves to be any way guilty of such, unless we have hardened our hearts against the fear of God, or make doubt of the undoubted truth of God's word, it would be very much better for us now to believe the truth after wise and careful repentance than to find the truth in the hereafter by dreadful and woeful experience when it is too late for us to either believe or repent, to believe the truth of the one or to repent us of the other.

Chapter 12

An admonition to avoid divining lotteries, with answers to some arguments alleged in defence of them: and the Conclusion of the whole

§1. Ignorance no defence

These matters have now been weighed up and conclusions delivered. Those who have at any time taken part in these courses, perhaps not realising the greatness and grievousness of their sin should not try to justify their evil act or to soothe themselves in doing it. They are the first to be admonished here. As the apostle Paul said *(Act 3:7)* of himself that when he blasphemed and was persecuted and also Peter of the Jews that when they crucified Christ: "They did it in ignorance". Although that may lessen the sin, it does not save the sinner. Nor could the ignorance of the Jews avoid making them wicked when they were employed in that action, nor does Paul's ignorance privilege him from being a prime sinner. This is especially so if your ignorance is not just simple and naked *(Bernard, ~1120)*, but a wilful and affected ignorance; as if it was only a companion to and not the cause or occasion of your sin. It does not do much to lessen your sin and you therefore have more cause for repentance in that regard. Even if it was by being simple, you still have cause to repent, because if in it you were simple then you cannot now but repent of your sin. For if your ignorance was simple then so was the cause of your sin. If you did it therefore because you did not know it was a sin, you cannot now choose to come to see your sin, which you saw not before or to know your offence, which you knew not before and then bewail and lament, be sorry for and repent of it, seek pardon and forgiveness at the hand of God for it and be careful next time to avoid the like evils. If you do this (assure yourself) then Satan has you in a snare, entangled in his nets. It is by repentance alone that you can unwind yourself out of it. "The Devil holds you tight by the heel", as he speaks. *(Job 18:9)* This is like a bird-catcher, having the bird caught by one foot, is content to let her have the liberty of both wings and her whole body; that is enough to give him the command of the whole bird. Even though you might live blamelessly otherwise, this is one wicked course which is enough of itself to engage you body and soul to Satan. Alone it is sufficient to give the Devil title and interest to the whole. In a word, either you sinned ignorantly or knowingly. If ignorantly, your ignorance was either simple or affected; if it was from simple ignorance that you sinned, you cannot but repent now that you come to see your sin. If it was from an affectation of ignorance you have more cause to repent because that cannot lessen your sin. But if you sinned, not of ignorance but with knowledge then you have much more cause to repent because that aggravated the sin. You have good and just cause to repent in every way because there is no way that you can be freed from sin.

§2. Innocence no defence

Again, all those that give way to such superstitious conceits and courses are to be admonished. By this means they enthral their souls to Satan and incense the wrath of God against themselves. Their own conscience cannot but tell them that even if they deal sincerely with it and it with them, that they are devilish and abominable, wicked and unwarrantable. Consider this seriously: when some trifle is missing, do you go to work with your book and key, or with your sieve and shears for the finding of the thief? (And that maybe it has not been stolen either; but let us assume it is.) Firstly, do you think that a book and key, or a sieve and shears can be able either jointly or severally to do anything about this of themselves? Surely you are not so simple to suppose so, unless there is as little in you as in them! Are you able then to put any such power into them which they have not of themselves? Undoubtedly you can not. It is a thing utterly out of your power. What then? Do you think that your fooleries will cause God to do extraordinary and miraculous work for you? If so, it looks like you imagine you have a miraculous faith. If you think you have, try it for some better or some greater matter, in a matter of more moment such as the raising up in an instant of someone that is at death's door. Or rather, try it in neither; you should not tempt God. But suppose you do try Him, do you think He would do it? And what reason have you to imagine that God would work extraordinarily for you, more so in this one than in another cause? There may be like ground and warrant for either, but there is word of promise for neither. Nor can you easily be so foolish as to suppose that God would do anything about it, especially when for the most part there is no solemn seeking to God, whatever abuse of His name there might have been, or of the word of God now and then.

So if the thing itself is unable to do anything in and of itself and you are unable able yourself to give any such powers to it and God has no hand in it (other than in all actions else whatsoever), then what else can it be (if anything comes of it) but the work of the Devil, whose aid you have therefore implored and who you employ, yea, who you thereby show that you trust in and believe in, whatever you might pretend? If you supposed it was only a vain and idle thing of no certainty then you would never have used it. If you thought that it was the Devil who could and would tell you the truth then you would never resort to him or base anything on his answers. You would never use any such tricks of his nor conclude anything from their outcome. In fact your practice shows that you believe and trust in him whatever you might say. And by so doing you cross our Saviour. He warned us that the Devil is a liar and the father of lies. *(John 8:44)* You may suppose and assure yourself that by these means they not only can, but will and do tell you the truth. In your own heart therefore if you are serious and sincere, it cannot but inform you that you deal with the Devil, the first author of all evils, a liar and a murderer from the beginning; and what good or gain, what faith or truth, what help or health can be expected from him?

Do not let the wretched desire or love for things that have been lost, or of any other wealth whatever it may be, much less a vain curiosity and lusting to foreknow and be acquainted with future events, which God has reserved to Himself, prevail so far with you so as to persuade you to pass the limits that God has prescribed for you and to join with Satan in using satanical courses just to satisfy your worldly and fleshly desires against God. Remember that Shimei *(1 King 3:37),* when he went to seek his servant who had fled away from him, went beyond the bounds set him by Solomon. For his own purposes he used the same methods that you engage in when you seek to recover your losses and thereby would cause his and your own ruin, drawing destruction on yourself as he did. *Augustine* has truly said of those who seek the help of Satan in sickness, to recover their health either directly or by use of indirect courses, that they are strangely and strongly deluded by the Devil when they think him willing to help them. He is far readier to destroy them and would undoubtedly do it if he had his own way. If there is anything to be done for them in that way then it is not done in God's name but in the Devil's. It would be better to remain sick than to be helped or healed in that way. If the Devil were to do anything for them when they ask, he heals the body only to slay the soul; he heals the body for a time so that he may slay soul and body for eternity; and accursed is that bodily health that is bought with so dear a price as the blood and death of the soul. *(Gersonides, ~1320)*

Here for the most part the Devil just deludes men, promising them that which he seldom performs and many times casting them into further losses instead of helping them to regain and recover the former. Or if he does help you find your gold or garment again it is dearly bought when it is recovered that way. He helped you to find your gold or garment again in order to get and gain your body and soul. By recovering it, even seeking so to recover it, you sell him your soul. Now, as our Saviour said *(Matt 6:25)*, "Is not the soul better than treasure; and the body than apparel?" And will you do it then, even against the Devil's own proverb *(Job 2:16)*, "skin for skin; but all that a man hath, will he give to save his soul"? Will you give up the one for the other, the better for the worse? "What", said our Saviour, "shall it avail a man to gain the whole world and lose his own soul?" Just as here, what shall it avail a man to regain his garment and cast away his body so that he should wear it again; or to regain his gold and cast away his body that should use it, to cast away his soul that may do well enough without the body, whereas the body cannot possibly do well without it? As our Saviour has said in another case, "If thy coat be gone, let gown go after" *(Matt 5:40)*; choose rather to lose both one after the other, than seek to regain either by such courses as these. "Better it is", said our Saviour *(Matt 5:29)*, "to go halt into heaven than to go with two legs whole, to hell". And better it is to go naked or thin-clad into heaven, than to go clothed or well-apparelled to hell; without money to heaven, than with money to hell; better to want for meat and money, than receive either from Satan; better lose clothes and coin, than recover either by Satan, or encompass either by any Satanical course whatsoever. We surely show little love for God if we do not hesitate to displease when seeking for such trifles as these. We should stick fast and close to Him even when thread-bare (as we say) when we might well be pulled away from Him or drawn out of the way that He has prescribed for us.

Let us therefore, fearing God, put such practices far from us as we have regard for our own good. We should not only forbear them, but we should abhor them, defy and detest them, not in word only but in deed also, not in tongue only but in truth too. So our hearts may be sincere and entire with God, not divided between God and Satan; our heads and brains busied with searching out the holy and acceptable will of God, not about curious inquiries into such secrets as the wisdom of God has hidden from our eyes; our hands should be employed only in the good works of God, not in the works of that wicked one, which he came to dissolve and destroy in those that be his *(1 Job 3:6);* and our feet should be walking in the straight and clear ways of God's word that lead to life and salvation and not in Satan's crooked and blind by-ways that lead to death and destruction.

§3. Did Augustine approve?

I will answer an idle objection or two and then all will be at an end. It is said by some *(Gersonides, ~1320)* that when using these methods there are many good words, even Scripture itself, often used. How then can they be anything other than good? Or at least how can they be so bad, as you seem to say of them?

Augustine indeed, (as bishop *King (1597)* has also observed) seems in this regard to be over-favourable to some of these and the like courses when he wished "that men would rather make lottery of the pages of the Gospel rather than run directly to enquire and ask advice of the Devil". There are some (*Gregory of Tours)*, (as I showed before Ch10, §10) of no very ill note who have been taken in by this. But Augustine himself disliked it and ancient canon-law has also condemned it on good grounds and warrant: God's holy oracles should not be used for such idle vanities nor applied to such superstitious uses as these. Holy things may be abused as well as profane ones. The Devil produced scripture to persuade our Saviour to sin. *(Matt 4:6)* And the sacrifices that the Gentiles offered to idols and to the devils that were in them were the same in substance as those that the Jews offered to Jehovah. The holiness of the thing used does not excuse the abuse of it. In fact it is rather the more heinous, the holier the thing is. (*Gersonides, ~1320)*

§4. If it sometimes works, why not use it?

Yes, some might say, often these observations fall out right and the outcome accords with the truth of the thing being enquired into. Was this not so in many of the examples already mentioned? Did not the lottery light correctly on Jonah and upon Jonathan? Did not the Philistine and the Babylonian lotteries *(Ezek 21:23)* answer the expectation of those who used them? Indeed we may have found, as some say, by our own experience, in ordinary practice they often prove to be true.

To this I answer: first, they make note of it when it proves to be true, but not how often it proves false. As the philosopher *Aristotle* said of dreams, that they seldom prove true and yet many men believe in them, because they remember only those that prove so. And as *Erasmus (1515)* said of relics and monuments hung up by those who had made vows to our Lady (as they term her) and by her help (for so they would have it) were delivered safely. There are relics like this in heathen temples of which there were many indeed, says *Diogenes,* but there were no monuments from those that had made the same like vows but were not delivered safely, but had either drowned or perished. If there were there would be many more relics to be seen! What we have here is a few outcomes scored up and recorded when they have sometimes hit it right, whereas there may be many more, ten or twenty (perhaps, as the learned *Seneca* said, above a thousand) for each success, if they had been observed and registered when they happened contrariwise. In earlier examples it proved alright for Nebuchadnezzar, but clean contrary with Haman. Yet so often do they fall out this way that, as *Minucius* well said, "though they may lie but by accident, they may seem to do it out of industriousness, with the set purpose to tell untruths".

As *Gersonides (~1320)* well observed, the blindness and madness of most men is both strange and miserable, who in other and better matters will be extremely hard of belief, refusing to give credit to a certain truth, even though it is confirmed by an infinite number of undoubted examples. But they will, if they can just once pick out any one singular precedent where things have fallen out otherwise. For instance, tell men about the many who have died ill that lived ill and then tell them that if they take the same course in their life they may justly look for same result in the end at their death. But yet they will accept nothing at all that is alleged in that kind so long as they can name but one counter-example, like that of the thief on the Cross who was saved at the last minute. *(Luk 23:40)* This is a single counter-example and a questionable one at that, but let it go for now. It was well said by *Augustine* "that no man should despair, but neither should any man presume". Whereas I would say that in important matters which more nearly concern them, men will reject a thousand truths for one untruth and this despite a thousand examples of outcomes which have fallen out alike and aright, just so long as a single one has fallen out extraordinarily otherwise. In these cases which go against the usual run of events, one truth they will excuse an hundred untruths, and the one outcome that randomly falls out right, a hundred maybe will be passed by that fall out otherwise. This shows how lightly we come to believe in such vain and hurtful things that we really ought to distrust; and are so hard of belief in good and profitable things and such as we stand bound by God to believe in. "A liar", said *Aristotle,* "is not believed even when he tells the truth, if he has once been found out telling untruths". But yet people are still prone to give credit to these kinds of liars, though they have been manifestly taken in by ever so many untruths and although they themselves evidently know it.

§5. Wise men know it is ridiculous

The outcome of an event does not argue for either its truth or certainty nor make it lawful and warrantable, something even the heathens *Plutarch* and *Pliny* had seen and observed. Are there not many to be found everywhere who thrive in sin and by sin? Have not many been conquerors in unjust wars? The length of the lance does not argued the equity of the cause nor the sharpness of the sword's-edge the lawfulness of the course or the quarrel. It did not follow that the Benjamites' cause was good or that the Israelites' case bad just because they beat down their brethren and their adversaries fell before them in two battles. (*Jug 20:21)*

But to come nearer home, take the comments of *Cicero,* that grave author and one of great authorities about divination: "How vain and idle, how frivolous and ridiculous was their method of divination by opening the bellies of beasts and poring over their entrails, or by observing the voices or the flight of birds and their feeding or refusing of their food?" As *Cicero* was also wont to say; that he wondered how their wizards and soothsayers could forbear laughing when they looked at one another when deluding the common sort of people by such methods. The wiser sort among the Romans scoffed at them and ignored them. *Pliny* affirmed that "these wizards and soothsayers can tell what the birds chirp and what wit and wisdom lies buried in the bellies and bowels of beasts; they may well be heard, but they are in no way to be hearkened unto". And *Cicero* and others said such things as: "The enchanters and spell-mongers of Marsum*, as well as the common sacrificers and bowel-searchers, the star-gazers and figure-casters, the Egyptian fortune tellers and dream-readers. They are all not worth a button. They do not have any divine art or skill at all, but are either superstitious wizards, blind blunderers, idle-headed, addle-brained, or arrant beggars. Like the fools that they are, they profess to tell other men their fortunes, when they are ignorant of their own (and to foretell things to come when they are ignorant of what, is at

* This is an obscure reference by Cicero to a tribe that lived in central Italy

present). They search the hidden corners of the heavens above even though they cannot see what is at their feet. They promise to help find hidden hoards of gold, for which they only beg to be paid, as we say, a 'grey groat' [coin], which groat, it could be said, they could well first take out of that hoard and then hand over the rest". So it was not without cause that the cynic *Diogenes* once said that when he considered "the art and skill of mariners, builders, physicians and philosophers", he deemed man to be the wisest and wittiest creature in the world. But on the other side again when he considered the extreme folly of these "dream-readers and fortune-tellers and those that gave heed to such fooleries" he was induced to judge man the most foolish and vainest creature that might be. Yet did not some of these prophecies sometimes come true? Did it not prove true, both in this and that other, when Nebuchadnezzar *(Ezek 21:19)* used them both together? We know that heathen stories are stuffed full of similar reports like: "The observations of eight hundred years and upwards", said *Cicero*, "confirming most with them". In this regard, the argument drawn by *Zwingli (~1523)* from the result which justified the act of Eliezer, Abraham's servant, though it may have had some good probability of happening, yet it was not of undoubted certainty. The sign that the Philistine sorcerers set themselves did come out rightly *(1 Sam 6:12)* and the witch of Endor told Saul much truth and that it is what shortly afterwards accordingly came to pass*. *(1 Sam 28:7)* And yet neither of their methods are justified by any author that I know. "Reasons and arguments", said *Cicero*, "must be produced for the confirmation of men's courses, not examples of uncertain and chance events". And well has a nobleman of ours, Lord *Howard,* Earl of Northampton said in a learned and elaborate work of his (1583) on a somewhat similar subject: "Examples which fall out by chance are never current, where the cause has to be justified by reason. And therefore until a man can as readily produce a certain ground to make his guesses good, as readily as he scores up a register of blind outcomes, we may rather commend his luck rather than his learning".

§6. Not magical but natural

And lastly, when these things prove true and fall out in accordance with the intent, desire or purpose of the user, it is not, as *Jerome* and others such as *Bede* have well observed, done by the force or from the nature of the thing itself that is used. Therefore, as is well said by *Peter Martyr (~1560)* that the argument drawn from the outcome is weak and feeble, mistaking the grounds for the matter, assigning a cause where indeed there is none. This is like the concepts of the superstitious papists and idolatrous heathens in ascribing God's usual bounty in ordinarily blessing the year with plenty to be a result of their idle processions, just because one followed the other. They both used such things and they were

* An equivocal biblical tale, where Saul deliberately sought the advice of a 'woman with a familiar' (witch), who first refused to use her black arts because her sort were not welcome, but then complied when Saul assured her that "God would not punish her for this".

equally useless for them both. There is also the practice of the unskilful empiricists *(Fernel, 1567)* that give medicines haphazardly one after another, so that when the disease breaks away by other means or of itself they ascribe the cure to the medicine they last gave, just because the disease went away at the same time it was used. But these things come to pass by other means and they may be either ordinary or extraordinary.

Ordinarily it happens so, either by mere randomness or maybe by human guile or subtlety. As *Heraclitus* said of unskilful physicians, that "it is chance and not themselves who cure their patients, if by any chance they are cured". Because they administer medicines without grounds or good reasons they may, by chance give some that sometimes do good. Those whom chance favours seem to prove true prophets; but when it fails them then they too fail and prove false. They were just as false at first even when what they claimed proved true because they had no grounds or knowledge or anything that they were aware of that should make it so. As *Cicero* said of fortune-tellers, "that the best diviner was the one that could give the best guess". They went by mere conjecture without any certain grounding in skill. Any man can as we say, 'hit the nail on the head' many times without any divine help or divining facility. And so these people go by blind, groundless and uncertain conjectures, but amid all this, (just as men may grope to and fro in the dark and then sometimes land on something that they had not looked for), they may stumble on the truth. *(Chysostom)* Similarly, those that play at odds-and-evens, even though they go merely by guess can often guess right. And as *Euripides* said of dreams and dreamers (and the methods we deal with now are no whit more certain than that) that though there might be no divine matter in them, yet they often fall out with answers for those who dreamed them. With men dreaming as they do, so often and about so many sundry things of all sorts (melancholy persons especially according to *Plutarch*) it is not strange if they light on some things that fall out accordingly by chance. This is like two boys throwing stones as they come to hand at each other and it is chance (though they did not intend it) when they throw the same stone twice. Or if a man keeps shooting, though with little skill, maybe even blind-folded, he may by chance sometimes hit the mark. And so by casting dice often, even dicing all day long, sometimes, by chance it is possible to score the highest chance that the dice have, maybe even twice or three times all together*. One of the Roman Emperors is reported by *Cicero* to have set the garland on a huntsman's head for the 'feat' of striking several times at a huge bull that was driven at him several times, but missing every time. It was a harder matter for one striking so many times to miss than for someone or other to have hit once.

It would be even more strange and wonderful if when dreaming of so many things as most men do, that your common fortune-tellers should not now and then find that by foretelling so many things from them they as claim to do, that it

---

* This represents a remarkably prescient statement by Gataker of the nature of randomness

sometimes comes to pass accordingly. Unlucky indeed is the dicer, that dicing all day should never once light on any one chance of the dice that he desired. And it would be a very unfortunate fortune-teller or lot-caster who in making a continual trade and practice of such things, should seldom or never by chance light on something which by chance would likewise fall out answerable to his foretellings. And though it was mere ravings when he spoke and it would be merely a chance outcome if it should ever should fall out so, it might seem otherwise to some.

Augustine tells of two young men who were travelling about and made many believe that they were astrologers, except they did not even know so much as the 12 signs of the Zodiac. When they perceived that the host of the inn where they stayed seemed to give them some credence by telling him about many strange matters they grew bolder. The inn-keeper then asked whether they could tell him anything about his son who was then out, staying later than his appointed time which made his father somewhat fearful that some evil had befallen him. Having little regard for how the matter would fall out in their absence and so they might please their host and get themselves something as a present, they bade him be of good cheer; his son, they would warrant, was safe and not very far off. Although they no more knew, as we say, than the post, or than their host himself, yet by mere chance against their expectation it fell out accordingly. The son came in just as they were leaving the inn, which made them to be thought of as men of extraordinary skill.

This story is like the physician who is said by 'Euphor. Satyr' to have handed out his prescriptions by lot. Though he killed many by that means, yet when he hit right or the parties by some means recovered, he was esteemed a man of great skill[#].

§7. The use of Fraud

Sometimes these methods take effect not by mere randomness but either in the ordinary course of events by some trickery of man, or in an extraordinary way by some secret work of Satan or even by some hidden hand of God Himself.

For as *Augustine* said of the miracles done or pretended to be done by the Donatists[*], that they were either of men's forging or of the devil's doing. A learned schoolman and our country-man *Alexander de Ales (1452)* wrote about the popish miracles wrought for confirmation of the mass: "That they were either procured by men or effected by Satan". So it often falls out in these lotteries and divinations by lot.

[#] This tantalising suggestion of randomised medical trials is probably apochryphal, may be taken from a satirical play by Aristophanes, but I could not find a source for it.

[*] The Donatist schism in Africa began in 311 and flourished just one hundred years, until the conference at Carthage in 411, after which its importance waned.

Sometime they take effect by means of some trick which seems chance when indeed is not. Although a lottery may be thought to be used, there is indeed none, just like those who cheat at dice. Sometimes an outcome that seems to be the result of skill is indeed but mere chance. Sometimes where there seems to be chance in the act itself it is based on trickery and skill. *Lyra (~1300)* testified to the falsity of the miracles in his time: "That many of them were wrought by the priests and their accomplices using trickery for gain to delude the people". In our times also, similar practices have been seen. *Bale (1560)* reports that Sir Nicholas Gervase, a priest of Surrey did penance at Paul's Cross in 1544 for bloodying the communion wafer by the pricking of his finger to make people think that the host bled. The heathen oracles were often cunningly and craftily carried out so as to speak to private men's purposes. Entrails from their sacrifices were made by art and crafty connivance to give signs of success for men's better encouragement which they could not do by themselves.

Thus we find in ancient story of *Pausanias* that whereas Aristomachus's sons Temenus and Cresphontes accompanied the forces of their uncle Aristodemus (who died leaving issue of twins Procles and Eurysthenes in the custody of his brother-in-law Theras) and had by a joint conquest recovered the Peleponnese, then held by the issue of Hercules, of whose linage they were, long before, until they were forcibly disposed by Eurystheus of it. And so to make a partition of it, they divided into three portions, Argos, Sparta (or Lacedaemon) and Messena. Cresphontes greatly desired to have Messena and persuaded his brother Temenus (who had already seized Argos and was chosen to make lottery for them, to assign the other two parts between Cresphontes and Theras, which was the right of the two orphans) to use some trick and fraud for him. This he accordingly did, as all agree in the report of it, though by what manner there is some difference among them. *Pausanias* said that it was agreed that he should have Messena, or his choice of all three, whoever's lottery came out first. Whereupon Temenus made two pellets of clay, the one dried in the sun for his nephews and the other baked in the fire for his brother, which being cast both at once into the water and lying there for some time, theirs being dissolved; his of necessity came forth first. Whereas *Apollodorus* reported that it was agreed among them all that whoever's lottery came out not first, but last, should have Messena and that when either of the other two cast in a white stone, Cresphontes cast in a piece of white clay, which being dissolved in the water was not drawn at all and so by that means he obtained his desire, not by chance, as it might seem, but indeed by craftiness and deceit.

In a similar vein, *Porta (1584)* who wrote about the secret techniques which were prescribed to be used, not so much for the finding out of a thief, as for drawing out a confession from someone that is suspected to be so on some good grounds. First put his name in a scroll of paper together with many others, all wrapped all up in lumps of clay, but his wrapped somewhat more loosely than any of the others. Then put all the scrolls into a basin of water so that it seems by chance that his unfold first and he may thereby suppose himself miraculously discovered and be induced to confess it.

In this kind of trickery imagination may oftentimes do much of the work. As *Delrio (1618)* says, "a strong imagination in either the agent or the patient, in the doer or the sufferer, can further an effect many times over". It can do so in the agent. When using the sieve-and-shears, if the names of many whom they think good to question are read out, because among that group they strongly suspect someone, then the strong imagination of the participants, particularly the one that holds the sieve-and-sheers between them (and even though no wilful tricks may have been played by either of them) may be a sufficient means to work an undetectable movement in the hand of the holder who becomes so strongly possessed that he will turn the sieve and shears so naming the party who was formerly suspected.

In the patient it was observed by *Gersonides (~1320)* that in some superstitious courses of cure, they may receive some strength from their imagination. But this *Gersonides,* a grave writer, wished physicians to be wary and beware; while they may cure other men's bodies they must not cast away their own souls. The author *Porta (1584)* prescribed a method for the discovery of a thief by making bread or paste of meal mingled with the powder of a stone said to be found usually in eagles' nests. The suspect, said he, while eating it together with others would feel fear arising from the expectation of the event which will dry his throat and hinder his swallowing so that he shall not be able to get it down as readily as the rest do. By that means he may be discovered. Whether this is true or not, it is certain that the imagination has much force in producing effects and making things seem to be chance or random when indeed they are nothing of the sort.

§8. 'Extraordinary', by Satan

These superstitious divinations sometimes take an ordinary course, but at other times again they hit on extraordinary means, either by diabolical cooperation or by divine permission and special appointment.

Sometimes, I say, with Satan's cooperation. He is said (by *Biel, ~1480)* to have had a hand in miracles that are reported to have been wrought by images of saints. There can be no doubt that he often does the same in some of these lotteries and other kinds of divination, which Christian writers *(Augustine)* have observed and heathens *(Socrates)* also themselves acknowledged.

But some say: how can the Devil come to know such things that are discovered by these means? I answer: the things discovered this way are contingent either on the past, present or the future. For hidden things in the past or present the Devil may well know many things, much more then men ordinarily do. In this regard he acts as a spirit and is either present at the doing of them or is a partaker in them.

First: as an example of being present at the doing of them, he was present when the sons of God, that is the angels, came one time to appear before God. *(Job 1:6)* No doubt he is often with us when we have little awareness of it. By this means therefore the Devil, being of a swift and subtle nature, can take notice of many things done in secret while he an unseen presence. Thus he can give advice in one place from what he knows is going or was to be done in some other place, even though it was far distant from there. *Augustine* gives an example of a person possessed, who said he could tell his house-companions when one of them set out from 12 miles away to come towards them and how far he had come on every foot of the way forward until he came to him and from whose hand alone he would take sustenance. But this was no divination or prophecy, as *Peter Martyr (~1560)* a good divine put it. Think of a soldier standing sentinel; if he was to spot of a troop of horse that he could see coming towards him he could tell how far they had come forward and how near they approached to the place where they were expected.

Secondly as a partaker in them, either instigating or assisting in them: this was what happened with Judas who knew well what he was doing in betraying his Master Christ Jesus. *(John 13:2)* So too when the Chaldeans and Sabeans *(Job 1:12)* were robbing and spoiling Job. So first the Devil incites men to sin and then accuses them to God of that sin. So often here he sets men on sinning and it is their public shame or bane afterwards which berates and betrays them when they have sinned.

For future contingent events the Devil would ordinarily not know them for certain, but only extraordinarily or uncertainly.

First uncertainly: probably it is because of his natural skill (which gives the Devil his Greek name 'diabolos' – to hurl across) and his long experience using it. And no wonder. Any skilful physician could by reason of his skill say much more about the state of his patient and the likelihood or unlikelihood of his recovery than could an ignorant man or any other ordinary person. Old men by reason of their long experience can tell and foretell many things with good grounds by pre-conjecture and by observation of men's usual courses and carriages than the younger sort commonly can. So it is no marvel if Satan can do this; he is called a serpent because of his subtlety or even an old serpent because of his antiquity, having being in existence for more than 5,000 years. *(1 Sam 28:15)* He will probably be able to guess at many of the things that men can see or say little about. And so he might have been able to foretell what was likely to befall Saul, seeing how things then stood with him, although that was something that any man of even middling and ordinary capacity might at that time have given a shrewd guess at.

Again extraordinarily: he may be able to fore-see and fore-show with more certainty because of what he had heard from God or the servants of God, or because of what he is permitted to do or is employed for by God.

So what might he have heard from God himself, from the angels or the prophets of God, who also learn some things from the angels? Just as one sitting on the ground or abiding within may hear the news privately imparted to him from the watchman standing on the sentinel or watch-tower outside, so he could then relate to others pretending it was by a vision or apparition that only he could see and discover himself. Thus he might have foretold his own fall as well as Saul's down-fall, which he is sometimes said to have done. Many future events may have come to his notice; so while pretending to have prophetical divination he can then use it to draw divine adoration to himself.

Secondly what is he permitted to do by God or what he is employed to do for God? Often evil spirits are permitted by God to do much mischief both corporally and spiritually, by inflicting maladies and infecting the air, inciting and egging men on to evil courses because he knows their disposition and they do not hesitate to prevail and to persuade themselves. Hence on occasion men will foretell what they themselves are about to do or will draw others into it. To take men in hand when they can do no more mischief being near the end of their tether, so that they can help or heal them but only because they leave off hurting them. Or because they cannot get leave to molest them any longer and their evils at this time should be at an end if such and such fooleries be performed.

Sometimes they are employed by God for this purpose: for the Devil is God's executioner and He often makes good use of. This was how He used an evil spirit (not the soul of Naboth, as the doting rabbi *Jonan* dreamt) to entice Ahab out to his ruin. So he used evil Spirits, as the most think, for the plaguing of Egypt (though some expound the Psalmist otherwise and it is against the rule that say that God is wont to afflict good men by bad angels and bad men by good angels). Now it is evident that he used one of them, an evil angel of God for the vexing of Saul, which still shows in the text. It was an evil spirit in regard of his malicious quality and yet a spirit of God because it was an executioner of God's justice, as the Ancients have well observed. And thus may the Devil further foretell what God himself has set him or sent him to do. He might as well by that means also read about Saul's destiny, such as the one that God had given over and given up into his hands.

Now in the cases where such evil spirits have a hand in the results, they are not always alike. Sometimes they fail notwithstanding their skill (as well as the wis est and best experienced men often do also) in those things that by their natural wisdom and subtlety they foresee in the secret causes or signs of them, when God by some extraordinary course turned things about and controlled the ordinary carriage of the creature. As the patient being treated sometimes dies through some inward unexpected accident where the physician, according to the rules and grounds of his art saw no signs of danger. Or if a mariner had good grounds from observation for his opinion that a storm of wind should last so long, until Christ had suddenly calmed it. Or that a gardener should promise so much fruit from a vine in a year by judging it according to his skill; but if it was afterwards blasted with lightning or rooted up by some wild beasts breaking into the vineyard. And so these unclean spirits, notwithstanding all their skill and experience, often fail in their predictions when some greater power overtook that which they built upon.

They also fail in those things that they are enjoined and set or sent about by God. When God altered His course and either revoked a sentence, as with Ezekias and as with the Ninevites; or when God gives a countermand, as to Abraham *(Gen 22:2)* about the sacrificing of Isaac. This would be like a judge who sends suddenly and unexpectedly to reprieve a prisoner that he had condemned and when the executioner was ready to do his office with him and had taken full account of the sale of his spoils.

§9. Extraordinary, by God

So far we have seen how by Satan's help in such superstitious divinations and predictions may either fail or hold. We now go further: in the last place are those things that take effect by God's permission and providence as always, but in this case by his permission for a special purpose which is sometimes and for various reasons by his special ordination and appointment which no devil or creature therefore can cross.

First by permission for a special purpose either for the trial and exercise of something or for the punishment of someone: for a trial of something, there are those who will try out such superstitions as the crowing and croaking of ravens, the shrieking of owls, various kinds of lottery and others too. God forewarned his people *(Deut 13:1)* to beware of people who try by evil courses to draw from God what He does not choose to tell them; that they should not heed them unless they see things fall out according to what they foretell. But if they do set some sign and it happens accordingly, even so they should not pay heed to them. God allowed this to happen to try them, to see whether they did indeed love Him and wish sit so close to Him so they would not use such superstitious means even though it happened as was foretold them, to be drawn away from Him.

Again it is for the just punishment of some: they may be whipped and scourged with a rod of their own making or with a cord of their own twisting. God allows these things to often take effect so that they that loved not the truth may be given up by strong delusions to believe in lies *(2 Thess 2:9)* so that they may be further entangled in Satan's snares and would rather heed him than heed God. Sometimes God's children have been God's prophets, confirmed in their holy faith by true miracles and predictions. Some wicked wretches may be hardened in their false belief by counterfeit miracles and diabolical predictions like the Pharaoh did.

And therefore we see that such superstitious courses often can take effect and have their outcome answerable to the expectations of those that use them. Remember that the more successful the sin is, the more dangerous it is for the sinner. So in this case, the oftener such courses work the more perilous they are, because they are more powerful to prevail unless we are not wiser and more wary. In this regard they are rather to be suspected and shunned by us.

Secondly by God's special ordination and appointment these things sometimes work out His own purposes by the wickedness of others. For God works through even those who work against Him. They fight His battles, even as they fight against Him. Now God gives success to these things, though evil in themselves and as they are used, sometimes for the punishment of those that deserve to be punished and his will is to have either destroyed or corrected; and those either the users of them or others.

To the users of them, as in the lottery that was cast by Saul which lighted on Jonathan to punish Saul *(1 Sam 14:38)* for his unadvised adjuration and presumptuous inquisition and to show what straits men wilfully cast themselves into by such idle, rash, unnecessary and inordinate oaths. For this cause also it seems that he allowed the Devil to foretell Saul's overthrow and thereby to punish him for his impious act, first by dejection afterwards by death.

Or some others: the lottery that lighted on Jonah, of which *Jerome* well said, "that we ought not in that regard to give heed or credit to a lottery in suchlike cases", (for how do we know that God has still the same work or purpose to that work; or that he is willing ever so to work?) "nor should he match it with that lottery that we read of in the Acts *(1:26)* which was used in the choice of Matthias", (reasoning from the lawfulness of the one to the other) "since that a singular privilege does not make common law". God well used that course that was familiar to them when they did evil in order to find out and fetch back his fugitive servant. As did Nebuchadnezzar's idolatrous divinations and his similar lottery, which he himself was foretold about by his own Prophets: that he would make good for the just and well deserved punishment of his perverse and perjured prince and people. *(Ezek 21:19)*

Again sometimes God gives a clear run to these courses to manifest His own glory, power and providence; to let men discover by their own projects, though evil and impious, who it is that plagues them and has power over them, though they either know not or do not acknowledge Him. And so it was in that sign that the Philistine soothsayers set themselves, whereby God put them out of their doubts concerning His hand on them which they had made some doubt of before. We may consider that as these courses took effect when God had a hand in them so the same courses used by others such as Haman and Senacharib, though at other times they failed and had no effect, falling out clean contrary when God was not pleased to give them success or had not (and who can tell when He had?) any such intention for them. Considering therefore that there can be no certainty in such a lottery, unless God himself has a special hand in it, which we have no reason to expect, unless it be for our evil, to plague us for our perverse courses in that kind. Also that the Devil, just as he may be deceived, so he may deceive us. From a professed and notorious deceiver we can expect nothing but deceit, whether he himself be has been deceived or not. Let us take heed how we give heed or credit to such deceits as they seldom prove true. However we regard them even though they often prove true, we remember that Saul's witchcraft was not therefore more allowable because the Devil told him nothing but truth. Nor were the Apostles of Christ one whit less spared from the unclean spirits because they told truly what they were. Bearing ever in mind that God has forewarned us beforehand that though they should prove true yet we should not believe them nor give credit unto them, because they are only the tricks of Satan to draw or drive us away from Him. These are such sorry flights that even the wiser sort of heathens have described and discovered the folly and vanity of them. And it is a foul shame for Christian men to be caught short in such. And thus much may suffice also for these latter sort of lotteries, namely the extraordinary and divinatory lotteries. Even if they might have been lawful at some times for some people yet none of them are lawful in these times for anybody.

§10. Final conclusion

To end where we began. "Take the dross", said Solomon, "from the silver and there will be a vessel fit for the sinner". *(Proverbs 25:4)* So take the ordinary abuse from the ordinary lottery and it will prove an ordinance of no evil use. Nor should the use and the abuse of them be so mixed together that men may not be able to separate one from the other. As for extraordinary lotteries, the very ordinary use of that sort of lottery is a mere abuse of lotteries. As dross it therefore will not endure the refiner's fire but run to smoke and ashes when it comes to the assay and be utterly rejected. There may be superstition too in condemning the one, while approving of the other. Let the one therefore go, as it well deserves, to the dunghill. Let the other be so wisely and warily used that God, who has given us the free use of them would not be dishonoured. Nor should our brethren be offended or wronged because God has given us these lotteries to use for our benefit. They do not hinder us from doing the better things that more closely concern us and as such they then should be a means of bettering ourselves.

FINIS.

[I have omitted a final page in Latin and Greek, as well as mistakes noted by Gataker in the text and the margins.]

BIBLIOGRAPHICAL NOTES

Gataker's references: As explained in the Editor's Preface, the original text included a vast amount of footnotes (or 'marginalia' as they are usually called). What appears here in these Biographical notes is an indication of the main references that Gataker used, together with some details about the authors, where appropriate.

BIBLE: I used: http://bible.cc/ which cross-references many versions of the bible including KJV (King James Version – not used by Gataker, but he was aware of it) and the GWT – God's Words in Translation. Citations are given in their abbreviated form, as given by Gataker, but they are not difficult to decipher.

Abraham, Rabbi (~1140) could be Rabbi Abraham ben Meir Ibn Ezra (~1089 – ~1164) born Toledo, Spain and educated in the 'Golden Age' of Muslim Spain. He excelled as a poet, philosopher, grammarian and Biblical commentator. The latter part of his life (after 1140) was spent wandering in poverty through Italy, Provence, France, England, Egypt and Israel. It was during his wanderings that he composed most of his many influential literary works.

Aldhelm, Saint (~ 639–709) *de laud. Virg*, West Saxon abbot of Malmesbury, the most learned teacher of 7th-century Wessex, a pioneer in the art of Latin verse among the Anglo-Saxons, and the author of numerous extant writings in Latin verse and prose. Aldhelm was trained in Latin and in Celtic-Irish scholarship by Malmesbury's Irish founder and went on to study at the famous school at Canterbury.

Alexander de Ales (1452) *Summa Theologiae* Nuremberg: Alexander of Hales, (called Doctor Irrefragabilis), a celebrated English theologian of the 13th century, trained in the monastery of Hales. His most celebrated work was the *Summa Theologiae*, undertaken by the orders of Pope Innocent IV and approved by Alexander IV, on the report of 70 learned theologians, as a system of instruction for all the schools in Christendom.

Alsius *de bello Carthaginae* N/K

Anti-Piscat N/K

Ambrose (338 – 397) *Virgines, Expositio evangelii secundum Lucam (de pontifico forte designato)* Bishop of Milan, he is counted (along with Augustine, Jerome and Gregory) as one of the great Latin Doctors of the Church. Gataker makes references to them all.

Ammianus Marcellinus (325 – 391) was a fourth-century Roman historian. His is the last major historical account of the late Roman empire which survives today: his work chronicled the history of Rome from 96 to 378 AD, although only the sections covering the period 353 – 378 AD are extant.

Appolodorus of Athens (b. ~180 BC, d. after 120 BC) son of Asclepiades, was a Greek scholar and grammarian. He was a pupil of Diogenes of Babylon, Panaetius the Stoic, and the grammarian Aristarchus of Samothrace. He left, or fled, Alexandria around BC 146, most likely for Pergamum, and eventually settled in Athens.

Aquinas, St Thomas (1270) *De sortibus ('of lotteries')* is a main reference. Also refers to *ad Dominum Jacobum de.* Saint Thomas Aquinas (1225 – 1274) was an Italian Dominican priest, a philosopher and theologian in the scholastic tradition.

He is the foremost classical proponent of natural theology, and the father of the Thomistic school of philosophy and theology. St. Thomas is held in the Roman Catholic Church to be the model teacher for those studying for the priesthood. One of the 33 Doctors of the Church, he is considered by many Roman Catholics to be the Catholic Church's greatest theologian. Consequently, many institutions of learning have been named after him. Publications: The work for which he is best-known is the *Summa Theologica.*

Aret. *in problem clas* cannot crack the code here! 6 refs to; could be Aretaeus de Cappedocia, Greek physician 2nd Century AD who wrote many extant books on medicine.

Arias Montanus, Benedict (1593) *Antiquitatum Iudaicarum (Treatise of Jewish antiquities) libri IX., in quîs, praeter Iudeae, Hierosolymorum, & Templi Salomonis accuratam delineationem, praecipui sacri ac profani gentis ritus describuntur ... Adiectis formis æneis Lugduni Batavorum: Apud F. Raphelengium.Maps* Antwerp 'learned linguist' says Gataker, Spanish, 1527 – 1598

Aristides several; not clear which.

Aristophanes (456 – 386 BC) Greek comic dramatist. Plays: include *Wasps, Lysistra Hesych Equit poul Athenesis, Euphorm sine Barcli satyr*, *Euphor. Satyr* Euphorides Pittalus may have been the random doctor.

Aristotle *Harpocr, apud Lacr Rhetoric.* No need for any explanation about tthis great Greek philosopher.

Augustine of Hippo (354 –430), was a very important figure in the early Church. He was a philosopher and theologian, and was bishop of the North African city of Hippo Regius for the last third of his life. Augustine is one of the most important figures in the development of Western Christianity, and is considered to be one of the church fathers. He framed the concepts of original sin and just war. In Roman Catholicism and the Anglican Communion, he is a saint and preeminent Doctor of the Church, and the patron of the Augustinian religious order. Many Protestants, especially Calvinists, consider him to be one of the theological fathers of Reformation teaching on salvation and grace. His books included *Civitas Dei (The City of God), On Christian Doctrine, Confessions, Retractions contra academe de gen ad lit lib de Mendac*

Babington, Gervase (1583) *A very fruitfull Exposition of the Commaundements by way of questions and answeres for greater plainnesse, etc* Henry Midleton, for Thomas Charde: London. Babington was successively Bishop of Llandaff, of Exeter, and of Worcester.

Bale, John (1560) *The actes of the English votaryes* London Bale (1495 – 1563), English dramatist and clergyman. An ardent proponent of the Reformation, he used the stage as a vehicle for his views. He is notable for his part in the religious strife of the 16th century and for his antiquarian studies, including the first rudimentary history of English literature.

Balmford, James (1593) *A short and plaine dialogue concerning the unlawfulnes of playing at cards or tables, or any other game consisting in chance* Richard Boile: London

Balmford, James (1623) *A Short and Plaine Dialogue concerning the vnlawfulnes of playing at Cards or Tables, or any other game consisting in chance, etc. with a reply to Gataker*
Balmford b. 1556 was a vicar in at St Olave's, Southwark, not far from Rotherhithe which was Gataker's parish. In 1603, his controversial failure to visit the sick during plague perhaps attuned him to such: 'Open graves where sundry are buried together': J. Balmford, *A short dialogue concerning the plagues infection* (London, 1603). Remarkably little on this main 'adversary' of Gataker.

Baronius, Cardinal Caesar *Annales* about 312 AD not much known about him.

Becon, Thomas (1560) *The relikes of Rome, concernynge church ware and matters of religion, faithfully gathered out of the most faythfull wryters, of histories and chronicles, etc* London : John Day. Becon (1512 – 1567) was Chaplain to Thomas Cranmer, Prebendary of Canterbury Cathedral.

Bede, Venerable (~ 672 – 735), was a Benedictine monk at the Northumbrian monastery of Saint Peter at Monkwearmouth, today part of Sunderland, in the English county of Durham. He is well known as an author and scholar, and his most famous work, *Historia ecclesiastica gentis Anglorum* (The Ecclesiastical History of the English People) gained him the title 'The father of English history'.

Bellarmino, Roberto Saint Cardinal (1610) *de cleric.* Belarmino (1542 – 1621) 'Doctor of the Church', Italian beatified 1923, clashed with Galileo and James I of England.

Bernard of Clairvaux (~1120) *Bern de divers serm 26* Saint Bernard of Clairvaux (1090–1153) was a French abbot and the primary builder of the reforming Cistercian monastic order. The voice of conscience, the dominating figure in the Catholic Church from 1125 to 1153, his authority helped to end the schism of 1130. Bernard was the main voice of conservatism during the Renaissance of the 12th century and the main opponent of rising scholastic theology. Devoted to promoting the veneration of the Virgin Mary, he was also the most influential advocate of the Second Crusade. He was canonized as a saint in 1174.

Ben-Gorion, doubtful might be Joseph Gorionid 'counterfeit' Joseph ben Gorion (in Hebrew, Yosef ben Gorion) a medieval Jewish historian best known as the author of the *Sefer Yosippon*, a history of the Jews from the time of the Creation to the destruction of Jerusalem in 70 AD, with historical accounts of Babylonia, Greece, Rome, and other countries.

Beza, Theodore (1564) *Vita Calvini, The Life of John Calvin.* Beza (1519 – 1605) was a French Protestant Christian theologian and scholar who played an important role in the early Reformation. A member of the monarchomaque movement, who opposed absolute monarchy, he followed John Calvin as leader of the reformed church in Switzerland.

Biel, Gabriel (~1480) *Misc lect* ~ 1410 – 95. Born at Speyer, studied at Heidelberg, Erfurt and Cologne; member of the cathedral clergy at Mainz. 'Thomist thinker'.

Bodin, Jean (1580) *De la demonomanie des sorciers.* Bodin (1530–1596) was a French jurist and political philosopher, member of the Parlement of Paris and professor of Law in Toulouse. He is best known for his theory of sovereignty. Bodin lived during the Reformation, writing against the background of religious and civil conflict – particularly that, in his native France, between the (Calvinist) Huguenots and the state-supported Catholic Church. Bodin recommended torture, even in cases of the disabled and children, to try to confirm guilt of witchcraft. He asserted that not even one witch could be erroneously condemned if the correct procedures were followed, suspicion being enough to torment the accused because rumours concerning witches were almost always true.

Bonfinus, Antonius (1568) *Rerum Vngaricarum decades quatuor, cum dimidia. Quarum tres priores, ante annos Ex officina Oporiniana*: Basileæ, Bonfin, historian, born Ascoli in 1427, d. 1502.

Bradshaw, W (~1590) 'a reverend Minister of our Church now with the Lord' (Gataker) 'a celebrated Puritan'. A friend and patron of Gataker at Cambridge.

Brerewood, Edward (1614) *De ponderibus, et pretijs veterum nummorum, eorumq; cum recentioribus collatione* London William Stansby. Brerewood (1565 – 1613), antiquary and first professor of astronomy at Gresham College, was a scholar in many fields who published nothing in his own lifetime. *De Ponderibus* is a treatise on the weights and values of Greek, Roman, Hebrew and Byzantine ancient coins.

Broughton, Hugh (1588) *Concent of Scripture (with maps)* London: Gabriel Simpson & William White. Broughton (1549 – 1612) English scholar and divine. At Christ's Cambridge he laid the foundation of the Hebrew scholarship for which he was afterwards so distinguished. From Cambridge he went to London, where his eloquence gained him many and powerful friends. In 1588 he published his first work, 'a little book of great pains,' entitled *A Concent of Scripture*. This work, dealing with biblical chronology and textual criticism, was attacked at both universities, and the author was obliged to defend it in a series of lectures. In 1589 he went to Germany, where he frequently engaged in discussions both with Romanists and with the learned Jews whom he met at Frankfurt and elsewhere. In 1591 he returned to England, but his Puritan leanings incurred the hostility of Whitgift. Accordingly in 1592 he once more went abroad, and cultivated the acquaintance of the principal scholars of Europe, including Joseph Justus Scaliger and Rabbi Elias. Such was the esteem in which he was held, even by his opponents, that he might have had a cardinal's hat if he had been willing to change his faith. In 1599 he published his 'Explication' of the article 'He descended into hell,' in which he maintained that Hades means simply the abode of departed spirits, not the place of torment. On the accession of James he returned to England; but not being engaged to co-operate in the new translation of the Bible (though he had for some years planned a similar work), he retired to Middleburg in Holland, where he preached to the English congregation. In 1611 he returned to England. Some of his works were collected and published in a large folio volume in 1662, with a sketch of his life by John Lightfoot, but many of his theological manuscripts remain still unedited in the British Museum. (A longer entry here, because I think this life shows the religious turmoil of the times)

Bucer, Martin (1541) *Acta colloquii Mompelgardensis anno 1586 habiti, ... merito jungas. Horum inventis inter se copulatis atque in unum systema* Regensburg 1541. Bucer (1491 – 1551) was a German Protestant reformer, born at Schlettstadt in Alsace (today Sélestat, in France). In 1506 he entered the Dominican order, and was sent to study at Heidelberg. There he became acquainted with the works of Erasmus and Protestant Luther, and was present at a disputation of the latter with some of the Romanist doctors. He became a convert to the reformed opinions, then abandoned his order, still by papal dispensation, in 1521, and soon afterwards married a former nun, Elisabeth Silbereisen. In 1522 he was pastor at Landstuhl in the Palatinate, and travelled hither and thither propagating the reformed doctrine of Protestantism. After his excommunication in 1523 he made his headquarters at Strassburg, where he succeeded Matthew Zell. Henry VIII of England asked his advice in connection with the divorce from his wife Catherine of Aragon. In 1548 he was sent for to Augsburg to sign the agreement, called the Augsburg Interim, between the Catholics and Protestants. His stout opposition to this project exposed him to many difficulties, and he was glad to accept Cranmer's invitation to make his home in England and assist with the Reformation of the Church of England. On his arrival in 1549 he was appointed Regius Professor of Divinity at Cambridge. Edward VI and the protector Somerset showed him much favour and he was consulted as to the revision of the *Book of Common Prayer*. But on February 28, 1551 he died, and was buried in the university church, with great state. In 1557 Catholic Queen Mary''s commissioners exhumed and burnt his body (along with that of Paul Fagius, also considered an heretic) and demolished his tomb; it was subsequently restored by order of Queen Elizabeth I. Bucer is said to have written ninety-six treatises, among them a translation and commentary of the Psalms (one of the first of its kind from the Hebrew text published in 1529), *Grund und Ursach* (a detailed account of Strassburg reforms to the Roman Mass published in 1524) and *De regno Christi* (his last major publication; written for Edward VI in 1550). His name is familiar in English literature from the use made of his doctrines by Milton in his divorce treatises (An interesting life-history!)

Caesar, Julius *de bello Gallico.*

Cajetan, Tomaso de Vio, Cardinal (1525) *Summula de peccatis* Rome Cajetan 1468 – 1534. Born at Gaeta, he entered the Dominican order in 1484 and studied at Naples, Bologna, and Padua until 1493. Italian cardinal best known for his opposition to the teachings of Martin Luther and the Protestant Reformation while he was the Pope's Legate in Wittenberg

Calvin, John (1584) *The Holy Gospel of Iesus Christ, according to Iohn, with the commentary of M. Iohn Caluine: Faithfully translated out of Latine ... by Christopher Fetherstone, etc*

Camden, William (1594) *Britannia* Camden (1551 – 1623) was an English antiquarian and historian. He wrote the first topographical survey of the island of Great Britain and the first detailed historical account of the reign of Elizabeth I of England. In 1577, with the encouragement of Abraham Ortelius, Camden began his great work *Britannia*, a topographical and historical survey of all of Great Britain. His stated intention was 'to restore antiquity to Britaine, and Britaine to its antiquity.' The first edition was published in 1586. The work, which was written in Latin, was very popular, going into seven editions by 1607. The first English language translation, prepared by Philemon Holland (probably under Camden's direction) appeared in 1610.

Cartwright, Thomas (1617) *Commentarii succincti & dilucidi in Proverbia Salomonis.* Lugduni Batavorum G. Brewsterum. Cartwright (1535 – 1603), English Puritan divine, was born in Hertfordshire. He studied divinity at St John's College, Cambridge.

Casaubon, Isaac *('editio princeps' 1589)* 2nd-cent. Greek guide to warfare. Casaubon (1559 – 1614) was a classical scholar, first in France then later in England, regarded by many at the time as the most learned in Europe.

Cassiodorus, Flavius Magnus Aurelius (485 – 585), was a Roman statesman and great writer, serving in the administration of Theodoric the Great, king of the Ostrogoths.

Chaucer, Geoffrey (1476) *Canterbury Tales* William Caxton: London

Cicero, Marcus Tullius (known as Tully) Roman statesman, lawyer, scholar and writer who vainly tried to uphold republican principles in the final civil wars that destroyed the republic of Rome. His writings include books of rhetoric, orations, philosophical and political treatises, and letters. He is remembered in modern times as the greatest Roman orator and innovator of what became known as Ciceronian rhetoric. Publications: *On Divination, Verres,* composed as supplement to his *De natura deorum* ('on the nature of the gods')

Chlothar I (Gataker spells it Clotharij) *decret Coter de Jur mil Barlam de Duc Ven Salmuth in Ital*,; (497 – 561), called the Old (*le Vieux*), King of the Franks, was one of the four sons of Clovis. On Childebert's death in 558 he became sole king of the Franks.

Chrysostom, John (349 – ~407) was the archbishop of Constantinople. He is known for his eloquence in preaching and public speaking, his denunciation of abuse of authority by both ecclesiastical and political leaders, the *Liturgy of St. John Chrysostom*, and his ascetic sensibilities. After his death he was given the Greek surname chrysostomos, meaning 'golden mouthed', rendered in English as Chrysostom.

Chytraeus, David (~1580) *A Soueraigne Salue for a Sick Soule ... Englished by W. F. [Extracted from Chytraeus's 'Regulae vitae.']* Chytreus.(1530 – 1600) protestant lawyer produced concords for various states (this is a doubtful reference, but no other fits) German name Kochhafe)

Clement of Alexandria *Stromateis* Clemens Alexandrinus, Greek Father of the Church. The little we know of him is mainly derived from his own works. In the *Stromateis,* while attempting to show that the Jewish Scriptures were older than any writings of the Greeks, he invariably brings down his dates to the death of Commodus.

Conon Mythographus grammarian and mythographer Rome in the time of Caesar and Augustus. Author of myths and legends, especially about the founding of colonies. Ref to *Photius.*

Contareno, Gaspere (1599) *The commonwealth and gouernment of Venice* Facsimile reprint of original: London, pr by Iohn Windet for Edmund Mattes, 1599. (This has a long history of republication.)

Cyprian, Saint (Thascius Caecilius Cyprianus) (d. 258) was bishop of Carthage and an important early Christian writer. He was probably born at Carthage, where he received an excellent classical (pagan) education. After converting to Christianity, he became a bishop (249) and eventually died a martyr at Carthage. (See also Pseudo-Cyprian.)

Dalton, Michael (1618) *The Countrey Iustice, conteyning the practise of the Iustices of the Peace out of their Sessions. Gathered for the better helpe of such Iustices of Peace as haue not beene much conuersant in the studie of the lawes of this realme* The Societie of Stationers: London. Several books explaining the law from this author.

Daneau, Lambert (1586) *True and Christian Friendshippe ... Written first in Latine ... and now turned into English. Together also with a right excellent Inuectiue ... against the wicked exercise of Diceplay and other prophane Gaming. Wherein, as Godly recreations and moderate disportes bee Christianly allowed and learnedly defended: so, all vaine, ydle, unlawfull, offensive, and prophane Exercises, bee sharply reproved and flatly condemned.* [Both Englished by Thos: Newton, the rector of Little Illford) also (1575 orig pub in French 1574). In his lifetime, Lambert Daneau (1530 – 1595) was one of the most famous Calvinist theologians in Europe. He was the Professor of Theology at Geneva and the chair of Theology at Leyden. In 1564, Daneau wrote *Les Sorciers, Dialogue trs utile et trs necessaire pour ce temps*. In 1575, an English version was published with an immensely long title: *A Dialogue of Witches, in foretime named Lot-tellers, and now commonly called Sorcerers. Wherein is declared breefly and effectually, whatsoever may be required, touching that argument. A treatise very profitable, by reason of the diverse and sundry opinions of men in this question, and right necessary for Judges to understand, which sit upon life or death.*

Dartes *in Bar Annal* (Venice) n/k *deonian dialect.*

Delrio, Martin (1618 posthumously) *Disquisitionem Magicarum* P Hengenitii: Mainz. Del Rio (1551 – 1608) Scholar, statesman, Jesuit theologian, from Antwerp, studied at Paris, Douai, Louvain and Salamanca where he received the degree of Doctor of Law in 1574. Returning to the Low Countries with the reputation of being 'the miracle of his age' (Catholic Enc.) He has been accused of being the principal cause of witch-hunts in the Southern Netherlands. Most historians, however, have noticed Delrio's relative moderation on the subject of witchcraft.

Demosthenes, Androth Demosthenes (384–322 BC), Greek: was a prominent Greek statesman and orator of ancient Athens. His orations constitute a significant expression of ancient Athenian intellectual prowess and provide a thorough insight into the politics and culture of ancient Greece during the 4th century BC.

Diogenes Greek 'the Cynic', Greek philosopher, was born in Sinope (modern day Sinop, Turkey) about 412 BC and died in 323 BC, at Corinth. Diogenes is said to have been a disciple of Antisthenes, who (according to Plato's *Phaedo*) was present at the death of Socrates. Diogenes, a beggar who made his home in the streets of Athens, made a virtue of extreme poverty. He taught contempt for human achievements; his was a relentless campaign to debunk social values and institutions.

Dionysius Chrysostomus Dionysius of Halicarnassus (~60 BC – after 7 BC) was a Greek historian and teacher of rhetoric, who flourished during the reign of Caesar Augustus.

Edmunds, Sir Clement (1600) *Observations, Upon the Five First Bookes of Caesar's Commentaries, Setting Fourth the Practise of the Art Military, in the Time of the Roman Empire*. London: Printed by Peter Short. Edmondes (1567/8?–1622), government official. Remembrancer of the City of London.

Elliot, Sir Thomas (1531) *The Boke Named the Gouernour*. Elliot (also Eylot), 'one of our countrymen'. Writer and diplomat, born in Wiltshire, England. In 1523 he became clerk of the King's council, was ambassador to Emperor Charles V in 1531–2 and became MP for Cambridge in 1542. His chief work, *The Boke Named the Gouernour* (1531), is the earliest English treatise on moral philosophy. He was a strong supporter of the use of English (as opposed to Latin and Greek) in scholarly work and added many new words to the language, including *encyclopaedia* (1539). He was knighted in 1530.

Erasmus (1515) *Sileni Alcibiadis* is one of his most direct assessments of the need for church reform. Desiderius Erasmus (1469 – 1536) was a classical scholar who wrote in a 'pure' Latin style. Although he remained a Roman Catholic throughout his lifetime, he was critical of what he considered the excesses of the Catholic Church. Using humanist techniques he prepared important new Latin and Greek editions of the New Testament which raised questions that would be influential in the Reformation. He also wrote *The Praise of Folly*, *Handbook of a Christian Knight*, *On Civility in Children*, *Copia: Foundations of the Abundant Style* and many other works.

Estey, George (~1603) *History of the Gospell:* BL only shows (1603) *Certaine godly and learned expositions vpon diuers parts of Scripture : As they were preached and afterwards more briefly penned by that vvorthy man of God, Maister George Estey, sometimes fellovve of Goneuill and Caius Colledge in Cambridge. Late preacher of the word of God in Saint Edmunds Burie.(Suffolk)(1560 – 1601)* Printed by J. R. for R. Banckworth: London. No other information about Eastie/Easty as Gataker spells it.

Euphor. Satyr. see Aristophanes

Euripides (480–406 BC) Greek tragedian, famous for sayings like 'Those whom the gods would destroy, they first make mad', quoted in Plutarch, Symposium.

Eustachius (~1150) *Ad Illiam.* Eustathius of Thessalonica (~1110 – 1198) was a native of Constantinople who became archbishop of Thessalonica. He wrote commentaries on ancient Greek poets, theological treatises, homilies, epistles and an important account of the sack of Thessalonica by William II of Sicily in 1185. Of his works, his commentaries on Homer are the most widely referred to.

Falkenberg, Gerard (1569) *Dionysiaca nunc primum in lucem edita ex bibliotheca Joannis Sambuci Pannonii / cum lectionibus et conjecturis G. Falkenburg* (from Nonnus q.v.)

Fenner, Dudley (1587) *A Short and Profitable Treatise, of lawfull and unlawfull recreations and of the right use and abuse of those that are lawefull, etc* Richard Schilders: Midleburgh, Netherlands (Re-published in 1977) Dudley Fenner (~ 1558 – 1587) was an English puritan divine. He helped popularize Ramist logic in the English language. Fenner was also one of the first theologians to use the term 'covenant of works' to describe God's relationship with Adam in the Book of Genesis. He was born in Kent and educated at Cambridge University. There he became an adherent of Thomas Cartwright, (see entry) and publicly expounded his presbyterian views, with the result that he was obliged to leave Cambridge without taking his degree. For some months he seems to have assisted the vicar of Cranbrook, Kent, but it is doubtful whether he received ordination. He next followed Cartwright to Antwerp and having received ordination according to rite of the Reformed church, assisted Cartwright for several years in preaching to the English congregation there. The leniency shown by Archbishop Grindal to puritans encouraged him to return to England and he became curate of Cranbrook in 1583. In the same year, however, he was one of seventeen Kentish ministers suspended for refusing to sign an acknowledgment of the queen's supremacy and of the authority of the Prayer Book and articles. He was imprisoned for a time, but eventually regained his liberty and spent the remainder of his life as chaplain in the Reformed church at Middleburgh.

Fenton, Roger DD (1611) *A Treatise of Vsurie, diuided into three bookes* Imprinted by Felix Kyngston, for William Aspley: London. This clergyman was a native of Lancashire. He was Fellow of Pembroke Hall, in Cambridge University. For many years, he was 'the painful, pious, learned and beloved minister' of St. Stephen's, Walbrook, London, to which he was admitted in 1601. His principal publication is described as a 'solid treatise' against usury

Fernel, Jean (1567) *Physiologia* Jean François Fernel (1497 – 1558) was a French physician who introduced the term 'physiology' to describe the study of the body's function.

Field, John (1580) *A Notable Treatise of the Church, in which are handled all the principall questions, that haue been mooued in our time concerning that matter*. Translated corrected. out of Frenche into Englishe by I. F(eilde) : London.

Foxe, John (1563) *The Book of Martyrs*, by John Foxe (first published by John Day in 1563, with many subsequent editions, also by Day), is an apocalyptically oriented English Protestant account of the persecutions of Protestants, mainly in England and other groups from former centuries who were seen by Foxe and others of his contemporaries, such as John Bale, to be forerunners of the Protestant Reformation through whom the lineage of the church of England could be traced. Though the work is commonly known as Foxe's Book of Martyrs, the full title is *Actes and Monuments of these Latter and Perillous Days, touching Matters of the Church.* The work was lavishly produced and illustrated with a large number of woodcuts and installed as propaganda in all English cathederals.

Fulke, William (1560) *Antiprognosticon, that is to saye, an Inuectiue agaynst the ... Astrologians* ... Translated [by William Painter] ... Whervnto is added by the author a shorte treatise in Englyshe, etc. Henry Sutton: London, 1560. Fulke (1538 – 1589), Puritan divine, was born in London and educated at Cambridge. As a Puritan controversialist he was remarkably active; in 1580 the bishop of Ely appointed him to defend puritanism against the Roman Catholics. In 1581 he was one of the disputants with the Jesuit, Edmund Campion, while in 1582 he was among the clergy selected by the privy council to argue against any Roman Catholic. Numerous polemical writings.

Galen *de Hippocrat Index* Galenus (129 – ~216 AD) of Pergamum was a prominent ancient Greek physician, whose theories dominated Western medical science for over a millennium.

Gellius *Noct Attic* Aulus Gellius, fl. 2nd cent., Roman writer. He was a lawyer who spent at least a year in Athens and wrote *Noctes Atticae* [Attic nights], a collection of discussions of law, antiquities and sundry other subjects in 20 books (of which 19 and a fraction survive). The work is chiefly valuable as a storehouse of quotations from lost works.

Gersonides (~1320) *Astral theol propos* Levi ben Gershom (1288 – 1344) French-born Jewish philosopher and astrologer who argued that reason and the Torah are not in contradiction. His major work *Sefer Milhamot Ha-Shem/The War of the Lord* (1329) is a synthesis of traditional Jewish teaching with Aristotelian philosophy, as interpreted by Averroës and Moses Maimonides, although Gersonides's philosophy tends to dominate and go against traditional theology. He emphasized empirical observation, invented an instrument to measure the height of stars above the horizon and challenged several of Ptolemy's principles of planetary movement.

Giraldus Cambriensus (1188) *Topographia Hibernica* (Topography of Ireland), Gerald of Wales (~1146 – ~1223), grandson of the notorius Princess Nesta, was a medieval clergyman and chronicler of his times. Born at Manorbier Castle in Pembrokeshire, he was of mixed Norman and Welsh blood.

Godwin, Thomas (1616) *Synopsis Antiquitatum Hebraicarum, ad explicationem utriusque Testamenti valde necessaria* Oxford (*Moses and Aaron; or the civil and ecclesiastical Rites used by the ancient Hebrews, observed and at large opened for the clearing of many obscure Texts throughout the whole Scriptures,* etc. (London, 1685, 12th ed.)
Godwin (1587 – 1643) was rector of Brightwell. His book (above) about ancient Hebrew and Jewish rituals was well-known and re-printed several times over the centuries.

Gregoire, Pierre Tholosain (1581) *Syntaxeων artis mirabilis alter tomus. In quo omnium scientiarum et artium tradita est epitome, etc* Lugduni (Lyon) Gryphium. At Toulouse, wrote about constitutional matters '*de Republica*'.

Gregory of Tours, Saint (~538 –594) was a Gallo-Roman historian and bishop of Tours, which made him a leading prelate of Gaul. He is the main contemporary source for Merovingian history. His most notable work was his *Historia Francorum* (History of the Franks), but he is also known for his credulous accounts of the miracles of saints, especially four books of the miracles of Martin of Tours. St Martin's tomb was a major draw in the 6th century and Gregory's writings had the practical aspect of promoting this highly organized cult

Grimston, Edward (1611) *in a tr fr French 'Estates & Empires'* of **Avity, Pierre** d', sieur de Montmartin, (1573 – 1635). *Estates, empires, & principallities of the world. Represented by ye description of countries, maners of inhabitants, riches of prouinces, forces, gouernment, religion; and the princes that haue gouerned in euery estate. With the begin[n]ing of all militarie and religious orders.*

Gritsch, Johannes. (1477), *Quadragesimale*, Ulm, Johann Zainer 'one of ours' (doubtful).

Hackluyt, Richard (1560) *Justice by lot in Russia letter from Lane* M. Richard Hakluyt of Eiton in the Countie of Hereford, Esquire, (mis-spelled Hackluit by Gataker). Hackluyt (1552 – 1616) from a Dutch (or Welsh) family long settled in Hereford. Educated at Christ Church, Oxford 1570, ordained. Published in 1582, *Divers Voy. touching the Discov. of Amer. and the Isl. adjacent.* based on Verrazzano of 1524. Many other books of geographical description followed. The Hakluyt Society is named after Richard Hakluyt and publishes historical books about early explorations.

Hall, Bishop Joseph (1606) *Characters of Virtues and Vices*. Hall (1574 – 1656) was born at Ashby-de-la-Zouch, educated at Emmanuel College, Cambridge, where he was part of the University Wits. He published his *Virgidemiarum*, six books of 'toothless satires', in 1597 and 1598. These verse satires were, along with those of his friend John Donne, the first English satires that followed. (Donne later followed Gataker as preacher at Lincoln's Inn.) Hall also published religious writings, notably *Meditations and Vows* (1605) and *Characters of Virtues and Vices* (1608). Hall was appointed chaplain to Prince Henry in 1608 and was made Dean of Worcester by James I, representing the King at the Synod of Dort. Next, Hall was made Bishop of Exeter in 1627 and of Norwich (1641). In 1642, Hall was among 13 bishops imprisoned by Parliament, his cathedral was desecrated in the Civil War and Hall himself was evicted from his palace in 1647. He retired to the village of Higham and continued writing until his death. Reduced to beggary, Hall nonetheless survived until 1656

Hecataeus could be Hecataeus of Miletus (~550 – ~476 BC), was a Greek philosopher of a wealthy family. He flourished during the time of the Persian invasion OR Pseudo-Hecataeus In his treatise *Against Apion.* Josephus gives a number of excerpts on Jewish history from a work he attributes to Hecataeus of Abdera – a well-known pagan Greek historian of the late fourth – early third century B.C

Heraclitus of Ephesus (~535 – 475 BC)

Herodotus of Helicarnassus (~484 – 425 BC) Greek historian known for his *Histories*

Heydon, Christopher (1603) *A Defence of Judiciall Astrologie, in answer to a treatise lately published by M. John Chamber* (Cambridge), (re-pub in facsimile 1977). Heydon, (1561 – 1623), was an English soldier and writer on astrology. Educated at Cambridge, where he knew the young Earl of Essex and after proceeding BA in 1579 travelled widely on the continent. Heydon was famous as a champion of astrology. His best-known work was *A Defence of Judiciall Astrologie* (1603), the most substantial English defence of astrology of its day, rebutting John Chamber's *A Treatise Against Judiciall Astrologie* (1601), which had called for parliament to outlaw astrology. Heydon argued that it was a valid science, compatible with Christianity. He drew upon Tycho Brahe and others He also wrote but did not publish *An Astrological Discourse with Mathematical Demonstrations* (~ 1608), a further defence of astrology drawing on Kepler, with a short account of the 1603 conjunction of Saturn and Jupiter. The manuscript passed to the astrologer Nicholas Fiske, whose attempts to publish it failed, but it appeared in an edited form in 1650, subsidized by Elias Ashmole, with a preface by William Lilly (The notorious astrologer, butt of Gataker's ire in his last publication). Heydon's work was given weight by his social standing and the lack of challenges to it. No reply by Chamber appeared and George Carleton's *The Madnesse of Astrologers* (1624) was published only twenty years later. He remained a champion of militant Protestantism to the end. He wrote a treatise on the comet of 1618 and described his own astronomical observations with instruments made by his friend Edward Wright.

Higden, Ranulph (~1340) *Polychronicon. Description of England*; pub. by Caxton in 1480 Higdon (or Higden) (~1280 – ~1363), was an English chronicler and a Benedictine monk of the monastery of St. Werburg in Chester and seems to have travelled over the north of England. *Polychronicon* is a long chronicle written for the amusement and instruction of his society. For two centuries it was an approved work.

Holinshed, Raphael (1577) *The firste volume of the chronicles of England, Scotlande and Irelande, conteyning the description and chronicles of England, from the first inhabiting unto the Conquest. The description and chronicles of Scotland, from the first originall of the Scottes nation, till the yeare 1571. The description and chronicles of Yrelande, from the firste originall, untill the yeare 1547. (The laste volume ... conteyning the chronicles of Englande from William Conquerour untill this present tyme.)* London: Imprinted for John Harrison. Holinshed (d.1580) was an English chronicler, whose work, commonly known as Holinshed's *Chronicles*, was one of the major sources used by William Shakespeare for a number of his plays. Holinshed, or Hollingshead, probably belonged to a Cheshire family.

Homer is the name given to the purported author of the early Greek poems *the Iliad* and *the Odyssey*. It is now believed by Classicists (especially after the studies by Milman Parry) that they were composed by illiterate aoidoi (rhapsodes) in an oral tradition in the 8th or 7th century BC. However, there remains much argument between 'analysts' and 'unitarians' over whether *the Iliad* and *the Odyssey* were the product of one man or of many. Homer's works begin the Western Canon and are universally praised for their poetic genius. By convention, the compositions are also often taken to initiate the period of Classical Antiquity

Horace: Quintus Horatius Flaccus (65 BC – 8 BC**)** Horace was the leading Roman lyric poet during the time of Augustus.

Howard, Henry, Earl of Northampton (1583) *A defensative against the poyson of supposed prophecies, not hitherto confuted by the penne of any man, etc.* 'He was one of the most unscrupulous and treacherous characters of the age, but was nevertheless distinguished for his learning, artistic culture and his public charities'.

Howden, Roger of (1178) (an unusal instance where Gataker gives a date) *Epistle to Henricus Clarewell.* Roger of Hoveden, or Howden (fl. 1174 – 1201), was a 12th century English chronicler.

Isocrates (436 – 338 BC) Greek rhetorician, was one of the ten Attic orators. In his time he was probably the most influential rhetorician in Greece and made many contributions to rhetoric and education through his teaching and written works. *Areopagiticus* 'A study of Democracy' which contains a wealth of information about Athenian selection by lottery.

James I, King (of England); he of the KJV, was anti-tobacco and gave advice to his son Henry who died young.

James I, King (1603) *A Prince's Looking-Glasse; or, a Prince's Direction, ... Excerpted ... out of that most Christian ... or, his Majesties instructions to ... his ... sonne Henrie the Prince,* John Legat; Cambridge.

James I, King (1604) *A counterblaste to tobacco* London R B

Jerome (~347 – 420 AD); Greek: also known as Hieronymus, is best known as the translator of the Bible from Greek and Hebrew into Latin. Church father and Christian apologist, wrote many texts.

Jonan, Rabbi 'doting': perhaps Yonah ben Abraham Gerondi.

Josephus (37 – ~100 AD), who became known in his capacity as a Roman citizen, as Titus Flavius Josephus, was a 1st-century Jewish historian and apologist of priestly and royal ancestry who survived and recorded the Destruction of Jerusalem in 70 AD. His works give an important insight into first-century Judaism.

Junius, Franciscus (~1590) *Theologe* Junius (1545 – 1602), also known as Franz Junius and François du Jon, was a French Huguenot scholar and theologian and the father of Franciscus Junius the younger.

Justinius, Marcus *Epitome (of Trogus) Epitome of the Philippic History of Pompeius Trogus.*

Keckermann, Bartholomew (1612) *Resolutio Systematis logici in tabellas pleniores quam antehac fuerunt* Hanover, G A Haeredes: Keckermann (1572 – 1609) German philosopher, historian at University of Dantzig (Gdansk, Poland).

King, Bishop John (1597) *Lectures upon Jonas* Jonas (or Jonah as we now say) was a topic for Bishop, later Archbishop King's lectures in 1597, 1599, 1600, 1611 and 1618.

Krakewitz, Berthold von (~1610) *Pomeranian confessions* (1582–1642). Lutheran, theologian; educ. Wittenberg and other German universities; professor at Greifswald.

Lacon, Demetrius of. Greek, was an Epicurean philosopher of the late 2nd century BC and a disciple of Protarchus. Relatively little remains of his work. Sextus Empiricus quotes part of a commentary by Demetrius on Epicurus, where Demetrius interprets Epicurus' statement that 'time is an accident of accidents'.

Lactantius, Lucius Caelius Firmianus (~240 – 320). North African, an early Christian author taught rhetoric in various cities of the Eastern Roman Empire, ending in Constantinople. He wrote apologetic works explaining Christianity in terms that would be palatable to educated pagans while defending it from pagan philosophers. His *Divinae Institutiones* ('Divine Institutions') is an early example of a systematic presentation of Christian thought. He was considered somewhat heretical after his death, but Renaissance humanists picked up renewed interest in Lactantius, more for his good elaborately rhetorical Latin style than for his theology.

Lampridius, Aelius *The life of Antoius Heliogablus*; some confusion with a 15th century Croatian poet of the same name.

Landulfus (~1498) Coimbra, Spain a monk and forger of Cyprian.

Lavater, Ludwig (1586) *In Librum Prouerbiorum siue Sententiarum Solomonis* C. Froschouerum: Zurich. Lavater (1527 – 1586) was archdeacon at Zurich Grossmunster Church.

Lemnius, Levinus (1559) *De gli occulti miracoli. & uarii ammaestramenti delle cose della natura* Venice, appresso Lodouico Auanzo. An 'extraordinarily popular' book first published in 1559. Lemnius (1505 – 1568), a Dutch physician from Zierikzee in Holland and pupil of Vesalius, Dodoens and Gesner. 'The book, which is a disorderly miscellany of little value, with entertainment rather than instruction the author's aim. Bits of medical and natural lore are thrown together hit-or-miss.... It will not do, however, to dismiss this farrago too cavalierly, since it was often cited by subsequent learned authors and since the numerous editions and translations of it show that it well suited the taste of the century'. Lemnius also wrote on astrology and the prolongation of life. According to Valerius Andreas, he was an affable practitioner who cheered his patients up by telling them jokes and funny stories.

Leo, Brother (1318) *Mirror of perfection; Speculum perfectionis status fratris Minores Speculum Perfectionis seu S. Francisci Assisiensis legenda antiquissima* (The story of this allegedly first life of St Francis is a bit of a saga in itself!)

Linschoten, Jan Huygen van (1598) *The voyage of John Huyghen van Linschoten to the East Indies : From the old English translation of 1598* : The First book, containing his description of the East was published in Works issued by the Hakluyt (q.v.) Society First series in 1885. Linschoten (1563 – 1611) was a Dutch Protestant merchant, traveller and historian. He is credited with copying top-secret Portuguese nautical maps thus enabling the passage to the elusive East Indies to be opened to the English and the Dutch. This enabled the British East India Company and the Dutch East India Company to break the 16th century monopoly enjoyed by the Portuguese on trade with the East Indies.

Littleton, Sir Thomas (1480) *Tenores Novelli. Norman-French Litleton's Tenures. Conferred with divers true wrytten copies and purged of sondry cases, etc. B.L. MS. notes 1557 version; London Richard Tottil.* Littleton (1407 – 1481), English judge and legal author, was born, it is supposed, at Frankley Manor House, Worcestershire. (Several Littletons from this area were involved in the Gunpowder Plot of 1605.)

Livy, Horatias Titus Livius (traditionally 59 BC – AD 17), known as Livy in English, was a Roman historian who wrote a monumental history of Rome, *Ab Urbe Condita*, from its founding (traditionally dated to 753 BC) through the reign of Augustus in Livy's own time.

Lopez de Gomara, Francisco (1552) *Historia de la conquista de Mexico* Saragossa (reprinted in 2003) Editorial Oceana de Mexico. Gómara (1511 – 1566) was a Spanish historian at Seville, who is particularly noted for his works in which he described the early 16th century expedition undertaken by Hernán Cortés in the Spanish conquest of the New World.

Lucian *Decasier Hermotim* Lucian of Samosata, Greek: (~125 – ~180) was an Assyrian rhetorician and satirist who wrote in the Greek language. He is noted for his witty and scoffing nature.

Lyra, Nicholas of (~1300) *Hostensis Preceptory.* Lyra (1270 – 1340) was a Franciscan teacher and was among the most influential practitioners of Biblical exegesis in the Middle Ages. He was a doctor at the Sorbonne by 1309 and ten years later was appointed the head of all Franciscans in France. Luther made much use of Lyra's works. Publications: *Num Postillae perpetuae in vetus et novem testamentum* Rome

Macarius of Egypt (~300 – 391) was an Egyptian Christian monk and hermit. He is also known as Macarius the Elder, Macarius the Great and The Lamp of the Desert.

Macrobius *Saturnalia* Ambrosius Theodosius Macrobius was a Roman grammarian and Neoplatonist philosopher who flourished during the reigns of Honorius and Arcadius. (395 – 423 AD).

Maimonides, Moses (~1200), (b. 1135 Córdoba, Spain – d. 1204 Fostat, Egypt), was a Jewish rabbi, physician and philosopher in Andalusia, Morocco and Egypt during the Middle Ages. He was one of the various medieval Jewish philosophers who also influenced the non-Jewish world. Although his copious works on Jewish law and ethics were initially met with opposition during his lifetime, he was posthumously acknowledged to be one of the foremost rabbinical arbiters and philosophers in Jewish history. Today, his works and his views are considered a cornerstone of Jewish thought and study.

Malderus, Joannes (~1610) *de superstis* Malderus (1563 – 1633) Bishop of Antwerp, was a 'popish' writer on lotteries and a Jesuit.

Malmesbury, William of (1120) *Deeds of the English kings* Malmesbury (~1080/1095 – ~1143), English historian of the 12th century. His father was Norman and his mother English. He spent his whole life in England with his most productive working years as a monk at Malmesbury Abbey. William produced about 1120 the *Gesta regum anglorum* (*Deeds of the English kings* (449 – 1127), now considered by modern scholars to be one of the great histories of England.

Marbury, Francis (1602) *Notes of the Doctrine of Repentance. Gathered by occasion of opening the fift petition of the Lords Prayer.* Deliuered in the Church of Alford in Lincolne-shire, by way of catechising. Peter Short London *Psalms* 32. Marbury (1555 – 1611) was ordained a deacon in 1578, but was soon in trouble with the authorities for his views and was tried before Bishop Aylmer in London and imprisoned. For years he was unable to preach. In 1590, he appealed to Lord Burleigh, Sir Francis Bacon's uncle, to help him get his preaching license back and he was preaching again by 1594. He died in 1611 and was long remembered as a preacher and was referred to as such in the writings of Sir Francis Bacon.

Martial, Marcus Valerius Martialis, known in English as Martial, was a Latin poet from Hispania (the Iberian Peninsula) best known for his twelve books of *Epigrams*, published in Rome between AD 86 and 103, during the reigns of the emperors Domitian, Nerva and Trajan. In these short, witty poems he cheerfully satirises city life and the scandalous activities of his acquaintances and romanticises his provincial upbringing. He is considered the creator of the modern epigram.

Masius, Andreas (~1570) *ad Josh Didact; Phys* perhaps Andreas Masius (1514 – 1573) Belgian catholic cleric, humanist and first European expert in Syrian studies.

Minucius, Felix Christian apologist, flourished between 160 and 300.

Mornay, Philippe Duplessis (1581) *Traité de la verité de la religion chrétienne contre les athées, épicuriens, payens, juifs, mahométans et autres infidèles* Antwerp. Mornay (1549 – 1623). Educated a Protestant, he spent several years in Italy and Germany after completing his education, returning to France. Adviser to Henry of Navarre, he lost influence when Henry converted to catholicism (to claim the throne of France).

Moses, Rabbi n/k jewish writer *Munsteri praecept* ref to Slavs so he is not Moses Maimonides.

Nonnus paraphrase of the *Gospel of John.* Greek epic poet, Nonnus a native of Panopolis (Akhmim) in Egypt, probably lived at the end of the 4th or early 5th century. He produced the *Dionysiaca*, an epic tale of the god Dionysus, a paraphrase of the *Gospel of John* and two poems which are lost.

Olevianus 'of old' N/K

Origen, Adamantius, (~185 – ~254) was an early Christian scholar, theologian and one of the most distinguished of the early fathers of the Christian Church. His writings are important as one of the first intellectual attempts to describe Christianity. He espoused a Platonic view of eternal souls achieving perfection while escaping the temporary, imperfect material world. He imagined even demons being reunited with God. His views of a hierarchical structure in the Trinity, the temporality of matter, 'the fabulous preexistence of souls,' and 'the monstrous restoration which follows from it' were declared anathema in the 6th century.

Osorius, Hieronymus (~1590) *de Regis infinitus* (dubious ref the Canon of Evora)

Ovid: Publius Ovidius Naso (43 BC – 17 AD) was a Roman poet known to the English-speaking world as Ovid who wrote on many topics, including love, abandoned women and mythological transformations. Ranked alongside Virgil and Horace as one of the three canonical poets of Latin literature, Ovid was generally considered a great master of the elegiac couplet. His poetry, much imitated during Late Antiquity and the Middle Ages, had a decisive influence on European art and literature for centuries.

Pacuvius, Marcus *Paruv apud Conif ad Heron* (~220 – 130 BC) was one of the greatest tragic poets of ancient Rome.

Palat n/k

Panson *in Attica Lacon* N/K, but ancient Greek

Paris, Gdo (date n/k) forged Cyprian sermon *Hazard after Astoroath*

Parker, Rev R. n/k

Paschasius, Justus (1618) *Alea, sive de curandi in pecuniam ludendi cupiditate libri duo* Herzog August Bibliothek, Wolfenbüttel Frankfurt-am-Main. The physician Paschasius Justus (Joostens Pashier) was a deplorable instance of an incorrigible gambler. This otherwise most excellent and learned man having passed three-fourths of his life in a continual struggle with vice, at length resolved to cure himself of the disease by occupying his mind with a work which might be useful to his contemporaries and posterity. He began his book, but still he gamed; he finished it, but the evil was still in him. 'I have lost everything but God!' he exclaimed. He prayed for delivery from his soul's disease; but his prayer was not heard; he died like any gambler – more wretched than reformed.

Patrum. consist (~1550) Orat *habitat Patrus consist;* seems to be the Papal Consistory which allowed catholics to kill heritics, for example Queen Elizabeth I. I cannot identify the specific Consistory referred to, but it must have been ~1550.

Pausanias was a Greek traveller and geographer of the 2nd century AD, who lived in the times of Hadrian, Antoninus Pius and Marcus Aurelius. He is famous for his Description of Greece.

Pepin, Gulielmus (1530) *de confess super Confiteor, novissime pereũdem recognitum et emendatum.*: Luthetie. Pepin was the 'silly friar' who misquoted Cyprian; lived in Paris as a priest

Perkins, William (1555–1602) His collected works were said to be by 'that famous and worthy minister of Christ in the Universitie of Cambridge'. Perkins was a prominent English demonologist and widely regarded Puritan preacher. (Gataker was educated at Christ's, Cambridge, so they may have known each other)

Perkins, William (1590) *Armilla aurea, id est, Miranda series causarum et salutis & damnationis iuxta verbum Dei: eius synopsin continet annexa tabula* John Leggat: Cambridge

Perkins, William (1592) *A Case of Conscience, the greatest that euer was; How a man may knowe whether he be the Child of God or no. Resolued by the worde of God. [The text of the First Epistle of John and Psalm XV with a commentary by William Perkins.] Whereunto is added a brief discourse, taken out of Hier. Zanchius. (Wherein the foresaid case of conscience is disputed and resolued.) [Translated by W. Perkins.]* Robert Walde-graue: Edinburgh, 1592

Perkins, William (1608 posthumously) *A discourse of the damned art of witch-*

craft; so farre forth as it is revealed in the Scriptures and manifest by true experience ... Published by T. Pickering, Printed at Londonby C. Leggat, Printer to the Universitie of Cambridge His Discourse was published posthumously in 1608. Like several other witch believers such as Henry More and Henry Hallywell, he was a fellow of Christ's College, Cambridge. A primary English authority on witchcraft, Perkins ignored the work of the European demonologists, basing his work almost exclusively on the Bible. The book is divided into seven chapters covering true and false miracles, the league between Satan and a witch, divination, good witches and the discovery and punishment of witches. It was influential throughout the 17th century because of its distinctions between false and uncertain signs of witchcraft, presumptions of guilt and just and sufficient proofs. Perkins was the first to introduce into English experience the concept of familiar spirits. As cats and mice abounded, this meant it was never difficult to discover or 'prove' a witch.

Peter Martyr, in Italian Pietro Martire Vermigli (1500 – 1562), Italian Protestant reformer. He was born in Florence. After becoming an Augustinian monk, he read and was impressed by the works of the German reformer Martin Bucer and the Swiss reformer Huldreich Zwingli. After introducing reformed doctrines into his sermons, Vermigli was charged with heresy and was temporarily suspended from preaching He founded no church and his life north of the Alps was itinerant. Although his wide-ranging education in Italy enabled him to engage in learned debates, he did not write popular treatises in vernacular languages. Vermigli was superbly educated as a philosopher, theologian and scriptural commentator before his flight to Zurich. Active as a teacher and exegete in Strassburg, Oxford and eventually in Zurich, he tied together the embryonic Italian Reformation with the Protestant theologies of northern Europe. His knowledge of biblical languages together with his command of the early fathers and Aristotle enabled him to make important contributions to Protestant thought and to serve as a formidable opponent of Catholic critics.

Petrarch, Francesco (1304 –1374) Italian poet and humanist.

Petronius, Gaius (~27 – 66 AD), the author of the *Satyricon*, was the emperor Nero's advisor in matters of luxury and extravagance (his unofficial title was arbiter elegantiae). As befitted his office, he slept days and partied nights. He was a lover of style, manners and literature and his personality was characterized by freedom, a lack of self-consciousness, a loose tongue and an attitude. A rival's jealousy turned Nero against Petronius and he was forced to commit suicide. However, before his death, he lampooned Nero in his will and sent the emperor a copy.

Peucer, Caspar (1572) *Commentarius De praecipuis generibus divinationum, in quo a prophetiis autoritate divina traditis & a physicis coniecturis, discernuntur artes & imposturae diabolicae atque observationes natae ex superstitione & cum hac coniunctae. Et monstrantur fontes ac causaephysicarum praedictionum. Diabolicae vero ac superstitiosae confutatae damnantur ea ferie, quam tabella praefixa ostendit.* Johannes Lufft: Wittenburg. Peucer (1525 – 1602) was a German reformer, physician and scholar. Born in Bautzen, Peucer studied mathematics, astronomy and medicine at the University of Wittenberg since 1540. In 1543, he became a lodger in the house of one of the most famous professors in Wittenberg, the theologian and humanist Philipp Melanchthon, whose daughter Magdalena he married in 1550. In 1554, he became professor of mathematics at Wittenberg and in 1560 professor of medicine, leading the Wittenberg faculty in that field. Until 1574, he also served several times as dean and rector. In spite of his medical profession – in 1570, he became even personal physician to the Elector of Saxony – he was, after the death of Melanchthon, one of the leading Protestants in Saxony. However, in 1574 Peucer was officially charged with Crypto-Calvinism in an inter-Lutheran fight for power and put in jail in the famed Königstein Fortress for twelve years. Released in 1586, he went to the Duchy of Anhalt, where he became Councillor and personal physician of the Prince of Anhalt. He died in the capital of Dessau in 1602.

Pindar (b. 522 BC Boeotia; d. 443 BC in Argos), was a Greek lyric poet. Of the canonical nine lyric poets of ancient Greece, Pindar is the one whose work is best preserved and some critics since antiquity have regarded him as the greatest.

Piscatorius, Johann (~1600) *'ad Rami dialect'* (1546 – 1625) seems to be a Protestant German theologian and philosopher; 'rami' see *Fenner*

Plato *de leg, Hyprbolo* Plato (~428 – ~347 BC), was a classical Greek philosopher. Together with his teacher, Socrates and his student, Aristotle, Plato helped to lay the philosophical foundations of Western culture. Plato was also a mathematician, writer of philosophical dialogues and founder of the Academy in Athens, the first institution of higher learning in the western world. Plato was originally a student of Socrates and was much influenced by his thinking as by what he saw as his teacher's unjust death

Pliny *Imper*, *Hist epist 22* Gaius or Caius Plinius Secundus, (23 –79 AD), better known as Pliny the Elder, was an ancient author, naturalist or natural philosopher and naval and military commander of some importance who wrote *Naturalis Historia.*

Plutarch, (46 – 120 AD) Greek historian biographer and essayist. Titles quoted include: *ad Apollon;Pedagog Lycurg, Apopht, Grachae Prob, de Pyth* Grat. *Conjectis in sortem Symp Crasso Stoic de Pyth Orac.*

Pollux the Roman who produced the *Onomasticon* a guide to Greek phrases.

Pomponius *in Dig* on Roman Law. Sextus Pomponius was a jurist who lived during the reigns of Hadrian, Antoninus Pius and Marcus Aurelius. He wrote a book on the law up to the time of Hadrian. (Not to be confused with lots of other Pomponiuses.)

Porta, John Baptista (1584) (1658 in English) *Natural Magick: herein are set forth All the Riches and Delights Of the Natural sciences* London. (Giambattista della Porta) (1535 – 1615) A Neapolitan.

Proclus, Lycaeus (412 – 485), surnamed 'The Successor' or 'diadochos', was a Greek Neoplatonist philosopher, one of the last major Greek philosophers. He set forth one of the most elaborate, complex and fully developed Neoplatonic systems. He stands near the end of the pagan Greek development of philosophy and was extremely influential on later Christian (Greek and Latin) and Islamic thought. 'Wherever there is number, there is beauty.'

Prochorus. 'counterfeit bastard' (according to Gataker!) 'Tradition calls Prochorus the nephew of Saint Stephen and a companion of John the Evangelist, who consecrated him bishop of Nicomedia in Bithynia (modern-day Turkey). He was traditionally ascribed the authorship of the apocryphal Acts of John and was said to have ended his life as a martyr in Antioch in the 1st century.

Pseudo-Cyprian *Adversus aleatores Athen Hist de aleat* The work was first propagated throughout Europe by Irish missionaries in the 8th century. Its authorship was attributed at different times to Saint Patrick, Saint Augustine, but mainly Saint Cyprian of Carthage – men of such authority that it explains its acceptance and popularity. It was not until 1909 that Siegmund Hellmann revealed its Pseudo-Cyprian origins to an anonymous Irish author of the 7th century. Hellmann points out the extensive influence of the work upon Carolingian and later political literature.

Fardinando Pulton (1536 – 1618) was an English legal writer, the first to attempt a comprehensive book treating criminal law. Pulton belonged to Lincoln's Inn (where Gataker was preacher) but he was a Roman Catholic, so that at that time a legal career was denied to him.

Pulton, Fardinando (1612) *A Kalender, or Table, comprehending the effect of all the Statutes ... until the end of the Session of Parliament holden anno 4. R. Iacobi ... Collected by F. Pulton and by him againe augmented, sithence the Session of Parliament* holden anno quarto Regis Jacobi. B. Company of Stationers: London.

Pulton, Fardinando (1618) *A Collection of sundrie Statutes, frequent in use: with notes in the margent and references ... Together with an abridgement of the residue which be expired ... Whereunto be added certaine materiall statutes, neuer printed before in English. Also a necessarie table or Kalender ... By Fardinando Pulton.*

Sallust letters of to Caesar Gaius Sallustius Crispus, generally known simply as Sallust, (86 – 34 BC), a Roman historian, belonged to a well-known plebeian family and was born at Amiternum in the country of the Sabines.

Salmuth, Heinrich (1607) *The history of many memorable things lost, which were in use among the ancients : and an account of many excellent things found, now in use among the moderns, both natural and artificial:* Hamburg. Salmuth (1522 – 1576) Lutheran theologian, Leipzig.

Scacchus, Fortunatus (1635) *Sacrorum Elæochrismatωn Myrothecium Sacro-prophanum; in quo ... quidquid ad nomina, antiquitatem, usum et abusum oleorum et unguentorum ex sacris habetur litteris, ... explicatur.* A popular interpreter of some biblical passages (doubtful ref.).

Scaliger, Joseph Justus (~1610) *orbibus Hieraticis.* Scaliger (1540–1609) was a French religious leader and scholar, known for expanding the notion of classical history from Greek and Ancient Roman history to include Persian, Babylonian, Jewish and Ancient Egyptian history.

Schindler, Valentin (1612 posthumously) *Lexicon Pentaglotton, Hebraicum, Chaldaicum, Syriacum, Talmudico-Rabbinicum, et Arabicum, etc.* Hanover (re-pub London, 1635). Schindler, d. 1604, was a Lutheran Hebrew scholar and professor at Wittenburg, Germany.

Scopeliano di Clazomene (~1250) *Philostatum* (not much about this Italian).

Seneca *in satyr patre mathematicos; Sen de benef*: Lucius Annaeus Seneca (~4 BC – 65 AD) was a Roman Stoic philosopher, statesman, dramatist and in one work humorist, of the Silver Age of Latin literature.

Serarius, Nicholas (1609) *Iosue ab vtero ad ipsum us Deuteronomio; &̃e proprio ipsius libro toto, ac paralipomenis, libris quin explanatus, etc. [With the text of and a commentary on, the Book of Joshua.]* E I. Albini typographeo: Moguntiæ (Mainz, Germany). Serarius (1555 – 1610) born in Lorraine, was a 'learned Jesuit and commentator'. He wrote many books on biblical themes, including anti-Luther tracts.

Sidonius, Gaius (or Caius) Sollius (Modestus) Apollinaris *Epist,* the ancient French bishop Sidonius or Saint Sidonius Apollinaris (~430 – ~489), poet, diplomat, bishop, is 'the single most important surviving author from fifth-century Gaul'. He was one of four 5th to 6th century Gallo-Roman aristocrats whose letters survive in quantity.

Sigon *de rep Athen* N/K

Socrates no comment needed.

Solomon, Rabbi (~1090) Jewish writer Solomon ben Isaac, commonly known as Rashi (a Hebrew acronym) for Rabbi Shlomo Yitzhaki (1040 – 1105), was a rabbi from France, famed as the author of the first comprehensive commentaries on the Talmud, Torah and Tanakh (Hebrew Bible). Acclaimed for his ability to present the basic meaning of the text in a concise yet lucid fashion, Rashi appeals to both learned scholars and beginning students and his works remain a centerpiece of contemporary Jewish study. His commentaries, which appear in many printed editions of the Talmud and Torah (notably the Chumash), are an indispensable companion to both casual and serious students of Judaism's primary texts.

Sophocles (~496 – 406 BC) was the second of the three ancient Greek tragedians whose work has survived to the present day.

Stratonicus *Stato apud Athen dipnos*: Stratonicus lived in the 4th Century BC in Athens, was a distinguished musician, of whom scarcely anything is recorded, except the sharp and witty rebuke which he administered to Philotas, when the latter boasted of a victory which he had gained over Timotheus.

Suárez, Francisco *(1613) Defensio Fidei Catholicæ ... adversus Anglicanæ sectæ errores, cum responsione ad apologiam pro juramento fidelitatis, et præfationem monitoriam,... Jacobi Angliæ Regis, etc;* Coimbra Portugal. Suárez (1548 – 1617), Jesuit, was a Spanish philosopher and theologian, generally regarded as having been the greatest scholastic after Thomas Aquinas.

Suetonius, Gaius Tranquillus (~75 – ~130), was a prominent Roman historian and biographer.

Sylvester, Joshua, (1617) *Tobacco battered and the Pipes Shattered (poetry).* Sylvester was an excellent French and Latin scholar, his literary reputation was founded on his translation from French of Du Bartas's *The Divine Weeks and Works*. Later in life he was a friend of the satirist Joseph Hall, chaplain to Prince Henry and one of the bishops subsequently imprisoned by Parliament in 1642 (For an excellent analysis of the religious elements of the situation, see David Harley: The Beginnings of the Tobacco Controversy: Puritanism, James I and the Royal Physicians, *Bulletin of the History of Medicine* **67** (1993): 28 – 50)

Synod Basiliensis (1431) to resolve a number of complex issues. A synod is a council of the Christian church, convened to decide an issue of doctrine, administration or application.

Tacitus *Annal Sors ad Tacit annal, de mor German.* Publius (or Gaius) Cornelius Tacitus (~56 – ~117 AD) was a senator and a historian of the Roman Empire. The surviving portions of his two major works – the *Annals* and the *Histories* – examine the reigns of the Roman Emperors Tiberius, Claudius, Nero and those that reigned in the Year of the Four Emperors.

Tertullian Quintus Septimius Florens Tertullianus, anglicised as Tertullian, (~155 – 230) was a church leader and prolific author of Early Christianity. He also was a notable early Christian apologist. Tertullian, a Romanized African, was born, lived and died in Carthage, in what is today Tunisia. Tertullian denounced Christian doctrines he considered heretical, but later in life adopted views that themselves came to be regarded as heretical. He was the first great writer of Latin Christianity, thus sometimes known as the 'Father of the Latin Church'. He introduced the term Trinity and also old testament and new testament. In his *Apologeticus*, he was the first Latin author who qualified Christianity as the *vera religio* and symmetrically relegated the classical Empire religion and other accepted cults to the position of mere 'superstitions'. Tertullian adopted Montanist practices late in his life and was associated with the heretical Montanists. It is probably due to this association that he has never been acknowledged as a saint.

Theophanes, Confessor (~760 –, ~818) *Chronicles The Campaigns of Emperor Herakleios (620 – 6)*

Theophilus may be Theophilus of Alexandria, (d. 412) Coptic Pope of Egypt from 385 to 412. He is regarded as a saint by the Coptic Orthodox Church. He was a Coptic Pope at a time of conflict between the newly dominant Christians and the pagan establishment in Alexandria, each supported by a segment of the Alexandrian populace.

Thucydides (~460 – ~395 BC) was an ancient Greek historian and the author of the *History of the Peloponnesian War*, which recounts the 5th century BC war between Sparta and Athens to the year 411 BC.

Tilenius, Daniel (~1610) *Syntagm.* Tilenius (1563 – 1633) was a protestant theologian at Sedan University, France. Also wrote *Parænesis ad Scotos, Genevensis disciplinæ zelotas* (1620)

Timberlake, Henry (1603) *A true and strange discourse of the Travailes of two English Pilgrimes: what admirable accidents befell them in their journey to Jerusalem, Gaza, Grand Cayro, Alexandria and other places: Also what rare Antiquities, Monuments and notable memories (concording with the ancient remembrances in the holy scriptures) they saw in Terra Sancta, with a perfect* *description of the Countries about them. A discourse of no less admiration then well worth the regarding: written by one of them, on behalf of himselfe and his fellowe Pilgrime* London: Thomas Archer Timberlake was raised in Gloucester, as the son of a well-to-do seafaring merchant. His father, Alexander Timberlake, was a member of the Merchant Adventurers of England, which Henry joined later in his life.

Toletus, Franciscus, Cardinal (1610) *Summa Casuum Conscientiæ, sive Instructio Sacerdotum in libros VIII. distincta. Quæ denuo* Coloniæ Agrippinæ (Cologne, Germany). Toletus (~1533 – 1596) was among the first generation of Jesuit theologians in the Collegio Romano – the Jesuit university in Rome founded in 1551 – who read and commented on the *Summa Theologica* in his course of theology during the 1560s. His biography contributes to our understanding of the career patterns of other Jesuit philosopher-theologians of his age (among them de Molina, Bellarmino (q.v.), Suarez (q.v.)), all of whom spent the first decades of their career in intense teaching and writing while being chosen, later on, by kings or popes, to perform delicate political missions of mediation within the Church establishment, or between the pope and other political rulers. Toletus' commentary, entitled *In Summa Theologica . . . Enarratio*, was first published in the nineteenth century (Paris, 1869). One of its questions contains an elaborate discussion of ultimate truth – the object of faith – and the different modes of its reception by the believers (In the hands of other than Gateker, Tolet did not fare so well. Witness: 'I know that Popish Casuists who in matters of Morality, as well as in matters of Faith, are many times corrupt, do justify the impleaded Games as Lawful. So Tolet, A Lapide, Delrio and others.' 1687 *A Testimony Against several Prophane and Superstitious Customs, Now Practised by some in New-England* by Increase Mather, of Harvard University.)

Torreblanca Villapando, Francisco (1618) *Epitomes delictorum in quibus aperta, vel oculta inuocatio dæmonis interuenit, libri III, etc. Including the 'Defensa de los libros de Magia.'* Hispali. Torreblanca (d.1645), a jurist of Cordoba.

Travers, Walter (1574) *Ecclesiasticæ disciplinæ, et Anglicanæ Ecclesiæ ab illa aberrationis, plena è verbo Dei, & dilucida explicatio.* Rupellæ (La Rochelle, France). Travers (d. 1635) was a Puritan theologian. He was at one time chaplain to William Cecil, 1st Baron Burghley and tutor to his son Robert Cecil. He is remembered mostly as an opponent of the teaching of Richard Hooker. He was educated at the University of Cambridge and then travelled to Geneva to visit Theodore Beza (q.v.). He was ordained by Thomas Cartwright (q.v.) in Antwerp. He was a lecturer at the Temple Church in London in 1581, until he was forbidden to preach by Archbishop Whitgift in March 1586. He was provost of Trinity College, Dublin from 1595 to 1598.

Turnebus, Adrian (1580) *Advers Adversariorum libri triginta ... Ascripta sunt in margine auctorum loci qui in his sine certa nota appellantur studio & labore* I. Furdini, Paris. Turnebus was born at Les Andelys in Normandy. At the age of twelve he was sent to Paris to study and attracted great notice by his remarkable abilities. After having held the post of professor of *belles-lettres* in the University of Toulouse, in 1547 he returned to Paris as professor (or royal reader) of Greek at the College Royal. In 1562 he exchanged this post for a professorship in Greek philosophy.In 1552 he was entrusted with the printing of the Greek books at the royal press, in which he was assisted by his friend, Guillaume Morel. Joseph Justus Scaliger (q.v.) was his pupil.

Ulpian (Ulpianus), Domitius (d 228 AD) was a Roman jurist. *ad Demosthenes in Timar* He is credited with the production of tables used for life annuities – a form of lottery.

Valerius Maximus was a Latin writer and author of a collection of historical anecdotes. He flourished in the reign of

Tiberius. Nothing is known of his personal history except that his family was poor and undistinguished.

Virgil *Aeniad bucol* Publius Vergilius Maro (70 – 19 BC) known in English as Virgil was a classical Roman poet. He was the author of epics in three modes: the *Bucolics* (or *Eclogues*), the *Georgics* and the substantially completed *Aeneid*, the last being an epic poem in the heroic mode, which comprised twelve books (as opposed to 24 in each of the epic poems by Homer) and became the Roman Empire's national epic.

Vitoria, Francisco de (1593 based on 1989 450th anniv of pub) *De Indis et De ivre belli relectiones.* Vitoria (1486 – 1546) Basque, born at Vitoria in Alava, entered the Dominican order at Burgos before proceeding to the College de St Jacques in Paris where he stayed. He is best remembered for his defence of the rights of the Indians of the New World against Spanish colonists and for his ideas of the limitations of justifiable warfare.

Vives, Lewis (1522) *Commentary on Augustine Civitas Dei.* Vives, Juan Luis b. 1492, Valencia, Aragon d. 1540, Bruges.

Vopiscus, Flavius *Life of Probus.*

Voragine, Jacobus de (~1260) *The golden legend: or, Lives of the saints, as Englished by William Caxton,* 1483. Varagine (Giacomo da Varazze) (~1230 – 1298) was an Italian chronicler and archbishop of Genoa. He was the author of the Golden Legend, one of the most popular religious works of the Middle Ages, a collection of the legendary lives of the greater saints of the medieval church. Historians interested in the 'real lives' of individual saints value the earliest texts above all others. But for assessing the later cult of saints in Western Europe the *Golden Legend* achieved dominance in later western hagiographical literature – about 900 manuscripts of his Golden Legend survive. From 1470 to 1530 it was also the most often printed book in Europe.

Walther, Rudolph the Elder (1550) *Joannis Cantacuzeni ... contra Mahumeticam fidem Christiana et orthodoxa assertio ... per R. Gualtherum ... Latinitate donate.* Swiss theologian.

White, John (1614) *Defence of The Way to the true Church, against A. D., his Reply. Wherein the motive leading to Papistry and questions, touching the Rule of Faith, the Authority of the Church ... are fully ... disputed* London 1614 Co-authored with Wootton (q.v.) White (d. 1615), Minister at Eccles.

Wootton, Anthony (1605) *An Answere to a popish pamphlet, of late newly forbished and the second time printed, entituled: Certaine articles, or forcible reasons discouering the palpable absurdities and most notorious errors of the Protestants religion. [With the text of the Articles. By Thomas Wright catholic priest]* William Timme: London. Wooton was a protestant divine and penned many virulently anti-catholic polemics.

Xenophon *ped libr 8* Xenophon (~431 – 355 BC), son of Gryllus, of the deme Erchia of Athens, was a soldier, mercenary and a contemporary and admirer of Socrates. He is known for his writings on the history of his own times, the sayings of Socrates and the life of Greece.

Yates, John (1622) *A modell of divinitie catechistically composed, etc.* London, Yates, one of Brook's puritans, fl 1611 – 1618 in Cambridge, vicar of Stiffkey.

Zanchius, Jerome (~1580) *de fort* Jerome Zanchius (1516 – 1590) was an Italian Protestant Reformation clergyman and educator. He was born Jerome Zanchi in Alzano Lombardo, the son of a nobleman. At age 15 he entered the monastery of the Augustinian Order of Regular Canons, where he studied Aristotle, languages and divinity. He also attended the lectures on Romans given by Peter Martyr Vermigli (q.v.), the greatest of the Italian Reformers.

Zenodotus Greek grammarian, literary critic and scholar on Homer; first librarian of the Library of Alexandria; pupil of Philitas of Kos; a native of Ephesus. He lived during the reigns of the first two Ptolemies and was at the height of his reputation about 280 BC.

Zwingli, Ulrich (~1523) *de form adoles* Zwingli or Ulricus Zuinglius (1484 –

1531) was the leader of the Protestant Reformation in Switzerland and founder of the Swiss Reformed Churches. Independently of Martin Luther, who was *doctor biblicus*, Zwingli arrived at similar conclusions by studying the Scriptures from the point of view of a humanist scholar.

INDEX